Geology of the pegmatites and associated rocks of Maine, including feldspar, quartz, mica, and gem deposits: USGS Bulletin 445

Edson Sunderland Bastin

DEPARTMENT OF THE INTERIOR

UNITED STATES GEOLOGICAL SURVEY

GEORGE OTIS SMITH, DIRECTOR

BULLETIN 445

GEOLOGY OF THE PEGMATITES AND ASSOCIATED ROCKS OF MAINE

INCLUDING

FELDSPAR, QUARTZ, MICA, AND GEM DEPOSITS

BY

EDSON S. BASTIN

WASHINGTON

GOVERNMENT PRINTING OFFICE

1911

CONTENTS.

	Page.
Introduction	9
Definition of pegmatite	10
Geographic distribution	10
Geology	10
Bordering rocks	10
Pegmatites in foliated rocks	11
General statement	11
Sedimentary foliates	11
Igneous foliates	12
Pegmatites in massive granites	13
Age	15
General character	15
Mineral and chemical composition	15
Mineral constituents	15
Relative proportions of minerals	18
Quartzose phases	18
Fluidal cavities	19
Sodium and lithium phases	20
Muscovite phase	22
Texture	22
Irregularity of grain	22
Graphic granite	22
Feldspar brushes	23
Intergrowths of minor constituents	25
Mica	26
Gem-bearing pegmatites	26
Origin of the Maine pegmatites	27
Relations to granites	27
External conditions	28
Dominant constituents	28
Minor constituents	29
Gaseous constituents	30
Viscosity and gas content	32
Miarolitic cavities	32
Contact-metamorphic effects	33
Forms of the intrusives	35
Temperatures of pegmatite crystallization	36
Experiments of Wright and Larsen	36
Application to Maine pegmatites	39
Eutectics in pegmatites	39
Mineralogical provinces	43
Geographic relations	43
Summary	45

Page.

Local descriptions.. 46
    Androscoggin County.. 46
        Auburn... 46
            Character and distribution of the pegmatites............. 46
                Auburn Falls.. 46
                Auburn reservoir.................................... 46
                Danville Corners.................................... 47
                Danville Junction................................... 48
                Mount Apatite....................................... 49
            Quarries... 50
                Maine Feldspar Company quarry and mill.............. 50
                Turner feldspar quarries............................ 54
                Towne feldspar and gem quarry....................... 55
                Wade and Pulsifer gem quarries...................... 56
        Minot.. 59
        Poland... 59
    Cumberland County.. 61
        Brunswick.. 61
        Westbrook.. 62
    Hancock County... 63
    Lincoln County... 63
        Edgecomb... 63
            Edgecomb feldspar quarry............................... 63
            Geologic relations..................................... 64
        Boothbay Harbor.. 64
            Character and relations of the pegmatites.............. 64
            Schists associated with pegmatites..................... 68
            Syenite porphyry....................................... 69
    Oxford County.. 70
        Albany... 70
            French Mountain beryl locality......................... 70
            Bennett mica prospect.................................. 70
            Pingree mica prospect.................................. 70
        Andover.. 71
        Buckfield.. 71
        Greenwood.. 71
        Hebron... 72
            Hibbs feldspar and mica mine........................... 72
            Mount Rubellite.. 74
            Streaked Mountain...................................... 74
            Mills feldspar quarry.................................. 75
        Newry.. 76
        Norway... 78
        Paris.. 79
            Hill north of Crocker Hill............................. 79
            Mount Mica... 81
                History.. 81
                Gem-bearing zone................................... 83
                Pockets.. 85
                Minerals... 86
                Gems... 89
                Production and method of mining.................... 92
        Peru... 93

CONTENTS.

Local descriptions—Continued.

Oxford County—Continued.   Page.

Rumford ... 93

    Vicinity of Rumford Falls ... 94

    Black Mountain mica mine ... 95

Standish ... 98

Stoneham ... 98

    Geology ... 98

    Gem localities ... 98

        Sugar Hill ... 99

        Harndon Hill ... 100

Stow ... 102

Waterford ... 102

    South Waterford mica mine ... 103

    Beech Hill mica mine ... 104

Sagadohoc County ... 105

    Georgetown ... 105

        Georgetown Center ... 105

        Hinckleys Landing ... 105

        Goldings feldspar quarry ... 105

        Small Point feldspar quarry ... 108

        Schist-pegmatite contacts on Bay Point Peninsula ... 108

    Topsham ... 109

        Distribution of the quarries ... 109

        Products of the quarries ... 110

        Mount Ararat feldspar quarries ... 110

        Fisher's feldspar quarry ... 112

        William Willes feldspar quarry ... 113

        Maine Feldspar Company's quarry ... 115

        G. D. Willes feldspar quarry ... 115

        North Topsham feldspar quarry ... 116

        Mill of Trenton Flint and Spar Company ... 117

        Vicinity of Topsham village ... 117

Economically important pegmatite minerals ... 119

Feldspar ... 119

    Potash-soda feldspars ... 119

    Lime-soda feldspars or plagioclases ... 120

    Graphic granite ... 124

    Mining ... 125

    Commercial availability of deposits ... 126

    Milling ... 127

    Uses ... 129

    Grades and prices ... 130

    Production ... 132

Quartz ... 133

    General statement ... 133

    Massive crystalline quartz ... 133

        Occurrence ... 133

        Milling ... 133

        Uses ... 134

        Production ... 136

        Prices ... 137

    Smoky quartz ... 137

    Rose quartz ... 137

    Amethyst ... 138

Economically important pegmatite minerals—Continued.   Page.
    Mica... 138
        Types.. 138
        Physical and chemical properties................................. 139
        Occurrence.. 140
        Mining and manufacture.. 141
        Uses.. 141
        Prices and production.. 142
    Tourmaline.. 143
        Chemical and physical properties................................. 143
        Occurrence.. 143
        Mining, prices, etc.. 144
    Beryl... 144
        Chemical and physical properties................................. 144
        Opaque beryl.. 145
        Emerald... 145
        Aquamarine.. 146
        Golden beryl.. 146
        Cæsium beryl.. 147
    Topaz... 147
  Index... 149

ILLUSTRATIONS.

Page.

PLATE I. Map of southern and eastern Maine, showing distribution of granites and allied rocks and locations of developed pegmatite deposits.. In pocket.

II. Microphotograph of fine-grained pegmatite from Lewiston........... 10

III. A, Highly inclined dike of pegmatite on schists at Pemaquid Point; B, Flat-lying or sill-like dike in pegmatite in bed of Androscoggin River, Auburn–Lewiston..................................... 10

IV. A, Injection gneiss, McMahon Island; B, Injection gneiss, Georgetown.. 10

V. A, Lenses of quartz diorite in porphyritic granite, St. George River; B, Flow gneiss, same locality.................................. 12

VI. Zone of strain, fracture, and recrystallization in rose quartz from Norway.. 18

VII. Graphic intergrowth of microcline and quartz, Auburn........... 22

VIII. Photomicrograph of graphic granite from Topsham................ 24

IX. A, Muscovite-rich zones in pegmatite, Topsham; B, Pocket in pegmatite, Mount Mica.. 26

X. A, Deflection of schist folia near pegmatite, Paris; B, Development of feldspar crystals in schist near pegmatite, Rumford Falls....... 34

XI. General view of Mount Mica tourmaline mine..................... 82

XII. Early workings at Mount Mica.................................... 84

XIII. Largest pocket in pegmatite at Mount Mica...................... 86

XIV. Largest crystal of tourmaline ever found at Mount Mica.......... 88

XV. Large single tourmaline from Mount Mica......................... 90

XVI. A, Diabase dike network, Stoneham; B, Quartz dike in pegmatite, South Glastonbury, Conn... 98

XVII. Microphotograph of thin section of feldspar from Golding's Sons' quarry, Georgetown... 120

XVIII. Intergrowths of feldspar and quartz............................. 124

XIX. Muscovite from Topsham, showing wedge structure................ 138

FIGURE 1. Pinch and swell structure in pegmatite dike.................. 11

2. Gradation of granite into pegmatite, Boothbay Harbor........... 14

3. Quartz offshoot from pegmatite, Paris.......................... 19

4. Fluidal cavities in pegmatitic quartz.......................... 20

5. Diagram showing composition of graphic granite................ 40

6. Relations of pegmatite and wall rock at Hibbs feldspar and mica mine, Hebron.. 73

7. Fluidal cavities in spodumene from Newry....................... 77

8. Diagram showing geologic structure at Mount Mica tourmaline mine, Paris.. 84

GEOLOGY OF THE PEGMATITES AND ASSOCIATED ROCKS OF MAINE.

By Edson S. Bastin.

INTRODUCTION.

The field studies which form the basis of this report were made by the writer during July and August, 1906, under the general supervision of George Otis Smith, of the United States Geological Survey. The writer wishes to acknowledge the valuable advice and kindly assistance of the late Prof. Leslie A. Lee, state geologist of Maine, at the time the field work for this report was done, and the cordial cooperation of many persons interested in the deposits concerned, without whose aid these studies would not have been possible.

The expenses of the work were shared equally by the Survey Commission of the State of Maine and the United States Geological Survey.

On account of the brief time at the writer's disposal in the field, it was impossible to attempt anything like a prospecting of the whole State for the minerals here considered. Visits were made, however, to nearly all of the localities which had been or are at the present time operated commercially, and numerous observations were made on the geology of the intervening territory.

With the exception of a few of the gem deposits, most of the minerals here described have been exploited commercially only within the past fifty years. They belong neither to that class of natural resources, such as coal and limestone, which are useful to a pioneer civilization, nor (with the exception of the gems) to the class of highly precious materials which attract the explorer or the adventurer. Their utilization was possible only after a very considerable development in the arts and industries of New England had taken place.

9

DEFINITION OF PEGMATITE.

The granite-pegmatites, in which are found feldspar, quartz, mica, and gem minerals, are composed of the same mineral constituents as the ordinary granites of the State, and differ from these principally in their greater coarseness and in their very uneven texture.

Among themselves the granite-pegmatites differ greatly in coarseness, some being little coarser than ordinary coarse-grained granite and others showing single masses of feldspar or of quartz 20 feet in diameter. Their distinguishing feature is, therefore, not coarseness of grain but extreme irregularity of grain. In a granite different grains of the same mineral species differ in size, but usually only within rather narrow limits. In a pegmatite, on the other hand, they appear to differ without limit, a crystal of feldspar an inch across perhaps having a neighbor which is several feet across. This textural feature is illustrated on a microscopic scale in Plate II, which is a reproduction of a photomicrograph of fine-grained aplitic pegmatite exposed in the river bed at Lewiston.

Pegmatite usually forms dikes or sill-like masses in areas occupied principally by rocks of other kinds. (See p. 11.)

GEOGRAPHIC DISTRIBUTION.

Pegmatites occur throughout the Appalachian Mountain region from Alabama to New York and thence northeastward into Connecticut, Massachusetts, New Hampshire, and Maine. In most of these States they have been worked commercially to a greater or less extent. In Maine the commercial deposits are confined largely to Cumberland, Sagadahoc, Lincoln, Androscoggin, and Oxford counties, though pegmatites also occur to some extent in Franklin, Kennebec, Waldo, Knox, Hancock, and Washington counties. Their general distribution, as well as that of the granites, is shown on Plate I, on which are also indicated the localities which have been worked commercially for various pegmatite minerals.

Excellent opportunities for studying the character and relationships of the pegmatites are afforded by many of the quarry openings, by numerous glaciated rock surfaces, and by almost continuous exposures along the seashore. The shore in the Boothbay region especially is an excellent field for study.

GEOLOGY.

BORDERING ROCKS.

The geologic relations of the Maine pegmatites show that most of them are distinctly intrusive into the surrounding rocks, although the conditions of intrusion are somewhat varied; and that in origin they are closely connected with the granites (p. 27). The rocks

MICROPHOTOGRAPH OF FINE-GRAINED PEGMATITE FROM RIVER BED AT LEWISTON.
MAGNIFIED ABOUT 34 TIMES.

Illustrates the extreme irregularity characteristic of the commonest type of pegmatitic texture.

A. HIGHLY INCLINED DIKE OF PEGMATITE IN SCHISTS AT PEMAQUID POINT, MAINE.

Showing characteristic swelling and pinching of dikes.

B. FLAT-LYING OR SILL-LIKE DIKE IN PEGMATITE INTRUDING GENTLY INCLINED
SEDIMENTARY SCHISTS. BED OF ANDROSCOGGIN RIVER, BETWEEN RAILWAY
AND HIGHWAY BRIDGES, AUBURN-LEWISTON, MAINE.

Showing lenslike form characteristic of many of these pegmatite masses.

A. INTIMATE INJECTION OF SEDIMENTARY SCHISTS BY PEGMATITE, FORMING AN
INJECTION GNEISS.

South shore of McMahon Island.

B. PEGMATITE MASS, SENDING OFF STRINGERS OF PEGMATITE AND QUARTZ INTO THE
BORDERING SCHIST AND THUS FORMING AN INJECTION GNEISS.

Bay Point Peninsula, Georgetown.

into which they are intruded are in some places granites, but are generally foliates,[a] either schist or gneiss. The foliates are in many places dynamically metamorphosed sediments, but in others are unquestionably primary.

PEGMATITES IN FOLIATED ROCKS.

General statement.—Though showing minor irregularities of form, most of the pegmatite masses in the foliated rocks are of sheetlike character and lie parallel or nearly parallel to the schist or gneiss folia. If the foliates are steeply inclined the pegmatite exhibits a dikelike form (Pl. III, *A*); if they are flat-lying the pegmatite mass assumes a sill-like form (Pl. III, *B*).

Another feature highly characteristic of pegmatite masses in foliates is their tendency to swell and thin along their trend so as to form virtually a series of connected lenticles. (See fig. 1.)

The contact between pegmatite and foliate is in nearly all areas very sharp, whether the pegmatite lies parallel to or cuts across the folia and whether its mass is large or small. In many places (see Pl. IV, *A*, *B*) the pegmatitic intrusion is so intimate that the bordering schist becomes an injection gneiss. Such gneisses

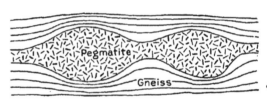

FIGURE 1.—Pinch and swell structure in pegmatite dike.

are very characteristic features of many districts in southern Maine, particularly in Oxford County.

Sedimentary foliates.—The sedimentary origin of many of the foliates associated with the pegmatites is shown beyond question at a number of localities by the preservation of distinct bedding in the more quartzose layers. Notable examples are the schists exposed at the Graphite mine at Crocker Hill (near Paris) and at many places in Auburn village and studied particularly at the new reservoir site, where the layers in which bedding is preserved are shown on microscopic study to be micaceous quartzite.

Since the pegmatite frequently cuts across the folia of the sedimentary schists and does not notably change the latter along the contacts, it is plain that the foliation of the schists is not a contact effect of the pegmatite intrusion. It is to be attributed mainly to regional metamorphism previous to the pegmatite intrusions. Since these foliates bear no traces of fossils, their age is indeterminate, but certain of them may be correlated with the Penobscot for-

---

[a] The term "foliates" was proposed by the writer (Jour. Geology, vol. 17, p. 449) as a convenient comprehensive term to include all rocks showing foliated structures other than bedding planes. Its use avoids frequent repetition of the terms schists and gneisses, and avoids any postulate as to the primary or secondary character of the foliated structure.

mation of the Penobscot Bay region.[a] As the last great dynamic metamorphism which affected southern and central Maine took place probably near the close of Ordovician time, these dynamically metamorphosed sediments are probably not younger than Ordovician.

Igneous foliates.—Others of the foliated rocks with which the pegmatites are associated are probably primary or flow foliates; that is, igneous rocks that owe their foliated structure to differential movement within their mass before complete solidification. To this class probably belong many of the foliates in the Boothbay Harbor region and about Brunswick and Topsham. Many of them are very similar in their general appearance to foliates of sedimentary origin but upon microscopic study are found to be indistinguishable in mineral composition from igneous rocks. One of the most instructive exposures of a foliate of this type occurs on the east shore of St. George River, near the extreme southern edge of the Rockland quadrangle, where porphyritic granite of normal composition, with feldspar phenocrysts from one-half to three-fourths of an inch in length, contains a number of elongated parallel lenses of much finer grained rock of dioritic composition. (See Pl. V, *A*.) The largest of these lenses is about 6 feet long and 1 foot wide. The inclosing granite shows a decided grain parallel to the direction of elongation of the lenses, and in other similar occurrences in this region the feldspar phenocrysts of the bordering granite show a tendency toward orientation with their long axes parallel to the axes of the basic lenses. Within a few rods of this exposure occurs another which presents the appearance shown in Plate V, *B*, the light-colored bands having about the texture and composition of normal granite and the darker bands being quartz diorite similar to the lenses at the exposure shown in Plate V, *A*.

Under the microscope the dioritic and granitic bands are both seen to be feldspathic and of interlocking granular texture without any cataclastic structures. The basic bands, however, besides being finer grained than the others, contain a much larger percentage of green hornblende and a smaller percentage of quartz. Both phases contain abundant titanite in grains, many of which show well-defined crystal form. The feldspar in both has the composition of oligoclase-andesine.

It seems evident that the gneiss of Plate V, *B*, represents merely the next step of the process of combined flowage and magmatic differentiation which developed the relations shown in Plate V, *A*, and that the two represent two stages in the making of a flow gneiss. At the time when the whole mass was in a molten condition the basic portions were presumably more fluid than the acidic portions, and the process is probably to be regarded as an intimate intrusion of

---

a Penobscot Bay folio (No. 149), Geol. Atlas U. S., U. S. Geol. Survey, 1907.

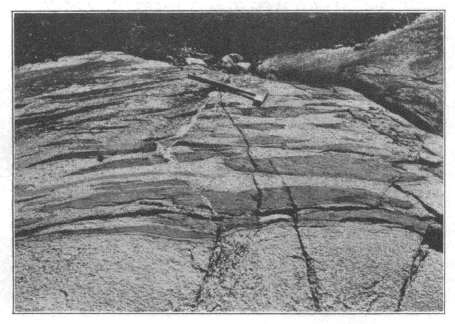

A. LENSES OF QUARTZ DIORITE IN PORPHYRITIC GRANITE. PROBABLY THE RESULT OF COMBINED FLOWAGE AND BASIC SEGREGATION ABOUT MANY CENTERS.

East shore of St. George River, near south border of Rockland quadrangle.

B. COARSE IGNEOUS GNEISS OF ALTERNATE LAYERS OF GRANITE AND QUARTZ DIORITE.

Same locality. Showing a further step in the process illustrated above.

the more viscous by the less viscous portions of the same magma when both were under lateral compression.

At an old road-metal quarry in the city of Brunswick schists of probable igneous origin are also well exposed in association with pegmatite. The schists show very even and regular foliation and an alternation of broad light-gray layers with narrower ones which are dark gray to nearly black. The lighter bands are seen under the microscope to be a hornblende granite of interlocking granular texture and without cataclastic structures. The foliated structure is due to a greater abundance of hornblende along certain planes than along others and to subparallel elongation of the hornblende grains. The dark-gray phases of the schist have the mineral composition of quartz diorite, the feldspar being largely andesine. A few bands up to one-eighth inch or so across are a more coarsely crystalline association of quartz with a little feldspar. These schists carry none of the minerals, such as staurolite and andalusite, frequently observed in metamorphosed sediments, and though their derivation by metamorphism from arkoses or graywackes is conceivable it is not probable. The pegmatite associated with these schists locally cuts across their foliation, but in other places grades into them so completely as to suggest that the schist was not completely solidified at the time the pegmatite was intruded.

Here and at a number of other localities a slight foliation parallel to the schist folia is visible in some of the pegmatites; it suggests a slight flowing movement in the schist subsequent to the intrusion of the pegmatite. The thickening of the schist folia opposite the nodes of pegmatite dikes and their thinning opposite the bulges (see fig. 1) is also indicative of flowing movements in the schists at the time the pegmatite was intruded. Many of the pegmatite bodies associated with the primary flow foliates are probably to be regarded as intrusions under high pressure of a less viscous into a more viscous magma.

PEGMATITES IN MASSIVE GRANITES.

The relationships exhibited at a number of localities between the pegmatites and the granites throw much light on the origin of the former. Of broad significance is the fact that granite is present in all of the districts in which pegmatite occurs. The reverse relation also holds, though to a lesser degree. The similarity in mineral composition between the granites and the pegmatites will be considered later.

The detailed relationships existing between the two rocks are various. At the Woodside quarry in the town of Brunswick, $2\frac{1}{2}$ miles southeast of Hillside station, a rather fine-grained muscovite-biotite granite has been quarried for flagging and underpinning. In it the pegmatite often forms lens-shaped or wholly irregular bodies, the two rocks being characterized by the same minerals and grading into each other in the most gradual and complete manner. In such cases there can be no question that the two rocks crystallized from the same magma and that the pegmatitic masses are to be regarded as segregations within the granite. In other places, however, even at this same quarry, pegmatite, which in general appearance and mineral composition is indistinguishable from that described above, forms sharp-walled dikes in the granite.

An exposure on the shore of the first point west of Boothbay Harbor shows a dike of fine-grained granite 1½ feet wide cutting schist and pegmatite. A few feet farther north the same granite dike is itself cut by pegmatite that is wholly similar in appearance to the pegmatite which the granite intrudes. These relations show that the pegmatites are not precisely contemporaneous. Since, however, there is no evidence here or elsewhere in Maine of very wide divergence in the age of different pegmatites or different granites (see p. 15), the exposure also shows the broad contemporaneity of granite and pegmatite.

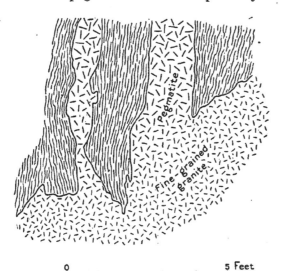

FIGURE 2.—Gradation of granite into pegmatite, Boothbay Harbor.

On the island of Southport, on the shore near the south entrance of Townsend Gut, the schist, granite, and pegmatite are associated in the manner shown in figure 2. Both are distinctly intrusive, the schist contacts being everywhere sharp and in many places very ragged. The main mass of the intrusion is granite of normal texture, but the narrower branches sent off by the granite parallel to the foliation of the schists become typical pegmatite a short distance from the granite mass. The gradation between the two rocks is gradual and complete.

Under the microscope the granite shows an interlocking granular texture and consists principally of quartz and microcline, with minor amounts of orthoclase, of biotite altering to chlorite, and of muscovite, in part primary and in part a product of feldspar alteration. Micrographic granite is present in small amounts, as are scattered small grains of oligoclase. The minerals of the pegmatite are identical with those of the granite but occur in much larger crystals, with much greater range in size among individuals of the same mineral species. Oligoclase and micrographic intergrowths of quartz and feldspar are also more abundant in the pegmatite than in the granite.

For detailed descriptions of other instances of gradations or close relationship between granite and pegmatite the reader is referred to locality descriptions of the Rumford Falls region (p. 94), Stow (p. 102), Edgecomb (p. 64), Boothbay Harbor (p. 67), and the South Waterford mica mine (p. 103).

The granites and associated pegmatites are the youngest known rocks occurring in notable abundance within the State. Here and there, however, they are cut by younger small dikes of diabase, usually aphanitic and sharp walled. Usually these occur only as individuals, but on the shore of Keewaydin Lake (Lower Stone Pond), near the village of East Stoneham, schist and associated pegmatite are intruded by a remarkable network of fine-grained diabase. (See Pl. XVI, *A*.)

AGE.

The field studies in Maine have afforded no evidence of great diversity in age among the pegmatite deposits. Although all of them are not strictly contemporaneous, it seems probable that all were formed within the limits of a single period of geologic time. As it has been shown (p. 27) that the pegmatites are broadly contemporaneous with the granites with which they are invariably associated, the age of the pegmatites may be inferred from that of the granites.

The evidence thus far available indicates that all of the granites of the State are of approximately the same geologic age. In the Penobscot Bay region granite is intrusive in rocks of Silurian (Niagaran) age.[a] In the Perry Basin,[b] in the extreme eastern part of the State, granite pebbles are absent from the late Silurian sediments but are present in the conglomerate of the Perry formation, which is probably of Upper Devonian age. The granites were therefore intruded in late Silurian or in Devonian time, and the pegmatites are also probably of that age.

GENERAL CHARACTER.

MINERAL AND CHEMICAL COMPOSITION.

Mineral constituents.—The pegmatite deposits in all parts of the State show great similarity in their principal minerals, although exhibiting notable differences in their minor constituents. Essentially they are coarse granites, their principal light-colored constituents being potash and soda feldspars, quartz, and muscovite,

---

a Penobscot Bay folio (No. 149), Geol. Atlas U. S., U. S. Geol. Survey, 1907.

b Smith, G. O., and White, David, Geology of the Perry Basin: Prof. Paper U. S. Geol. Survey No. 35, 1905.

and their principal dark-colored constituents black mica (biotite) and black tourmaline. In pegmatites in which black mica is abundant black tourmaline is almost always rare or absent, and vice versa. Accessory constituents present in almost all pegmatites are garnet, magnetite, and green opaque beryl. Accessory minerals present only in certain pegmatites number over fifty species, the most important probably being lepidolite or lithium mica; amblygonite; spodumene; blue, green, and pink tourmaline; transparent green, pale-blue, or golden beryl; colorless to amber-colored topaz; and rose and amethystine quartz.

The following minerals have been reported from the pegmatite deposits of Maine:

Albite.—Common in many of the pegmatite deposits; in some places massive, but usually occurring as the white lamellar variety clevelandite. Especially abundant in gem-bearing pegmatites.

Allanite.—Reported from pegmatite at Mount Apatite, in Auburn.

Amblygonite.—An original constituent of many of the pegmatite deposits, especially those bearing gem minerals.

Apatite.—Occurs as an original pegmatite constituent wholly inclosed by other minerals in many pegmatite deposits. The fine purple apatites of Mount Apatite, in Auburn, occur on the walls of pockets and were probably deposited by aqueous or pneumatolytic agencies during the latest stages of the pegmatite crystallization.

Arsenopyrite.—Reported from pegmatite at Mount Rubellite, in Hebron.

Autunite.—Occurs at the Dunton tourmaline mine in Newry, Oxford County, in crystals seldom over $\frac{1}{16}$ inch across, embedded in or lying between plates of clevelandite. Mostly decomposed. Found also at Harndon Hill, in Stoneham.

Bertrandite.—Occurs with herderite and hamlinite in cavities in pegmatite at Stoneham.

Beryl.—Translucent to opaque varieties, wholly inclosed by other constituents, occur in nearly all the coarser pegmatite bodies. A few crystals reach gigantic proportions. In a few coarse pegmatites transparent pale-green gem varieties (aquamarine) occur completely embedded or projecting from the walls of cavities.

Beryllonite.—Not found in place, but occurring in the soil in Stoneham. It is attached to typical pegmatite minerals and is plainly an original pegmatite constituent.

Biotite.—One of the abundant constituents of most of the pegmatites.

Calcite.—Not observed as an original pegmatite constituent, but occurs occasionally as a secondary deposit in fissures and cavities.

Cassiterite.—An original constituent in pegmatite at Paris, Hebron, Stoneham, and Auburn.

Childrenite.—Reported as an original constituent of pegmatite at Mount Rubellite, in Hebron, occurring in minute hair-brown prismatic crystals with amblygonite.

Chrysoberyl.—An original pegmatite constituent at a large number of localities, though nowhere abundant.

Clevelandite.—See Albite.

Columbite.—An original constituent of certain pegmatites. Present only in small amounts.

Cookeite.—Abundant as a coating in most of the pockets in the coarser pegmatites. Not an original constituent but secondary and due to water deposition.

Damourite.—Occurs at Mount Rubellite, in Hebron, as an alteration product of tourmaline. Also reported from Mount Apatite, in Auburn.

Emerald.—Gem beryl found in Maine is usually so pale that it is classed as aquamarine. One fractured crystal found by the writer at the Dunton mine in Newry could properly be classed as a pale emerald.

Feldspar.—One of the principal pegmatite minerals. See albite, orthoclase, and microcline.

Fluorite.—Small crystals occur as an original constituent in a few of the pegmatites, but in general fluorite is much rarer in the Maine pegmatites than in those of certain other regions.

Garnet.—A common constituent of most of the pegmatites. Frequently occurs in graphic intergrowth with quartz, muscovite, or feldspar. Garnet of gem clearness is extremely rare.

Graphite.—Absent from most of the Maine pegmatites. Occurs in pegmatite injected into sedimentary schists at a few localities.

Gummite.—Reported in minute particles from pegmatite at Mount Apatite, in Auburn. An alteration product of some uranium mineral.

Halloysite.—Reported from Mount Mica. Probably a decomposition product of feldspar.

Hamlinite.—Occurs sparingly at Stoneham, associated with herderite and bertrandite.

Hebronite.—See Amblygonite.

Herderite.—Found at Stoneham, Me., on quartz crystals in pockets in the pegmatite. Found sparingly in Hebron and Greenwood, at Mount Apatite in Auburn, and at Berry's quarry in Poland.

Kaolinite.—A decomposition product of feldspar. Common in pockets in the coarser pegmatites.

Limonite.—A secondary mineral in some pegmatites, resulting from the decomposition of other iron-bearing minerals.

Lepidolite.—Common in pegmatites which bear gem tourmalines.

Löllingite.—Occurs in narrow stringers cutting feldspar at Mount Mica, in Paris, as an original pegmatite constituent.

Magnetite.—Common in many pegmatites in well-developed step-crystals.

Microcline.—One of the commonest constituents in the pegmatites. Most of the potash feldspar present is microcline rather than orthoclase.

Mica.—See Biotite, Muscovite, and Lepidolite.

Molybdenite.—Abundant as an original constituent in granite and associated pegmatite at Catherine Hill in Hancock County, and reported in small amounts in similar rocks elsewhere. Reported from pegmatite in Auburn. Rare in most pegmatite bodies.

Montmorillonite.—Associated with cookeite and other secondary minerals in the pockets of several of the coarser pegmatite masses. A product of feldspar decomposition.

Muscovite.—One of the principal constituents in nearly all pegmatites.

Orthoclase.—Present with microcline in nearly all of the pegmatites, the two being commonly intergrown in the same crystal.

Phenacite.—Reported from pegmatite at Noyes's tourmaline mine in Greenwood.

Plumbago.—See Graphite.

Pollucite.—Occurs in pockets in pegmatite at Mount Rubellite in Hebron.

Pyrite.—An original constituent in many Maine pegmatites.

Pyrrhotite.—An original pegmatite constituent at Mount Mica, in Paris, and at a few other localities.

Quartz.—White or gray; one of the principal constituents of all the pegmatites. Massive rose quartz occurs in a few places and crystal groups of amethystine and smoky quartz are developed here and there on the walls of pockets in the pegmatite.

Rhodochrosite.—An original pegmatite constituent at the Towne quarry in Auburn.

Schorl.—See Tourmaline.

Spinel.—Reported from pegmatite at Cobble Hill in Norway.

Spodumene.—Common in many of the coarser pegmatites, especially those that carry gem tourmalines, lepidolite, and other lithium minerals.

Titanite.—A minor original constituent of many of the pegmatites.

Topaz.—An original constituent of a few of the coarser pegmatites. Usually forms crystals on the walls of cavities. A massive constituent of some of the solid pegmatites.

Tourmaline.—Schorl or black tourmaline is a common constituent of many of the pegmatites. Colored tourmalines occur in some, in many places completely inclosed by other minerals, but in others implanted on the walls or lying on the floors of cavities.

Triphylite.—An original pegmatite mineral at Harndon Hill in Stoneham. Associated with spodumene in Peru.

Triplite.—An original constituent of pegmatite in Auburn and Stoneham. Present only in small amounts.

Vesuvianite.—Reported from pegmatite at Mount Rubellite in Hebron.

Yttrocerite.—Reported from pegmatite at Mount Mica, in Paris.

Zircon.—Reported from pegmatite in Auburn and Norway and from Mount Mica, in Paris.

Relative proportions of minerals.—Not only are a great variety of minerals present in the pegmatites, but there is also much variability in their relative proportions. In the vast majority of deposits the pegmatite minerals appear to be present in very nearly the same proportions as in the associated granites. Variations in their proportions are principally along two lines, the first involving an increase in silica, the pegmatite becoming more quartzose; and the second involving an increase in both sodium and lithia, the pegmatite becoming rich in albite (variety clevelandite) and in the lithium minerals, lepidolite, spodumene, colored tourmaline, and amblygonite. A minor variation involving an increase in the fluorine content is shown by the presence of the fluorine minerals topaz, fluorite, herderite, hamlinite, certain types of apatite, etc. Increase in soda and lithium and increase in fluorine are both usually accompanied by some increase in the phosphorus content. Cavities which were probably originally filled with water are more abundant in the soda-lithium rich pegmatites than in the normal pegmatites. As shown later, the magmas from which the former solidified were presumably more aqueous than those of the normal pegmatites.

Quartzose phase.—The first type of variation, increase in the quartz content, is not as common a phenomena in Maine as in certain other regions where pegmatites are abundant, and it commonly takes place on a small scale only.[a] Quartzose phases of the pegmatite are particularly well shown on a nearly bare hilltop 2½ miles northeast of Paris in Oxford County, where the pegmatite is cut by a number of quartz veins or dikes mostly under 6 inches wide and mostly parallel to a rather poorly defined system of joints in the pegmatite. Some

---

[a] Certain large quartz dikes may be genetically connected with the pegmatite magmas. Such connection has not as yet, however, been proved.

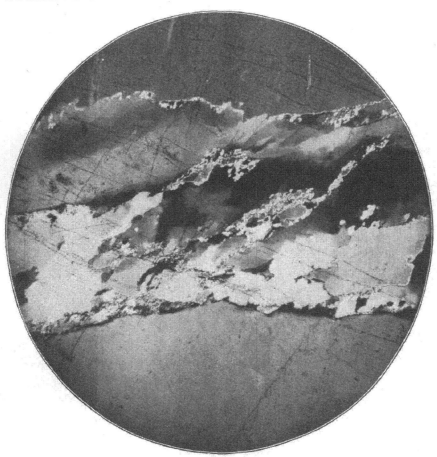

ZONE OF STRAIN, FRACTURE, AND RECRYSTALLIZATION IN ROSE QUARTZ FROM NORWAY,
MAINE.

Magnified about 34 diameters. Shows the continuance of certain of the straight bands of inclusions from
the unstrained quartz into the strained zone.

of these quartz veins possess very sharp boundaries, but others are only vaguely delimited from the pegmatite. The quartz veins of the latter type are particularly likely to contain scattered crystals of orthoclase-microcline and some muscovite and black tourmaline. Black tourmaline is also in some of the veins associated with quartz alone, the two minerals being in many places intimately intergrown. In some narrow veins the black tourmaline may be more abundant than the quartz. In one place the genetic relation between a quartz vein and the pegmatite was shown in the unequivocal manner illustrated in figure 3. Contemporaneous quartz dikes in pegmatite are also well exposed in the Boothbay Harbor region. (See p. 166.)

At a large number of localities, where injection gneisses are associated with pegmatite, quartz stringers in the gneiss can be traced into continuity with the pegmatite. A striking instance of this is illustrated in Plate IV, *B*.

In the Maine deposits quartz is very rarely found in distinct bands in dikes or sills of pegmatite. In a single small dike in Topsham some concentration of quartz in the central portion of the dike was observed, the feldspar being concentrated mainly along the walls.

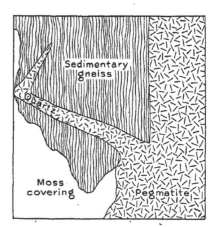

FIGURE 3.—Quartz offshoot from pegmatite, Paris, Me.

Four thin sections of rose, white, and gray quartz from the larger quartz masses in the pegmatites were examined under the microscope. One of these consisted of a single quartz individual, but the other three showed several interlocking quartz grains within the small area covered by the microscope slide. The quartz in all of these showed little or no strain except along an occasional zone of fracturing and recrystallization such as that shown in Plate VI. In one specimen of quartz from a quartz-rich pegmatite near Cumberland Mills (see p. 62) all of the grains are much strained and are granulated along their borders. Like the development of mica-coated shear planes in certain pegmatites, this indicates slight local shearing movements subsequent to some of the pegmatite crystallization. Such phenomena are the exception, however, and not the rule.

Fluidal cavities.—Fluidal cavities of microscopic dimensions are abundant in most of the pegmatite quartz examined. They are very similar in character in almost all the quartzes, characteristic forms being shown in figure 4. Nearly all contain a vacuole or gas bubble, which in the larger cavities reverses its position in the cavity when the slide is rotated in a vertical plane, moving always slowly toward the top of the cavity and thus indicating that the vacuole is of lower density than the inclosing fluid. An examination of a number of thin sections of Maine granites shows that the inclusions in the quartzes of both pegmatites and granite are similar in character and distribution and are not noticeably different in abundance. In both types of rocks the fluidal cavities are generally arranged in bands, most of which are nearly straight, though some are wavy. Some of these bands terminate abruptly at the border of a quartz grain, but others pass without change or deflection from one quartz grain to another.

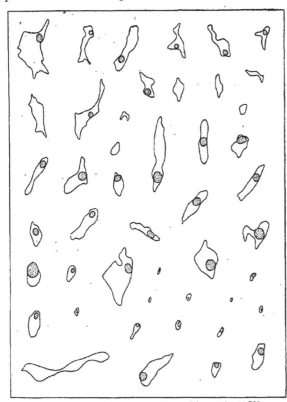

FIGURE 4.—Fluidal cavities in pegmatitic quartz, × 360.

In the rose quartz illustrated in Plate VI some of the bands of fluid inclusions in the larger quartz grains terminate abruptly at the sheared and recrystallized zone and others continue into it. Bands of inclusions also pass from grain to grain within the sheared zone. It appears therefore that some of the bands of inclusions are not only later than the original crystallization of the quartz but are later even than the straining, granulation, and recrystallization which subsequently affected it.

The tint and degree of opacity exhibited by the quartz seems to be dependent in some measure on the abundance and distribution of the inclusions. In several pieces of dirty-gray, opaque quartz, inclusions were particularly abundant and were not confined to bands but were also scattered irregularly through the quartz. A thin section of transparent smoky quartz from the Berry quarry in Poland was seen under the highest available power of the microscope (540 diameters) to be clouded with inclusions so minute that their character could not be made out. They were not arranged in bands and the usual type of fluidal cavities was entirely absent. It is not uncommon for the inclusions in pegmatite quartzes to be in two dominant sets of bands nearly at right angles to each other and showing considerable uniformity of trend throughout the area of the thin section. A thin section of an intergrowth of quartz and garnet from Mount Apatite showed well-developed bands of inclusions in both minerals, though the bands were most abundant and regular in the quartz. The inclusions appeared to be of the same type in both, but none were observed to pass from one mineral to the other. Alternating bands of clear and opaque quartz conspicuous to the unaided eye in the quartz of certain pegmatites are due to the much greater abundance of fluidal cavities in the opaque areas.

Dale[a] reports fluidal cavities ranging from 0.00285 to 0.062 millimeter in Redstone, N. H., granite. Fluid inclusions in the quartz and garnet intergrowth described above ranged from 0.0015 to 0.0068 millimeter. Those in the quartz of fine-grained granite associated with pegmatite at Rumford Falls ranged from 0.0015 to 0.01 millimeter in diameter. In the associated pegmatite from the same locality inclusions similar in character occurred in bands and showed the same range in size. In both of the Rumford Falls rocks the bands of inclusions in the quartz terminate abruptly against bordering feldspars. In the latter mineral no fluidal cavities were observed.

Sodium and lithium phases.—Increase in the proportions of sodium and lithium in the pegmatites results in the formation, in regions where most of the pegmatite is of normal character, of a few bands or zones characterized by the presence of clevelandite, lepidolite, spodumene, and colored tourmalines in addition to the more common pegmatite minerals. The rich tourmaline-bearing pegmatites of Mount Mica and Mount Apatite are of this type. Increase in the phosphorus content is shown by the presence of amblygonite in nearly all such deposits. The sodium and lithium rich pegmatites are confined almost exclusively to the western part of Androscoggin County and to the central and eastern part of Oxford County; practically all occur within a radius of 30 miles from Mount Mica, the richest discovered locality. Although it is true that the pegmatites within this area are richer than the normal pegmatites in sodium and lithium their average composition is but slightly different, since even within this area the sodium and lithium rich phases constitute only a small proportion of the total mass of the pegmatite.

Fluorine phase.—Some sodium and lithium rich pegmatites carry fluorine minerals, but pegmatites carrying fluorine and phosphorus minerals alone in addition to the normal pegmatite constituents are confined largely to the western part of Oxford County. Even there they constitute but a small proportion of the total mass of pegmatite present.

a Dale, T. N., Commercial granites of Massachusetts, New Hampshire, and Rhode Island: Bull. U. S. Geol. Survey No. 354, 1908, p. 42.

Muscovite phase.—A few deposits showing local increases in the proportion of muscovite have been worked for this mineral in the past, but have not been commercially successful.

TEXTURE.

The pegmatites show remarkable differences in coarseness, some, especially the narrower dikes and sills, being but little coarser than medium-grained granites, though differing strikingly from the latter in texture, and others containing single crystals of nearly pure feldspar 20 feet across and single beryl crystals the diameter of a hogshead. The majority of the deposits are nearer the lower limit than the higher. Only the coarsest deposits are commercially valuable for their feldspar, quartz, mica, or gem minerals, and these constitute a relatively small percentage of the total mass of pegmatitic material present in any district. In most of the pegmatites worked commercially the feldspar and quartz crystals will not average more than 4 or 5 feet in diameter.

Irregularity of grain.—The most striking characteristic of the texture of the pegmatites, with the exception of the graphic intergrowths described below, is their irregularity. Typical granites show considerable uniformity in the size of grains of the same mineral species, but the pegmatites show no such regularity, a feldspar crystal, for example, being as likely to be two or three or even ten times as large as an adjacent crystal as to be of equivalent size. This feature is shown on a microscopic scale in Plate II.

Graphic granite.—Most of the pegmatites contain much graphic granite, formed by an intimate intergrowth or interpenetration of large single crystals of quartz and feldspar. In certain directions through these intergrowths the quartz forms an angular pattern somewhat resembling the cuneiform inscriptions of the ancients. (See Pl. XVIII.) Fine-grained phases pass in the most gradual manner into coarser graphic granite (Pl. VII); and the latter, by decrease in the percentage of quartz, may pass into masses of pure feldspar, or by decrease in the percentage of feldspar into masses of pure quartz. Much of the material mined as "spar" is coarse-grained graphic granite containing from 10 to 20 per cent of free quartz.

On casual inspection the coarser types of graphic granite appear to contain a somewhat larger proportion of feldspar than the finer-grained types. Chemical analyses of graphic granites of different coarseness from Maine and from other districts indicate, however, that the proportion of feldspar to quartz bears no marked relation to the coarseness. Such variations as do occur are within relatively narrow limits and appear to be dependent on the composition of the feldspar and on other factors not yet understood. Analyses of graphic granites of widely different coarseness from the Fisher

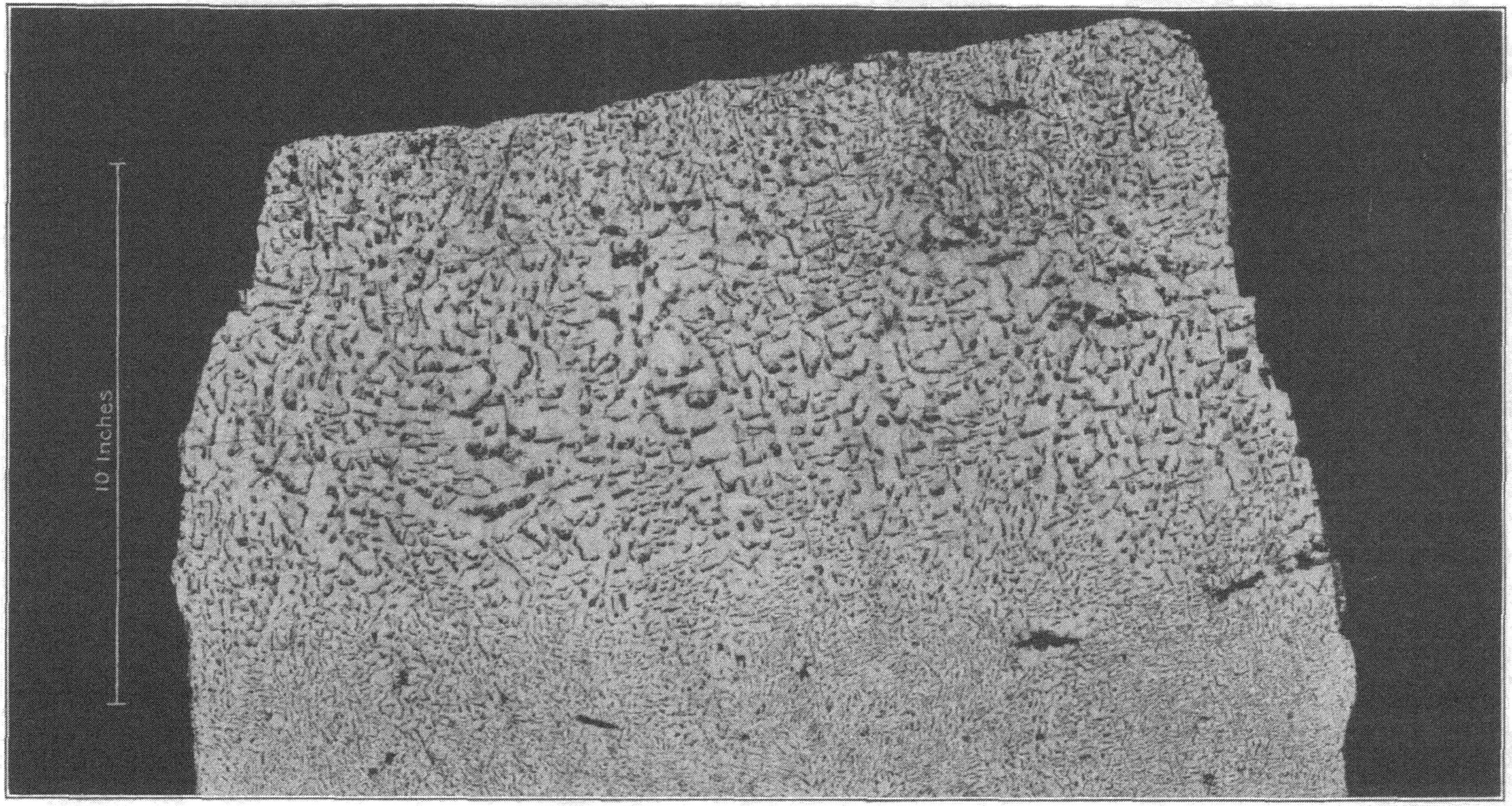

BULLETIN 445   PLATE VII

GRAPHIC INTERGROWTH OF MICROCLINE AND QUARTZ OF GRADUALLY VARYING COARSENESS.

Mount Apatite, Auburn. From specimen in U. S. National Museum.

feldspar quarry in Topsham are given on page 124. In the quarry these two rocks graded gradually into one another, and as shown by the analyses the proportion of feldspar to quartz is nearly identical in both. The samples analyzed were obtained by grinding five or six pounds of each granite and quartering down the product to a quantity convenient for analysis. Some allowance must, of course, be made for the difficulty in procuring a sample that is truly representative of the rock mass. This difficulty was greater in the case of the coarser rock.

Feldspar "brushes."—A very uncommon type of graphic granite was observed only in Topsham, in the G. D. Willes feldspar quarry, where it was exposed on the extreme southern wall in dikelike bands in the normal pegmatite up to a foot or so in width. These bands appear to the unaided eye to consist largely of buff-colored feldspar with different though minor amounts of biotite. The feldspar forms an aggregate of brush-shaped or long fan-shaped crystals placed with their long axes at right angles to the general trend of the dikelike band. A faint banding in these layers parallel to their general trend and at right angles to the trend of the feldspar brushes somewhat simulates bedding.

This banding is the combined effect (1) of a greater abundance of biotite along certain layers than along others; (2) of the presence of zones quite even in width, characterized by a coarser intergrowth of feldspar and quartz than the adjacent layers, though generally showing crystallographic continuity from one layer to another and even into a third layer; and (3) of the presence of some parting along planes parallel to the *a* pinacoid and resulting slight clouding of the feldspar by alteration along these fractures.

Single feldspar brushes range in length from a fraction of an inch to 3 inches. The biotite forms thin knife-blade crystals which range in lenght from microscopic dimensions up to three-fourths of an inch and are oriented in about the same direction as the feldspar brushes, penetrating or lying between them.

Under the microscope the brush-shaped crystals are seen to be made up not of feldspar alone but of a graphic intergrowth of quartz and feldspar of microscopic dimensions. The brushlike form represents, however, the form of the feldspar crystal. Quartz having one optical orientation frequently extends from one feldspar crystal into a neighboring one. The microscope shows also that the feldspar is not all of one variety. That forming the brush-shaped crystals is largely microcline, but some plagioclase, mostly in aggregates of irregular grains between the brush-shaped crystals, is associated with it. The plagioclase is albite and is in places graphically intergrown with quartz. Quartz with the same optical orientation in many instances continues from a crystal of microcline into a neighboring one of albite.

The long straight blades of biotite are idiomorphic with respect to the quartz and feldspar grains and their intergrowths. The biotite blades are paralleled in many specimens by an abundance of microscopic blades of muscovite alternating with thin layers of quartz. Other blades of muscovite traverse the rock in the same manner that biotite does, though they are much smaller.

The coarseness of the graphic intergrowth of quartz and feldspar described above varies notably, even where only one quartz and one feldspar individual are involved. There does not appear, however, to be any important difference in the relative proportions of the minerals involved. On the contrary, it is notable that the areas of graphic intergrowth, whether coarse or fine, terminate very abruptly against areas of pure feldspar that are crystallographically continuous with the feldspar of the intergrowth (Pl. VIII) and that show no transition through intergrowths characterized by progressively smaller proportions of quartz. The quartz and feldspar thus appear to be intergrown in rather definite proportions or not at all.[a]

Very little is known of the physical-chemical conditions that produce the peculiar types of crystallization described above. The mode of occurrence in the Alaskan and New Mexican examples suggests, however, that the brush-shaped crystals developed rapidly in a border portion of the magma where the temperature gradient was

[a] Adolph Knopf, of the U. S. Geological Survey, in a personal communication states that he has observed radiating graphic intergrowths identical with those of the Maine specimens in rocks from the Cape Mountain region near Cape Prince of Wales in Alaska. The specimen brought from the field was indistinguishable in appearance from the Maine specimens except that the graphic intergrowth was slightly finer grained. Its mode of occurrence, however, was wholly different. It occurs at the border of sills of microcline-orthoclase-biotite granite which radiate from a central granite massif at their contact with limestones. The latter have been metamorphosed by the granite with the development, within 3 feet of the contact, of numerous contact-metamorphic minerals. The contact zones of micrographic granite range up to 8 inches or so in width, though the individual brush-shaped crystals are not over 4 inches in length. In a microscopic section parallel to the long axis of one of the "brushes" and about parallel to the c (001) pinacoid of one of the feldspar crystals, the cross sections of the quartz bands are for the most part elongate rod-shaped. In some of these the long axis is the direction of fastest light transmission; in others it is the direction of slowest. Single microcline crystals may be intergrown with several quartz crystals, each with slightly different orientation and slightly different trend of their blades, which repeat in miniature the brushlike forms assumed by the microcline crystals. A feature observed in both the Maine and Alaskan specimens is the frequent abrupt termination of the quartzes along planes transverse to the axes of the brushes, other sets of intergrown quartzes beginning with equal abruptness farther on. The microcline is crystallographically continuous across these hiatuses. In other places the fine graphic intergrowths are succeeded abruptly along planes at right angles to the length of the brushes by coarse ones. As in the Maine specimen, grains of albite, usually graphically intergrown with quartz, occur between some of the quartz-microcline "brushes," and between others occurs a granular aggregate of quartz, microcline, and albite. There are occasional short blades of biotite.

Bands of brush-shaped intergrowths of feldspar and quartz, similar in appearance to the Maine and Alaska occurrences but of microscopic dimensions, were also studied in a microscope slide in the collection of the United States Geological Survey. This shows the contact between a coarse quartz diorite and an intrusive aplite dike from New Mexico. For 0.15 millimeter from the diorite contact occurs a granular aggregate of quartz and feldspar so fine that it may represent a devitrified glass; the next zone, 0.60 millimeter in average width, is made up of brush-shaped intergrowths of feldspar and quartz radiating from the finely crystalline zone mentioned above into the main mass of aplite.

Frank C. Calkins, of the United States Geological Survey, reports in a personal communication the occurrence near Anaconda, Mont., of borders 1½ inches or so in width similar to the Alaskan and Maine occurrences in general appearance, at the contact between diorite and an intrusive mass of biotite granite. No specimens of these were collected for study but presumably they are similar in structure to those here described.

PHOTOMICROGRAPH OF GRAPHIC GRANITE FROM TOPSHAM, MAINE.

Magnified about 34 diameters.   Note the abrupt termination of areas of graphic intergrowth against areas
of pure feldspar, even where the feldspar is crystallographically continuous from one to the other.

steep. In general the brushes are elongate in the direction probably
characterized by the most rapid temperature variation, that is, at
right angles to the bordering wall. It is possible that progressive
differences in concentration of the magmatic solution as the wall
rock was approached were also in part the cause of the faster growth
of the crystals in that direction. The brush-shaped crystals noted
in Maine unquestionably represent a phase of the pegmatite crystallization, evidently one of its later stages.

In addition to the graphic intergrowths of feldspar and quartz the
quartz in many of the Maine pegmatites assumes branching or
arborescent forms in the feldspar.

Intergrowths of minor constituents.—Graphic intergrowths are not
confined to feldspar and quartz but even in the same pegmatite mass
may often be found between several of the less abundant constituents. The most common of these are intergrowths of muscovite and
quartz in which a single crystal of muscovite is penetrated both
parallel to and across its laminæ by quartz. The quartz in some
specimens seems to be one crystal, in others, several. The pattern
produced on surfaces parallel to the muscovite cleavage resembles
that of graphic granite but is somewhat less regular. In some specimens these intergrowths are fine-grained in their centers and become
progressively coarser outward, terminating occasionally in blade-
shaped crystals of muscovite. In some places the intergrowths are
brush or rosette-shaped, and in others the graphic intergrowths form
borders about sharply bounded hexagonal crystals of muscovite, the
muscovite of the intergrowth being crystallographically continuous
with that of the crystal core.

Intergrowths of quartz and garnet are also common and in certain
directions through them have a more or less graphic pattern. Some
of these intergrowths are 2 to 3 inches across and they commonly
possess well-defined crystal faces, their outer portions being almost
entirely garnet. When broken open, however, they are seen to be
intergrowths of garnet with quartz, the rods and blades of the latter
in many places radiating toward the crystal faces. Garnet is locally
intergrown with the quartz of the quartz-muscovite intergrowths.

Intergrowths of quartz and black tourmaline are also common,
the tourmaline usually radiating from a core composed wholly of
tourmaline. At Mount Mica clusters of nearly parallel black tourmaline crystals, mostly from one-eighth to one-half inch in diameter, embedded in a satiny matrix of very minute muscovite flakes
are occasionally found. The tourmaline rods of these intergrowths
commonly emerge from the end of a large tourmaline crystal.

Intergrowths occur of a character less regular and intimate than
those already described. Microcline feldspar is locally intergrown
to some extent with muscovite, lying between the mica folia or

cutting across them. Many small garnets with well-developed
crystal forms are partly or wholly inclosed by muscovite. Lath-
shaped crystals of biotite bordered by muscovite are sometimes
found, the cleavage planes of the two micas being absolutely coin-
cident. Crystals of tourmaline lying in somewhat flattened form
between the plates of a mica crystal are common, and some small,
colored specimens are of much delicacy and beauty. At Black
Mountain, in Rumford, spodumene was observed intimately intergrown with quartz.

Mica.—In many of the pegmatite bodies muscovite is not evenly
distributed throughout the mass but is most abundant in certain
zones. (See Pl. IX, *A*.) These zones appear to be distributed
through the pegmatite in a totally haphazard manner, bearing no
relation to the general form of the pegmatite mass nor to the position
of the wall rocks. The central portions of these muscovite belts for
a width of a few inches consist of an aggregate of heterogeneously
arranged muscovite plates, few of them more than one-fourth inch in
diameter. (The hammer head in the illustration, Pl. IX, *A*, rests
on one of these central fine-grained portions.) They are commonly
plane or only gently undulating throughout their length and, being
lines of weakness, are usually marked by a fracture plane. From this
fine-grained portion spearhead-shaped books of muscovite, showing
wedge structure (see p. 139), project in a direction nearly at right
angles to the general plane of the mica belt; some of these muscovite
books are a foot in length. This peculiar distribution of muscovite
is not readily explainable; but it seems to represent a muscovite
crystallization proceeding not from a single center, but from a plane
or from a large number of centers lying in nearly the same plane. In
the pegmatite of the Black Mountain mica mine in Rumford, where
the mica locally constitutes three-fourths of the pegmatite mass, the
elongate mica books near the schist wall rock tend to orient themselves
with their long axes perpendicular to the contact. In a number of
quarries muscovite crystallization about a center is exemplified by
the presence of nearly equidimensional aggregates, some of them 5
feet across, consisting of small heterogeneously arranged plates averaging about one-fourth inch in diameter. From their peripheries
these muscovite aggregates send off spearhead-shaped muscovite
books into the surrounding pegmatite.

Biotite may occur in isolated lath-shaped crystals penetrating the
pegmatite in all directions or in radiating aggregates of such crystals.

Gem-bearing pegmatites.—Pegmatites particularly rich in gem minerals exhibit peculiarities of structure not present in the normal rock.
Lithium minerals, such as colored tourmalines, lepidolite, spodumene, etc., and the soda feldspar clevelandite, are concentrated in a
zone which usually parallels the plane of greatest dimension of the

A. MUSCOVITE-RICH ZONES IN PEGMATITE. G. D. WILLES FELDSPAR QUARRY, TOPSHAM.

B. POCKET, ABOUT 3 FEET IN DIAMETER, IN GEM-BEARING LAYER AT MOUNT MICA. OPENED JUNE, 1904.

The giant compound tourmaline crystal shown in Plate XIV came from this pocket; also another similar but smaller compound tourmaline crystal; two large simple tourmaline crystals, one of which is shown in Plate XV; about $1,300 worth of red and pink gem tourmalines; and about $300 worth of green gem tourmalines. In all the pocket yielded about 75 pounds of tourmaline. Photograph by Mr. A. A. Norton, of Portland, Maine.

commonly lens-shaped pegmatite body. Within this zone pockets are also apt to be particularly abundant. Pockets are found in some of the normal pegmatites also, but their disposition seems to be wholly sporadic and most of them are barren of gem minerals, though some contain groups of fine quartz crystals or of small feldspar crystals on their walls.

In the richly gem-bearing pegmatites the zone of sodium and lithium minerals is generally separated from the normal pegmatite which borders it by a highly garnetiferous zone from an inch to several inches wide, the garnet being associated with a granular aggregate of quartz and feldspar. A few such bands are paralleled by a second one of similar character 1 or 2 inches away. These garnet bands are frequently of practical service in tracing the gem-bearing zone. The pegmatite outside them is invariably barren of gem minerals.

As explained in the detailed descriptions of Mount Mica and other gem localities, the gem tourmalines are usually found in pockets, having developed on their walls. The pockets, though confined mainly to the zone rich in soda and lithium minerals, may be wholly absent from considerable portions of such zones and are distributed with great irregularity through the remaining portions. The character and distribution of pockets is best illustrated at the Mount Mica tourmaline mine. Plate XII is from an early photograph of the workings at Mount Mica, taken at a time when only the outcropping portion of the gem-bearing zone had been worked. A stake with card attached marks the position of each pocket.

Most of the pockets are somewhat spherical in form, but others are oval or elongate and others exceedingly irregular. Their size ranges from a few inches across to a magnitude such as is shown in Plate XIII, which represents the largest pocket ever found at Mount Mica.

Minor details of structure of the gem-bearing pegmatites are discussed in the locality descriptions (p. 18).

ORIGIN OF THE MAINE PEGMATITES.

The writer does not purpose in this report to discuss the voluminous literature on pegmatites except in so far as it bears closely on those of the region under discussion. Previous writings and theories have been well summarized by George H. Williams [a] and especially by Brögger.[b]

RELATIONS TO GRANITES.

The geologic relations of the Maine pegmatites, as already pointed out (pp. 13–15), show beyond reasonable doubt that they are geneti-

---

[a] Williams, G. H., Fifteenth Ann. Rept. U. S. Geol. Survey, 1895, pp. 675–684.
[b] Brögger, W. C., Der Syenitpegmatit-gänge der sudnorwegischen Augit und Nephelinsyenite: Zeitschr. f. Kryst., vol. 16, 1890. Sections on genesis translated in Canadian Rec. Sci., vol. 6, 1894, pp. 33–46, 61–71.

cally connected in a most intimate manner with the granites. Evidence of this is found in mineralogical similarity, in the invariable presence of granite in all areas where pegmatite is found, and in many actually observed transitions from one to the other. (See fig. 2.)

If we admit a genetic connection between the pegmatites and granites, it is next of importance to inquire what evidence is afforded by the Maine pegmatites as to the physical and chemical conditions which resulted in the crystallization from related magmas of rocks of such widely varying character.

EXTERNAL CONDITIONS.

Differences in external conditions at the time of crystallization appear inadequate to explain the observed textural differences. This is shown by the close association of the two types of rocks—an association already cited as evidence of their genetic relationships. The field relations show that in many instances the external conditions, such as the nature and temperature of the wall rock, the depth at which solidification took place, etc., were similar for both types of rocks. In cases such as that shown in figure 2 the general external conditions must have been practically identical. A similar conclusion is justified in numerous other instances where granite and pegmatite grade into each other, and especially where pegmatite forms segregation-like masses wholly inclosed in granite. Conversely, the broad, general similarity of the pegmatites over very large areas where the external conditions were certainly not constant also indicates that the causes of their peculiar textures were in the main internal rather than external. It seems necessary to look, therefore, to differences inherent in the magmas themselves for an explanation.

DOMINANT CONSTITUENTS.

The characters shown by the Maine pegmatites accord with the evidence obtained from many other districts in indicating (1) that the pegmatite magmas were characterized as a general rule by the presence of certain components in amounts larger than occur in normal granite magmas, and (2) that to these differences in composition were in large measure due the differences in texture. The exact nature of such differences is, however, more largely a matter of inference than of direct field observation.

In the great mass of the normal pegmatite it is exceedingly difficult, if not impracticable, to make a satisfactory estimate of the relative proportions of the different mineral constituents. So far as can be judged without measurements the proportions are of the same general order as in the normal granites, except that the pegmatites are probably on the average slightly more quartzose, a conclusion that seems warranted by the numerous transitions from pegmatite masses into veins composed largely or wholly of quartz. The differences in the proportions of the principal mineral constituents in the normal granites and the normal pegmatites seem, however, insufficient to account for the great differences in their textures. It appears necessary to seek the cause of these contrasts in differences in the proportions of minor constituents or in the presence in the granite or pegmatite magmas of constituents which have since escaped or which, through occlusion, are not now visible to the unaided eye in the derived rocks.

MINOR CONSTITUENTS.

The presence in many pegmatites of unusual minerals, such as fluorite and other fluorine-bearing minerals, lithium minerals, boron and phosphorus minerals, and occasionally rare earth minerals, has led certain geologists [a] to attribute to some of these substances an important rôle in the production of pegmatite textures. It can not be doubted that when present in magmas such substances have some influence upon the texture of the resulting rock. It has not been demonstrated, however, that the presence of these unusual constituents is essential to the development of typical pegmatitic textures. In the opinion of the writer their presence is probably not essential. The pegmatites which earliest attracted the attention of American mineralogists and geologists, and which have been most often described in the literature, were naturally those in which unusual minerals were present in especial abundance or in perfection of crystal form. Such pegmatites constitute, however, only an exceedingly small proportion of the pegmatite in any district and must be regarded as unusual rather than as normal types. The writer is familiar with certain deposits showing typical pegmatitic textures, which have been worked for their feldspar for years with the discovery of few if any of the rarer minerals.[b] In by far the greater number of the pegmatites of Maine unusual minerals are so uncommon as ordinarily to escape detection. In pegmatites in which they are present their paucity or abundance seems to have small influence on the textures developed. Those inclined to attribute large influence in the development of pegmatitic textures to the presence of rare constituents usually contend that a more careful study will show that their scarcity is more apparent than real. Such an assumption is not in

---

[a] Certain French geologists in particular have supported this view. See De Lapparent, Traité de géologie, 4th ed., 1900, p. 639; De Launay, La science géologique, 1905, pp. 557–558, 582–583.

[b] The Andrews feldspar quarry in Portland, Conn., the Mitchell feldspar quarry in Maryland, and the Goldings feldspar quarry in Georgetown, Me., are examples. See Bull. U. S. Geol. Survey No. 420, pp. 50, 75, and this report, p. 105.

accord with the field observations of the writer in Maine and other parts of New England, and it appears to be unwarranted.

GASEOUS CONSTITUENTS.

If neither the dominant nor the rare minerals of the pegmatites have been controlling factors in the development of typical pegmatitic textures, it appears necessary to seek an explanation in the presence in the magmas of certain constituents which have subsequently escaped or at least are not readily recognizable in the resultant rock. The fact that large crystals can not be obtained at atmospheric pressures from simple dry melts of the commoner rock-forming minerals suggests at once that the crystallization of these minerals in nature took place either under widely different physical conditions (such as high pressure) or in the presence of certain substances which are scarce or absent in the rocks as now exposed. It has already been argued from field evidence (p. 28) that in many instances differences in pressure or other external conditions at the time of crystallization can not reasonably be adduced to explain the textural variations observed. In such cases an appeal to the escaped constituents of the magma appears unavoidable. The same conclusion appears necessary when the extreme viscosity exhibited (under atmospheric pressures) by silica, orthoclase, and albite near the melting temperatures is considered. The various forms of silica that have been artificially produced have all crystallized from a melt so viscous as to be virtually a glass.[a] As regards orthoclase the viscosity of its melt is so great that all attempts to crystallize the mineral from it have been unsuccessful. Since increase in pressure can hardly be appealed to as increasing molecular mobility[b] in magmas, it seems necessary again, in accounting for the large crystals developed in the pegmatites, to postulate the presence in the magma of some substance or substances not now recognizable in the derived rock. That the presence of volatile constituents in a magma does influence the viscosity is shown by the fact that certain obsidians may be readily melted with evident fluidity and the escape of gases, but that their refusion after such gases have escaped is much more difficult. Iddings[c] has also shown from a microscopic study of the obsidian of Obsidian Cliff, Yellowstone National Park, that where there was more dissolved gas the conditions were more favorable for crystallization than in other parts of the magma.

Among those constituents of magmas which might escape, leaving little record of their former presence, water gas and hydrogen are

---

[a] Day, D. T., and Shepherd, E. S., The lime-silica series of minerals: Am. Jour. Sci., 4th ser., vol. 22, 1906, pp. 271-273. Day, D. T., and Allen, E. T., The isomorphism and thermal properties of the feldspars: Pubs. Carnegie Inst., No. 31, 1905, pp. 28-29 and 45-55.

[b] Harker, Alfred, The natural history of igneous rocks, 1909, pp. 163-164.

[c] Iddings, J. P., Seventh Ann. Rept. U. S. Geol. Survey, 1888, pp. 283-287. Also Igneous rocks, 1909, p. 185.

probably the most abundant, as is plainly indicated by analyses of the gases still remaining in igneous rocks[a] and by studies of the gases emitted from volcanic vents.[b]

The presence of water gas in association with subordinate amounts of other gases and of certain unusual substances (mineralizers) has been considered by many observers to be the competent and effective cause in the development of pegmatitic textures. With this opinion the present writer is in general accord, though the persuasion is based more largely on the process of reasoning already outlined than on field evidence of high-water content or relatively low viscosity in pegmatite magmas. The field evidence gathered in the study of the Maine pegmatites is summarized later (p. 45), but must be looked on as merely suggestive; anything like a complete solution of the problem will in all probability wait upon synthetic laboratory experiments on the interaction between gases and rock-forming silicates.

The small weight of the gaseous and liquid constituents of most igneous rocks as compared with the total weight of the rock might lead one to question their competence to notably affect the viscosity of magmas and to produce large textural variations. In this connection it may not be out of place to call attention to a possible application of Raoult's law,[c] according to which if various substances are dissolved in equal amounts of the same solvent in the proportions of their molecular weights the resulting lowering of the freezing point of the solution will be the same in each case.[d] In other words, the effect produced is a function of the number of molecules concerned and is not primarily dependent on the nature of the substances introduced. It follows that a small amount by weight of a substance of low molecular weight (such as H_2O, molecular weight 18) will exert the same depressing influence on the freezing point of the solution as a much greater weight of a substance of high molecular weight (such as Fe_2O_3, molecular weight 160); and that given equal weights of the two the substance of lower molecular weight will exercise much the greater influence. This law has been found to apply strictly only to very dilute solutions where there is no chemical action between solvent and dissolved substance. It has been applied by Vogt[e] to rock magmas, but the wisdom of such extension to cover widely different and much more complex physical conditions may well be questioned. It seems not unreasonable, however, to attribute some general importance to this principle in rock magmas, to the extent that magmatic constituents of low molecular weight may exert

[a] Chamberlin, R. T., The gases in rocks: Pubs. Carnegie Inst. No. 106, 1908. This includes a summary of earlier investigations.

[b] For a review of the literature on volcanic gases, see Clarke, F. W., The data of geochemistry: Bull. U. S. Geol. Survey No. 330, 1908, pp. 212-236.

[c] Ostwald, Wilhelm, Outlines of general chemistry, 1895, pp. 136-137.

[d] Neglecting electrolytic dissociation, which is probably of small importance in rock magmas.

[e] Vogt, J. H. L., Die Silikatschmelzlosungen, vol. 2, 1904, pp. 128-135.

greater influence in lowering the freezing point, decreasing viscosity, and affecting textures, than do constituents of high molecular weight. They may thus attain an importance which appears disproportionate to the small part by weight which they form of the whole magma. The substances (hydrogen, water, fluorine, chlorine, and boron) commonly believed to exert the greatest influence upon the viscosity of magmas and the textures of the resulting rocks are all substances of much lower molecular weights than silica and the rock-making silicates and oxides, even if minimum values for the latter are assumed. The hiatus between the molecular weights of these two groups of substances is so marked as to justify the retention of the term "mineralizers" for the lighter group, in case the principle outlined above is eventually shown to be operative to an important degree in magmas.

VISCOSITY AND GAS CONTENT.

The field and laboratory data on the pegmatites of Maine that bear on the viscosity and gaseous content of the pegmatite magmas may be set forth as follows. As the pegmatite magmas crystallized at some distance below the surface, the gases which they contained must either have made their escape through the wall rocks or else must have remained in cavities or occluded within the solid pegmatite mass. The escape of such materials through the wall rocks should presumably leave some record in contact-metamorphic effects. Their retention within the rock should presumably be recorded in an especial abundance of miarolitic cavities and fluid or gaseous inclusions.

Miarolitic cavities.—The field studies of the writer in Maine and other parts of New England show that the granites are almost wholly devoid of miarolitic cavities of any kind. An isolated cavity of small size is occasionally found, but its walls are usually more or or less pegmatitic in texture. In the great bulk of the pegmatites of Maine, particularly the finer-grained ones, such cavities are also exceedingly rare. In the coarser pegmatites, however, they are a characteristic feature, though usually as far as can be judged constituting considerably less than 1 per cent of the total volume of the pegmatite. Within the very narrow gem-bearing zones of certain pegmatites miarolitic cavities may form a considerably larger percentage of the total volume. Such cavities have been attributed by various writers to shrinkage of the pegmatite mass in crystallization. This may in fact play some part in their formation, but that they are not entirely the result of shrinkage, but, on the contrary, were filled or partly filled with some material which has since disappeared, is shown by the presence of perfectly developed crystals of quartz, tourmaline, and other minerals projecting inward from the walls of the cavities. Some filling must have been present from which such crystals derived the materials for their growth. It is probable, therefore, that immediately after the crystallization of the main body of pegmatite the miarolitic cavities were completely filled with a gaseous solution, which may later have liquified and has since disappeared. Water carrying numerous other substances in solution probably formed the bulk of this cavity filling. The abundance of quartz crystals on the walls of these cavities indicates that silica was one of the most abundant of the dissolved substances.

If the crystallization of the rock with pegmatitic rather than granitic texture is due to the presence of larger amounts of gaseous constituents, greater size or abundance of microscopic fluidal or gaseous cavities might reasonably be expected in the pegmatite minerals than in those of the normal granites. With this idea in mind the writer attempted a microscopic measurement of these inclusions in pegmatites and associated granites from Maine. On account of the uneven distribution of the inclusions in bands traversing the minerals accurate estimates were found to be impracticable and the results were negative or inconclusive. It was found, moreover, that some of the bands of fluidal cavities in the quartz of pegmatite were formed later than shearing movements which had affected the quartz. (See Pl. VI.) The inclusions in the pegmatite were similar in character to those in the normal granites of the State and any differences in their size and abundance in the two types of rocks was not sufficient to be noted on casual inspection.

Contact-metamorphic effects.—If the pegmatite magmas are characterized by considerably larger proportions of gaseous constituents than are present in the granite magmas and hence by notably greater fluidity, notable differences might be expected in the contact-metamorphic effects produced by the two types of rocks, since such effects are believed to be produced largely by gaseous and fluid emanations from the cooling igneous masses. Field observations in Maine fail to show that contact-metamorphic effects due to the intrusions of pegmatite are notably greater than those produced by the granites. The effects produced by both are usually slight and in many instances almost nil. In many places masses both of pegmatite and granite cut across the foliation of schists without any distortion of the latter, the contacts being of knife-edge sharpness. In other places, however, pegmatite has produced a notable softening of the bordering rock, though this effect is usually apparent only close to the contact.

A striking instance of this effect was observed about $2\frac{1}{2}$ miles northeast of Paris village, where a pegmatite mass 2 to 3 feet across and several smaller masses are intrusive in schists of probable metamorphic-sedimentary origin. (See Pl. X, *A.*) Although the schist folia do not in general conform to the outline of the large pegmatite mass, as they would if any considerable amount of softening had occurred, still in a zone an inch or two wide along the immediate contact such softening has taken place with a deflection of schist folia toward parallelism with the pegmatite contact. The bending of the schist folia in the manner shown indicates also that the pegmatite when intruded behaved to a certain extent like a solid body capable of exerting differential thrust on the inclosing walls of schist. In a body behaving essentially like a liquid, pressure would be equalized in all directions and it is difficult to see how such bending of folia along the borders of the mass could occur.

Another instance of still more extensive softening of the schists bordering pegmatite, with the development therein of minerals derived from the pegmatite magma, was observed at Rumford Falls (Pl. X, B). The contact is very irregular and the schist folia near the contact curve around so as to conform rather closely to the outline of the pegmatite mass. Not only are there irregular protuberances of the pegmatite into the schist, but there are developed in the schist next to the contact a number of masses, mostly composed of feldspar but with some admixture of quartz, which in the plane of the section are not connected with the main pegmatite mass. There may, of course, have been some connection between them and the main pegmatite body, either above or below the plane of the present surface of exposure. A feature of especial interest is the development in some of these masses of well-defined crystal faces, as is clearly shown in Plate X, B, especially in the mass to which the hammer handle points. The straight faces on these masses are parallel to the cleavage directions in the feldspar and there can be no doubt that they are crystal faces. These relations plainly indicate a considerable permeation of the schist by the pegmatite magma and a sufficient yielding on the part of the schist to permit the development of very perfect crystal faces in the feldspar. This may have been accomplished through absorption or by metasomatic replacement of the schist, but other evidence of absorption is wholly absent, for the contacts though very irregular are very sharp, and no difference is noticeable between the pegmatite next the contact and that some distance away. It seems more probable, therefore, that the phenomena observed indicate a yielding of the schist through recrystallization to the pressures of various kinds exerted by the pegmatite.

Further instances of the softening of the schists as a result of the intrusion of pegmatite are exemplified by numerous occurrences of the type illustrated diagrammatically in figure 1 (p. 11), where the schist laminæ show a thickening opposite the nodes of the pegmatite dike or sill and become thinner opposite the bulges.

A. DEFLECTION OF SCHIST FOLIA ALONG THE IMMEDIATE CONTACT WITH A PEGMATITE
DIKE.

Two and one-half miles northeast of Paris village, Oxford County.

B. DEVELOPMENT OF FELDSPAR CRYSTALS IN SCHIST NEAR PEGMATITE, RUMFORD FALLS.

Such softening effects as those cited are confined, however, to the immediate vicinity of the pegmatite, usually to a zone a few inches in width, and are the exception rather than the rule, most pegmatite contacts being exceedingly sharp and free from all evidence of softening. Absorption (except in a few doubtful instances) appears to be wholly absent, the contacts even in the places where softening is shown being sharp, and the pegmatite next the contact showing no difference in composition from that at some distance away. Where schist fragments are inclosed in the pegmatite their sharp outlines are preserved. Contact-metamorphic effects of the pegmatite on schists are particularly noticeable at Black Mountain in Rumford. (See p. 96.)

Forms of the intrusives.—If the physical conditions of the pegmatite and granite magmas were notably different at the time of their intrusion, it would be natural to expect some differences in the forms assumed by the granite and pegmatite masses. Though in many cases those forms are similar, there is in general a tendency for the smaller pegmatite intrusions in the foliates to assume the form of a succession of lenses (fig. 1, p. 11) and for the granite intrusions of similar size to be more nearly parallel walled. This contrast is particularly noticeable in the Boothbay Harbor region and near Rumford Falls and is probably expressive of slightly greater rigidity in the granite than in the pegmatite magma and also of greater softening of the inclosing schist by the pegmatite than by the granite magmas. The great size of certain pegmatite masses, such as Streaked Mountain in Hebron, is, on the other hand, suggestive of degrees of viscosity in some pegmatite magmas not widely different from those prevailing in normal granite magmas. The crest of Streaked Mountain was examined for more than half a mile of its length and the width of outcrop examined across the trend of the ridge for about half a mile. The whole area traversed and the remainder of the mountain as far as it could be seen was underlain almost exclusively by coarse pegmatite, the mountain being a "boss" of this material. The pegmatite is of the usual granitic type and exhibits no more than the usual amount of variation in texture and composition from point to point. It is difficult to conceive of a mass of this size and general uniformity crystallizing under anything like vein conditions. With very high gaseous content and correspondingly high mobility it would be natural to expect more differentiation both in texture and composition. It seems probable that the viscosity of such a pegmatite magma was not so much below that of a granite mass intruded under similar conditions as has been commonly supposed.

Fragments of the wall rock are very frequently found inclosed by the border portions of the granite masses of Maine. The phenomenon is much less common in the case of the pegmatites but was nevertheless observed at several localities. On the highest portion of Streaked Mountain a number of patches of schist a few square yards in area were seen apparently entirely inclosed by pegmatite. Small schist fragments are also inclosed by pegmatite in the Boothbay Harbor region. W. H. Emmons, of the United States Geological Survey, who visited Mount Mica a year later than the writer, when the excavation had proceeded farther, observed, a few feet below the schist hanging wall, schist fragments which appeared to be wholly inclosed in the pegmatite. The schistosity of these fragments made large angles with the schistosity of the walls from which they had evidently been dislodged. The pegmatite shows no bending of the minerals nor other changes in character near the fragments. In the instances cited the schist fragments appear to have been caught up while the pegmatite mass was still partly or wholly fluid, and the density of the magma was sufficient, at least in the Mount Mica example, to float the fragments.

TEMPERATURES OF PEGMATITE CRYSTALLIZATION.

Experiments of Wright and Larsen.—Some evidence in regard to the temperatures of the pegmatites at the time they crystallized has been obtained from studies of quartz by Wright and Larsen, some of the specimens being collected by the writer from the pegmatites of Maine and other parts of New England. To quote from their paper—[a]

For * * * geologic thermometric purposes, quartz has been found by experience to be well adapted. It is plentiful in nature and occurs in many different kinds of rocks. SiO_2 in the form of tridymite melts at about 1,625° (centigrade); between that temperature and about 800° tridymite is the stable phase; below about 800° quartz is the stable phase. From evidence thus far gathered it is probable that pressure has but slight effect on raising or lowering such an inversion point, and that, therefore, whenever quartz appears in nature, it was formed at a temperature below 800°.

The studies of Wright and Larsen and of earlier observers have shown that at about 575° C. there is a sudden change from one form of crystal symmetry to another. Quartz developed below 575° crystallizes in what has been called the α form (the trapezohedral-tetartohedral division of the hexagonal system) and quartz developed above 575° appears to crystallize in the β form (the trapezohedral-hemihedral division of the same system).

Quartz itself undergoes a reversible change at about 575°. * * * Practically the only crystallographic change which takes place on the inversion is a molecular rearrangement, such that the common divalent axes of the high temperature β form become polar in the α form, and this fact involves certain consequences which can be used to distinguish quartz which has been formed above 575° from quartz which has never reached that temperature. At ordinary temperatures all quartz is α quartz, but if at any time in its history a particular piece of quartz has passed the inversion

---

[a] Wright, F. E., and Larsen, E. S., Quartz as a geologic thermometer: Am. Jour. Sci., 4th ser., vol. 28, 1909, p. 423.

point and been heated above 575°, it bears ever afterwards marks potentially present which on proper treatment can be made to appear just as an exposed photographic plate can be distinguished at once from an unexposed plate on immersion in a proper developer, although before development both plates may be identical in appearance.[a]

In addition to the change in crystal form at 575°, the quartz exhibits changes in its coefficients of expansion, in circular polarization, and in birefringence.

Briefly stated, the four criteria which can be used to distinguish, at ordinary temperatures, quartz which was formed above 575° from quartz which has never been heated to that temperature, are: (1) Crystal form, if crystals be available, the presence of trigonal trapezohedrons and other evidence of tetartohedrism, irregular development of the rhombs and the like, being indicative of the α form. (2) Character of twinning, as shown by etch figures on the basal pinacoid. In the α form, which crystallized from solutions at comparatively low temperatures, the twinning is usually regular and sharply marked, while in quartz plates originally of the β form and now α by virtue of inversion in the solid state, the lines are usually irregular, and the twinning patches are small and bear no relation to the outer form of the crystal. (3) Intergrowths of right and left handed quartzes are more frequent and more regular in boundary lines in the α than in the β form. (4) Plates of originally β quartz but now α quartz by inversion show the effect of the inversion by the shattering, which should be most evident on large plates. Into all these criteria an element of probability enters, and in testing quartz plates, with this end in view, a number of plates should be examined to strengthen the validity of the inferences drawn.[b]

The bearing of the experiments on the temperatures of crystallization of granites and pegmatites has been briefly discussed by Wright and Larsen, but the writer desires to amplify the discussion by a more detailed description of its relation to those specimens with which he is personally familiar.

No granites from Maine were tested by Wright and Larsen, but thirteen specimens of granites, granite gneisses, and porphyries which were tested from other regions show as a rule the characters of β or high-temperature quartz, thus placing their temperature of final solidification above 575° C.

Two specimens of rose quartz from Maine (Nos. 13 and 14, Wright and Larsen), one of them from Paris, Oxford County, now in the collection of the United States National Museum, were examined by Wright and Larsen and found to show the characters of α or low-temperature quartz. The specimens have the appearance of typical pegmatite quartz; and in Maine rose quartz, so far as known, occurs only as a pegmatite constituent.

A specimen of rose quartz (No. 12, W. and L.) collected by the writer from the feldspar and quartz quarry of P. H. Kinkle's Sons at Bedford, N. Y., also showed the characteristics of α or low-

---

[a] Wright, F. E., and Larsen, E. S., Quartz as a geologic thermometer: Am. Jour. Sci., 4th ser., vol. 28, pp. 423, 425.

[b] Idem, p. 438.

temperature quartz. This pegmatite has been described by the writer in another report [a] and is similar in most of its characteristics to the coarser Maine deposits. The quartz of this quarry is mostly white but is rose colored in places. It is associated with the feldspar in a wholly irregular manner and forms large masses in one pit, being the principal rock on two of the walls. These quartz masses at their borders are in intimate interpenetration with the feldspar and may even grade into the quartz of graphic granite. There is not the slightest doubt that they form an integral part of the pegmatite mass, though very likely they were the latest portion to crystallize.

Another specimen of quartz, collected by the writer from the pegmatite at an old feldspar quarry on the northwest side of Mount Ararat in Topsham, showed a quartz crystal about $1\frac{1}{2}$ inches across projecting with perfectly developed pyramid faces into a crystal of pink microcline. The crystal faces of the quartz were only shown when the feldspar was broken away. The two minerals formed intimate parts of a large mass of coarse pegmatite and plainly crystallized contemporaneously. The tests on this quartz (No. 20, W. and L.) indicate that it crystallized below 575°.

Another test (No. 18, W. and L.) was made upon quartz collected from the Berry feldspar quarry in Poland, Me. The deposit is a gem-bearing pegmatite and the quartz tested was irregularly intergrown with rounded lepidolite and bladed albite of the clevelandite variety. It occurred in the solid pegmatite but near miarolitic cavities. The tests, though not wholly conclusive, show that it probably belongs to the low-temperature variety.

Crystals of transparent smoky quartz (No. 15, W. and L.) developed on the walls of pockets in the pegmatite at the same quarry exhibited low-temperature characters. Similar results (No. 19, W. and L.) were obtained for a compound quartz crystal developed in one of the pockets at the G. D. Willes feldspar quarry in Topsham. At its proximate end this crystal mass was intergrown with the feldspar of the wall of the pocket. It was plainly a pegmatite crystallization, though a late one.

A specimen (No. 16, W. and L.), taken by the writer from a large mass of white quartz several feet across in the pegmatite at the Fisher feldspar quarry in Topsham, also showed the characters of the α or low-temperature variety. These quartz areas form an intimate part of the pegmatite mass, interlocking at their borders with crystals of the other constituents and in places grading without break into the quartz of coarse graphic granite.

In contrast to the above tests on specimens of quartz from the large quartz masses in the pegmatites and from the quartz in or near

---

[a] Bastin, E. S., Feldspar and quartz deposits of southeastern New York: Bull. U. S. Geol. Survey No. 315, 1907, pp. 395-398.

the cavities, tests of smaller masses of quartz in finer-grained pegmatite or intergrown with feldspar in graphic granite show that in these crystallization took place above the inversion point of 575° C. Quartz, for example, from a pegmatite dike 1 to 4 feet in width, cutting fine-grained biotite granite in a railroad cut near Rumford Falls (No. 22, W. and L.), proved to be of the β or high-temperature variety. The rock, in addition to quartz, contained microcline and biotite, few of the feldspars exceeding 2 inches in diameter. This dike in texture and coarseness is typical of very many of the smaller pegmatite bodies of the State. Similar results were obtained with quartz (No. 25, W. and L.) from the coarse graphic granite of Fisher's feldspar quarry in Topsham (see Pl. XVIII, and an analysis, p. 124). At this quarry much of the feldspar of the graphic granite is crystallographically continuous with large masses of pure feldspar, and much of the quartz of the intergrowths may be traced into the large pure areas. Graphic granite of similar composition and coarseness (No. 23, W. and L.) collected by the writer from the Andrews feldspar quarry in Portland, Conn., also showed high-temperature characters. Concordant results were obtained on quartz of graphic granite from the Urals in Russia.

Application to Maine pegmatites.—The results of these several tests are consistent among themselves and in accord with the order of crystallization of various portions of the pegmatite as established by field evidence. Though it is not safe to draw sweeping conclusions from the rather small number of tests they are nevertheless very suggestive and render it highly probable that, although many of the finer-grained pegmatite masses and most of the graphic intergrowths of the coarser pegmatites crystallized at temperatures above 575° C., the coarser and more siliceous portions—the portions characterized by the cavities and hence presumably richer in gaseous or fluid constituents—crystallized at temperatures below 575°. The portions characterized by high and by low temperature quartz are commonly so intimately associated in the same pegmatite mass that it seems unreasonable to assume great differences in the temperature of crystallization of different portions. It is probable, therefore, that the whole mass of many of the coarser pegmatites crystallized not far from the inversion point of quartz; that is, not far from 575° C.

EUTECTICS IN PEGMATITES.

Largely as a result of the extensive studies of Vogt,[a] many geologists[b] have been led to attribute to eutectics an important part in rock formation. One of the phenomena[c] that most obviously sug-

[a] Vogt, J. H. L., Die Silikatschmelzlosungen, vol. 2, 1903, pp. 117–135.

[b] Harker, Alfred, The natural history of igneous rocks, pp. 262–266, 270–272.

[c] Teall, J. J. H., British petrography, 1888, pp. 401–402.

gested such a relation was the graphic structure exhibited by many pegmatites, which closely resembled patterns formed by eutectic mixtures in alloys. Vogt [a] calculated the ratio between quartz and feldspar in a number of analyses of graphic intergrowths of quartz with microcline, the latter mineral being also perthitically intergrown with various amounts of soda plagioclase. The ratios were constant enough to lead Vogt to conclude that the graphic granites represented eutectic mixtures. Slight disparities between analyses he attributed to slight variations in the compositions of the feldspars and to variations in the pressures under which the granites had crystallized. In many specimens, especially in microscopic varieties, the graphic intergrowths are considered to be the end products of crystallization.

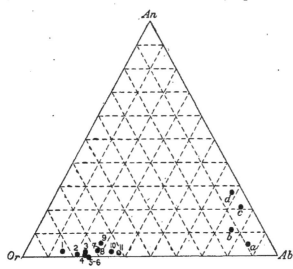

FIGURE 5.—Diagram showing composition of graphic granite.

In 1905 H. E. Johansson,[b] working mainly with Vogt's analyses, computed the molecular proportions of the quartz and feldspars present and concluded that these bore very simple numerical relations to each other. In graphic granites with dominant orthoclase the molecular ratio of feldspar to quartz was about 2:3. In an oligoclase graphic granite the proportion was about 1:2, and in an albite-quartz micropegmatite it was about 1:3.

Later Bygden[c] made a considerable number of other analyses of graphic granites with the special purpose of determining to what extent the quartz-feldspar ratio is dependent on the composition of the feldspar. He concluded that the ratio between quartz and feldspar bore no *regular* relationship to the composition of the feldspar. He believed that in most graphic granites definite ratios did exist between the proportions of feldspar and quartz, but that these ratios were not always so simple as Vogt and Johansson had supposed.

To supplement the small number of available trustworthy analyses the writer collected specimens of graphic granite from the Fisher

a Op. cit., pp. 120–121.

b Geologiska föreningens förhandlingar, Stockholm, vol. 27, 1905, p. 119.

c Bygden, A., Über das quantitative Verhaltnis zwischen Feldspat und Quartz in Schrift-graniten: Bull. Geol. Inst. Univ. Upsala, vol. 7, 1904, pp. 1–18.

feldspar quarry in Topsham, Me., and from Kinkle's feldspar quarry in Bedford, N. Y. These were analyzed by George Steiger in the laboratory of the United States Geological Survey. (See p. 124.) In order that the material analyzed should represent closely the true composition, about 10-pound samples of the Maine granites were taken. These were pulverized, carefully mixed, and quartered down to convenient size for analysis. The New York specimen was a cleavage piece about 1 by 2 by 3 inches in size.

The ratio of quartz to feldspar in the analyses published by Vogt and Bygden and in the author's analyses are given in the table below. In figure 5 the compositions of the feldspars are plotted on triangular projection. The numbers in the diagram correspond to those in the table.

Composition of graphic granites.

No.	Locality.	Feldspar.[a]	Quartz.[a]	Molecular percentages of feldspar components.			Reference.
				Orthoclase.	Albite.	Anorthite.	
		Per cent.	*Per cent.*				
1	Skarpö	70.5	29.5	82.5	15.1	2.4	Bygden No. 7.
2	Hitterö	66.0	34.0	77.6	21.6	.8	Bygden No. 8.
3	Voie, Arendal	74.7	25.3	73.8	24.0	2.2	Vogt No. 1.
4	Elfkarleö	79.2	20.8	74.8	24.5	.7	Bygden No. 6.
5	Topsham, Me.	72.9	27.1 }	74.4	25.6	None.	See p. 112.
6	....do	73.7	26.3				
7-8	Hitterö	75.3	24.7	69.1	28.5	2.4	Vogt Nos. 2 and 3.
9	Reade	72.7	27.3	66.1	28.2	5.7	Vogt No. 4.
10	Arendal	76.5	23.5	63.9	33.7	2.4	Vogt No. 5.
11	Bedford, N. Y.	76.8	23.2	61.7	37.0	1.3	See p. 112.
A	Rödö	56.0	39.0	9.6	85.4	5.0	Bygden No. 9 (Holmquist).
B	Evje	68.3	31.7	12.4	76.0	11.6	Vogt No. 6.
C	Ytterby	62.1	37.9	4.3	74.5	21.2	Bygden No. 11.
D	Beef Island	81.7	18.3	4.6	68.0	27.4	Bygden No. 12.

[a] Calculated from the analyses.

From the table and diagram it is at once evident that even among those graphic granites whose feldspars are almost identical in composition (such as Nos. 2 to 6) there are quite considerable variations in the quartz-feldspar ratio. In analyses Nos. 1, 2, 3, 7, 8, 10, and 11 (particularly in Nos. 1, 3, 7, 8, and 10) the percentage of anorthite is small and nearly constant, the only important variation being in the ratio between orthoclase and albite. No regular or consistent relationship is recognizable, however, between this ratio and the ratio between quartz and feldspar. The grouping of Nos. 1 to 11 near the lower line of the diagram signifies merely that the feldspar associated with the orthoclase (or microcline) in graphic granites as in normal granites[a] is usually albite or oligoclase.

Both analyses and microscopic studies show that most graphic granites are mixtures of three minerals—quartz, orthoclase or

[a] Clarke, F. W., The data of geochemistry: Bull. U. S. Geol. Survey No. 330, 1908, p. 369.

microcline, and a member of the isomorphous series of plagioclase feldspars. It should be pointed out, moreover, that if water or other gases were present, as it is almost certain they were, they formed additional components whose amount the analyses do not reveal, but whose influence on the proportions of the other constituents may have been great. If graphic granites crystallized from magmas of eutectic proportions these were therefore eutectics of at least four components. The series of analyses (p. 41), though suggesting that the proportions between the constituents of graphic granites are controlled by *some* laws, can hardly be regarded as proving their eutectic origin. The theoretical value of such analyses in elucidating the laws governing rock solutions is impaired by the fact that they take no account of the gaseous components of the magmas.

Vogt [a] states that many graphic intergrowths, especially when developed on a microscopic scale, represent the last portions of the magma to crystallize. This fact he cites as in harmony with the conception that they represent eutectic residues. Although this may be the true relation in some cases, in others the graphic granite was unquestionably not the last crystallization from the magma. In the Fisher feldspar quarry in Topsham, for example, where large masses of graphic granite pass gradually and irregularly into large areas of pure quartz and feldspar, the tests of Wright and Larsen (see p. 39) have shown that the quartz of the graphic intergrowths crystallized above 575° C., whereas the quartz of the large pure areas crystallized below 575°. The latter was therefore the later crystallization. Almost all the gem and cavity bearing portions of the Maine pegmatites grade into normal pegmatite containing abundant graphic granite. From the presence of cavities and of the rare minerals, from the general field relations, and from the fact that the quartz of the pockets and of the gem-bearing portions, wherever tested, is of the low-temperature variety, there can be no reasonable doubt that these gem and cavity bearing portions rather than the bordering graphic portions were the last parts of the pegmatite to crystallize.[b]

In considering the significance of the graphic intergrowths found in pegmatite, it is necessary to consider not only the intergrowths of feldspar and quartz, but also the almost equally regular intergrowths of muscovite and quartz, garnet and quartz, black tourmaline and quartz, etc. As muscovite, tourmaline, and garnet are less abundant than feldspar in the pegmatites, their intergrowths

---

a Op. cit., pp. 118–123.

b In the tourmaline-bearing pegmatites of California (according to W. T. Schaller, oral communication) the zones characterized by cavities and by the presence of the gems and other rare minerals, which were almost certainly the last portions to crystallize, grade laterally without sharp break into graphic granite which borders one wall of these pegmatite masses. Occasional stringers of pegmatite bearing lithium minerals branch off from the main gem-bearing layer and cut the bordering graphic granite.

with quartz are also less abundant and are usually of smaller size. Such intergrowths occur, however, scattered irregularly through practically all of the coarser pegmatite masses. If the eutectic be considered, as usual, as the residue of uniform composition and minimum freezing point which is the last portion to crystallize, it is manifestly impossible to regard each of these intergrowths as representing a eutectic mixture, unless indeed several portions of the pegmatite magma are regarded as crystallizing more or less independently of the remainder of the mass.

MINERALOGICAL PROVINCES.

It has already been pointed out that most of the known pegmatites which are rich in sodium and lithium minerals—that is, most of the gem-bearing pegmatites—are restricted to a zone about 25 miles long and 8 to 9 miles in width extending in a northwesterly direction from Auburn in Androscoggin County to Greenwood in Oxford County. A second and much smaller area includes the Newry and Black Mountain localities in the northern part of Oxford County and differs from the larger area in that the gem minerals are embedded in the solid pegmatite and are not in pockets. Within both areas the lithium-bearing phases form only a small proportion of the pegmatite present, most of which has the normal composition. The occurrence locally of certain masses of unusual composition is to be attributed either to the existence in the magma of sodium and lithium in very minute excess over their percentages in bordering pegmatite magmas, or else to differing degrees of segregation in magmas whose average composition was similar. As already explained, quartz associated with lepidolite and clevelandite from the gem-bearing portion of one of these pegmatites showed low-temperature characters, and the unusual abundance of pockets indicates that these portions were richer than the normal in gaseous constituents, probably mainly water vapor. In general, therefore, the gem-bearing pegmatites were characterized by a higher percentage of sodium, lithium, and phosphorus than the normal pegmatites, and probably by more water vapor and a slightly lower temperature of crystallization.

The region characterized by pegmatites rich in fluorine minerals but not in lithium minerals forms an area only a few miles across in the town of Stoneham and bordering parts of other towns in Oxford County, Maine, and Chatham, N. H.

GEOGRAPHIC RELATIONS.

The broad geographic relationships of the granites and pegmatites are also significant of their relationship and origin. As may be seen from Plate I, many of the granite areas of the eastern portion of Maine are characterized by *sharp* boundaries, and most of the granite areas of southwestern Maine show very *indefinite* boundaries and are bordered by large areas of slates and schists which have been intruded by various amounts of granite gneiss and pegmatite and by some granite and diorite.   The contrast between the two types of contacts is well shown within the Penobscot Bay [a] and Rockland [b] quadrangles.   In many parts of the former area, notably along the granite-schist contact from Bluehill village northward and from Bluehill Falls southwestward to Sedgwick, the granite preserves its normal medium grain up to the exact contact.   In most places this contact is so sharp that it is possible to stand with one foot resting upon typical Ellsworth schist and the other foot resting upon normal granite.   Dikes and irregular intrusions of granite are not very abundant in the schists near the main granite masses, and flow gneiss, pegmatite, and basic differentiations from the granite magma are almost entirely absent. In the Rockland quadrangle, on the other hand, the contact relations are wholly different, the change from pure granite to pure sediments taking place gradually through a transition zone of contact-metamorphosed and injected sediments 2 to 3 miles in width.   These transition zones include a great variety of rocks, slate, schist, injection gneiss, flow gneiss, diorite, diabase, pegmatite, and granites of various textures all associated in a manner so that it is impracticable to delineate them separately in ordinary geologic mapping.   In western and southwestern Maine these transition zones are much broader than in the Rockland quadrangle and contain larger amounts of pegmatite and granite gneiss and smaller amounts of basic igneous rocks.

The contrast between the sharpness of certain granite contacts observed in the Bluehill region and the very gradual transitions observed in the Rockland quadrangle and farther southwest seem to be best explained on the hypothesis that the broad injected zones represent portions of the "roof" of granite batholiths, whereas the sharp contacts represent the sides of similar batholiths.   The character of the rocks found in the two types of contacts lends support to this view.   The fact that water gas and other gases and their dissolved substances escape upward more readily than they do laterally may explain the great abundance of pegmatite in the broad transition zones, inasmuch as the presence of such gases is believed to be the most important factor in the development of pegmatitic texture.   It is a reasonable supposition that basic differentiation from the granitic magma would also be more rapid upward than laterally, and the abundance of diabase and diorite in certain of the transition zones may thus be accounted for.   The hypothesis is also in accord with the low temperatures at which certain portions of the pegmatites appear to have crystallized in comparison with the temperatures of

---

[a] Folio 149, Geol. Atlas U. S., U. S. Geol. Survey.
[b] Folio 158, Geol. Atlas U. S., U. S. Geol. Survey.

crystallization of normal granites; it also accords with the presence of numerous dikes of very fine-grained granite, some so fine as to be rhyolitic in certain of the contact zones, and with their absence about the sharper contacts.

SUMMARY.

Field and laboratory studies of the Maine pegmatites indicate that all are in a broad way contemporaneous and are genetically related to the associated granites.

External conditions, though locally having some slight influence, are not primarily the cause of the pegmatitic textures. The presence of the rarer elements seems to have had only a minor influence on the texture, for in many typical pegmatites such elements appear to be entirely absent. Theoretical considerations and the presence of miarolitic cavities in certain pegmatites point to the gaseous constituents of the pegmatite magmas, especially water vapor, as the primary cause of their textures.

Although certain facts, such as the pinch and swell phenomena observed in many pegmatite dikes in contrast with the parallel-walled character of most of the granite dikes, indicate somewhat greater mobility in the pegmatite than in the granite magmas, other facts, such as the sharpness of many of the contacts between pegmatite and schist, the absence of absorption along any of the contacts, the presence of angular schist fragments now surrounded by pegmatite, the small proportion by volume which the cavities bear to the whole pegmatite mass, the absence of notably greater contact-metamorphic effects near pegmatite than near granite contacts, and the batholithic dimensions of some pegmatite bodies, all suggest that the difference in average composition between the granite pegmatites and the normal granites was relatively slight and that the pegmatite magmas were not so greatly different in physical characters from the granite magmas as has been commonly supposed.

In his text-book on igneous rocks [a] Iddings, in discussing the pegmatites, says "the amount of gases concentrated in such magmas was not many times that of the gases originally distributed throughout the magma from which the pegmatite was differentiated; possibly not more than ten times as much." The present writer would be inclined, in the case at least of the granite pegmatites of New England, to estimate the gaseous content of these rocks at a still lower amount.

The experiments of Wright and Larsen on quartz from pegmatites from Maine and elsewhere indicate that some at least of the coarser pegmatites began to crystallize at a temperature slightly above the inversion point of quartz (about 575° C.) and completed their crystal-

---

[a] Iddings, J. P., Igneous rocks, vol. 1, 1909, p. 276.

lization somewhat below this temperature. It is probable that many of the finer-grained pegmatites crystallized wholly above 575° C.

The theory that the graphic intergrowths in pegmatites represent eutectic mixtures can not be regarded as proved by the published analyses. Certain field evidence is unfavorable to the eutectic theory.

The broader field relations suggest that the large areas characterized by particular abundance of pegmatite intrusions constitute in reality the roofs overlying granite batholiths. Where more extensive erosion has exposed the flanks of such batholiths, pegmatite masses in the bordering schists are not abundant.

LOCAL DESCRIPTIONS.

ANDROSCOGGIN COUNTY.

AUBURN.

CHARACTER AND DISTRIBUTION OF THE PEGMATITE.

Large areas in the town of Auburn, especially in the valleys of Androscoggin and Little Androscoggin rivers, are covered with sands of glacial origin which obscure the bed rock. Wherever the latter is exposed, however, it is found to be either quartz-mica schist or pegmatite intrusive in the schist or a coarse gneiss resulting from a very intimate injection of the schist by pegmatite.

Auburn Falls.—The prevailing rock types and the relationships between them are well shown in the river bed at the falls just above the bridge between Auburn and Lewiston. (See p. 11 and Pl. III, *B*.) The purplish-gray quartz-mica schists, which dip about 30° NE., in many places show distinct bedding and are of undoubted sedimentary origin. They are similar in every way to those at the Auburn reservoir. The pegmatite masses are intruded in general parallel to the trend of the schists. Just below the bridge both schists and pegmatite are cut by a dike of fine-grained diabase 3 to 4 feet wide.

The largest pegmatite mass exposed crosses the river bed at the falls, which are a result of the superior resistance to erosion offered by this pegmatite and its bordering intensely injected schists as compared with the ordinary phases of the schists. This pegmatite sill has a maximum thickness of about 20 feet and extends nearly across the river bed, though it forks at several places. It preserves about the same coarseness in the wide and narrow parts and in the center and next the walls. Its contact with the schist is everywhere sharp, and there is not the least evidence here or anywhere in this vicinity of any absorption of schist by the pegmatite.

Auburn reservoir.—Fresh exposures of the schists were also beautifully shown at the new reservoir site on Goff Hill in Auburn. This reservoir was under construction at the time of the writer's visit, and many exposures then showing have since been covered. The schists, which in general are purplish gray in color, have been intensely injected by pegmatite, though the largest pegmatite lens observed was 10 feet long and 2½ feet in greatest width. The injection does not in all places take the form of definite lenses or stringers of pegmatite, but in many the impregnation of the schist is so intimate as to obscure almost entirely the schistose structure and develop a speckled appearance. The sedimentary origin of the schist is shown by the general evenness and regularity of its trend and by the local preservation of bedding in its more quartzose layers.

Danville Corners.—An exposure of considerable interest was observed in a road cut about half a mile southeast of Danville Corners, where the rock, which has been recently blasted, is for the most part a gray granite of slightly gneissic texture. It is phanerocrystalline, most of its mineral grains ranging from 1 to 2 millimeters in diameter and its texture is typically granitic. The faint gneissic texture is due to a parallel orientation of many of the biotite plates, to their slightly greater abundance along some planes than along others, and to slight differences in the coarseness of certain bands as compared with others. Under the microscope the constituents are seen to be quartz, orthoclase and microcline, albite, biotite (altering to chlorite), and some muscovite, their relative abundance appearing from casual examination to be in the order given.

This granite gneiss is associated with subordinate amounts of pegmatite, which is not so coarse as much pegmatite found elsewhere, but is typically pegmatitic in texture. The pegmatite specimen collected for detailed study shows feldspar crystals up to one-half inch across and aggregates of feldspar crystals unmixed with other constituents 1 inch across and areas of smoky quartz one-half inch across. Muscovite crystals are one-eighth inch across and biotite crystals one-fourth inch. Garnets up to one-sixteenth inch in diameter occur. Texturally the pegmatite differs from the granite gneiss in showing a much greater range in size in the mineral grains of each species and much less evenness in their distribution. In the pegmatite there is a marked tendency toward segregation of the different mineral constituents, some areas being dominantly feldspar and others dominantly quartz. This feature is entirely distinct from mere increased coarseness of grain.

The constituents of the pegmatite are identical with those of the granite gneiss, being (1) quartz, (2) orthoclase and microcline, (3) oligoclase-albite with some border rims of albite, (4) biotite, and (5) muscovite, the numbers showing the order of their apparent abundance. The principal difference in their mineral composition is the much smaller quantity of biotite present in the pegmatite. Inclusions are abundant in the quartzes of both rocks and are of about the same size. The majority are under 0.005 millimeter, but a few are over 0.01 millimeter in greatest dimension. They are not notably more abundant in the pegmatite than in the granite gneiss.

In a few places the pegmatite is rather sharply delimited from the granite gneiss in dikelike masses, but for the most part it occurs in the granite in lens-shaped or roughly spheroidal masses from a few inches to a foot or more across, coarsest in the center and grading very gradually with increasing fineness into the surrounding granite gneiss. A few of the pegmatite "bunches" show a center composed largely of quartz, surrounded by a zone in which feldspar is dominant. In places the pegmatite masses send off irregular and vaguely bounded ramifications into the granite gneiss. The two types are associated in the most irregular manner. In places the pegmatite is very coarse and carries beryl and black tourmaline. One feldspar crystal in this portion measured 8 inches across.

The relation and mineral characters detailed above suggest the following inferences in regard to the genesis of the rocks described:

1. The presence of the same mineral species in the same order of abundance in both rocks and the many instances of complete gradation of one rock into the other show that they are products of the same parent magma.

2. The fact that the pegmatite masses in some parts of their length have rather sharp walls and in other parts grade gradually into the granite gneiss indicates that certain portions of the pegmatite crystallized after some of the granite was rigid enough to develop cracks into which the pegmatite magma penetrated, and that at the same time other parts were fluid enough to permit pegmatite and granite to solidify with gradual gradation and perfect crystallographic continuity between them.

3. The intimate and small-scale manner in which the pegmatite and the granite gneiss are associated, and the fact that these variations are so irregular and are not related in any way to any wall rock now observed or probably existent in the past, suggest that the causes operative in producing the variations in texture and composition were not of external origin, but were inherent in the magma itself.

Danville Junction.—In the extreme western part of the town of Auburn, about 3 miles west of Danville Junction, along the road to Poland Springs, conspicuous white ledges of pegmatite exemplify clearly certain common relationships of the pegmatites of this part of the State. In places this pegmatite grades gradually with perfect crystallographic continuity into a rather fine-grained granite gneiss. One pegmatitic band 1 inch wide in this granite gneiss shows contortions, which, in the absence of any regional metamorphism later than the granite-pegmatite intrusions, appear only explainable as the result of flowing movements in the granite gneiss at the time the pegmatite was intruded. A small mass of quartz-mica schist lying between two sill-like masses of pegmatite, though evidently molded somewhat during their intrusion, shows no evidence of absorption. Some of the narrower pegmatite bands in the schists can be traced continuously through portions showing successively larger proportions of quartz into "lit-par-lit" injections of pure quartz. Several diabase dikes at this locality strike N. 70° to 80° W. and dip vertical; they are about parallel to the most prominent joint planes in the granite and pegmatite.

The inferences which appear justified from the relations just described are as follows:

1. The complete and gradual gradation of pegmatite into granite gneiss and the presence of contorted bands of pegmatite in the granite indicate that portions at least of the granite gneiss were still more or less fluid when the pegmatite was intruded.

2. Certain quartz stringers in the schists are the end products of pegmatitic crystallization.

3. Neither the granite gneiss nor the pegmatite at this locality exercised any considerable absorptive action on the quartz-mica schists into which they were intruded.

Mount Apatite.—Pegmatite deposits are worked extensively for feldspar, and to some extent for minerals valuable as gems or as cabinet specimens, at Mount Apatite, a low prominence about 6 miles west of the city of Auburn near the road to Minot, and about 2 miles from Littlefield, the nearest railroad station on the Lewiston branch of the Grand Trunk Railway.

The interest in Mount Apatite as a mineral locality may be said to date back to 1868, when the Rev. Luther Hills called attention to a specimen of tourmaline found by G. C. Hatch on his farm. This crystal yielded a fine 2-carat gem of light-green color, but it was not found in place, and considerable searching having failed to reveal any further crystals the property remained unworked for some years. In 1883 N. H. Perry, of South Paris, found the tourmalines in place near the Hatch farmhouse, and in that year, from an excavation about 20 by 8 feet and 8 feet deep, took nearly 1,500 tourmaline crystals, ranging from very small ones 1 centimeter long to one $10\frac{1}{2}$ centimeters long. Thomas F. Lamb, of Portland, was also one of the pioneers at this locality, working intermittently for three or four years, part of the time with Loren B. Merrill, of Paris, now the proprietor of the Mount Mica tourmaline mine. He found a considerable number of gem tourmalines and some remarkably handsome groups of crystals of smoky quartz, besides much valuable cabinet-specimen material.

After the expiration of the leases of the persons mentioned, no mining of importance was done at Mount Apatite until 1902, when the Maine Feldspar Company, now the largest operator at this locality, commenced mining feldspar for use in pottery manufacture. Previously small amounts of quartz had been mined and shipped for use in the manufacture of sandpaper, and it is interesting to note that at this time the feldspar was considered to be of no value and was thrown on the dump piles. Although a few gems and cabinet specimens have been found in the course of the feldspar mining and by collectors paying short visits to Mount Apatite, regular mining for gems was not resumed until 1907, when J. S. Towne commenced operations at a new locality (p. 55).

operations at a new locality (p. 55).

QUARRIES.

Maine Feldspar Company quarry and mill.—The largest workings at Mount Apatite are those of the Maine Feldspar Company, of Auburn, which commenced operations in 1902 and has operated continuously to the present time (1909). The property was visited by the writer in August, 1906, and again in October, 1907.

The workings consist of a number of small pits 75 to 150 feet long, 50 feet in average width, and 10 to 20 feet in depth. These are either close together or partly connected and are located in a single mass of pegmatite which constitutes the summit of the hill. Much of the hilltop is bare, but in a few places as much as 6 feet of clayey till must be stripped in working.

The minerals present are those usually found in the granite pegmatites of the Atlantic States which are worked for feldspar but include many others that are characteristic only of the gem-bearing pegmatites.

Quartz varies from white to dark gray in color and from opaque to beautifully transparent. Its commonest occurrence is in graphic intergrowth with feldspar, but it is found also in large pure masses and in clusters of beautiful crystals projecting inward from the walls of pockets or fallen into the mass of kaolin, cookeite, etc., at their bottoms. Many of these groups of crystals are colorless and transparent, but others, notably some found by Thomas F. Lamb in one of the early workings near the Hatch farmhouse, though transparent, are smoky. Some of these latter are 20 centimeters in length and many are coated, especially at the tips of the pyramids, with thin white opaque quartz, which is plainly of more recent development than the main mass of the crystal. A few of the quartz crystals of the pockets are penetrated by small colored tourmaline crystals. The quartz obtained in the course of the present mining for feldspar is white and very pure and is of excellent quality for any of the many purposes for which crystalline quartz is now used. It is saved in stock piles, where it is allowed to accumulate until a sufficient amount is obtained to make its shipment worth while. The profit is very small in handling quartz so far from the principal markets in the Middle Atlantic States. At the time of the writer's visit, in 1906, about 300 tons of it was lying in stock piles.

The feldspar is mostly buff to cream colored with local bluish-gray spots and streaks due to minute inclusions. Microscopic study shows it to consist of the potash varieties, orthoclase and microcline, minutely (perthitically) intergrown with small amounts of the soda feldspar, albite. In certain narrow and irregular bands in the pegmatite, albite of a dirty olive-green color in irregularly bounded crystals up to 2 inches in length is almost the only feldspar present and is associated with quartz and muscovite. As is usual in all feldspar quarries, most of the material marketed under the commercial name "feldspar" is a graphic intergrowth of feldspar and quartz, though whatever pure feldspar may be found is mixed with this. In those portions of the pegmatite which bear pockets, the white-bladed variety of albite known as clevelandite is very abundant in radiating aggregates of thin plates. The standard or No. 2 grade obtained at this quarry consists principally of graphic granite with a subordinate amount of pure feldspar. Some No. 1 grade nearly free from quartz is also obtained; an analysis of a sample of this, made in the laboratory of the United States Geological Survey, is given below.

Analysis of No. 1 ground feldspar from Auburn, Me.

Silica (SiO_2)	65. 73
Alumina (Al_2O_3)	[a] 19. 28
Magnesia (MgO)	None.
Lime (CaO)	.22
Potash (K_2O)	10. 26
Soda (Na_2O)	4. 08
Water (H_2O)	.48
	100. 05.

The mineral composition of this sample, as calculated from the analysis, is as follows:

Mineral composition of No. 1 ground feldspar from Auburn, Me.

Quartz	2. 22
Orthoclase and microcline	60. 60
Albite	35. 69
Water	.48
Other constituents	1. 02
	100. 01

Muscovite is moderately abundant, but almost none of it is in clear transparent plates. Most of it is of the A variety (see p. 139) and some of the bladelike books are as much as a foot in length. It is common

---

[a] Includes traces of iron and any TiO_2 and P_2O_5 that may be present.

in graphic intergrowths with quartz. As described below, some small clear muscovite prisms are surrounded by a border of lepidolite. Mr. Lamb has also found some fine curved crystals of muscovite.

Biotite is abundant only locally and can in most areas be readily avoided in mining the feldspar. It forms typical lath-shaped crystals.

Lepidolite is not very abundant, but some occurs especially associated with clevelandite and muscovite near pockets. It is present in granular aggregates of small plates and prisms (in many places intergrown with some quartz) and also in larger plates. Its occurrence as narrow borders surrounding muscovite and in crystallographically parallel growth with it has been fully described and figured by Clarke,[a] who gives analyses of both of the muscovite and the lepidolite border.

Garnets of small size occur sparsely in all parts of the pegmatite. They are most abundant in the more quartzose and micaceous parts and are not present in injurious amounts in the more highly feldspathic portions.

Black tourmaline is present in all those portions of the pegmatite which carry colored tourmalines but is only locally abundant and is not particularly bothersome in feldspar mining. Most of the colored tourmalines which have been obtained have come, not from the feldspar workings, but from small pits near the Hatch farmhouse, worked at an earlier date solely for their gems and mineral specimens. Those found in 1883 by N. H. Perry ranged from 1 centimeter to $10\frac{1}{2}$ centimeters long, and differ from the majority of the Maine tourmalines in being mostly of lighter color. They were found colorless, light pink, lilac, light blue, light puce colored, bluish pink, and light green, some single crystals showing nearly all these colors. Gems from some of the paler crystals are said to have deepened very much in color after cutting. The majority of these crystals, of which nearly 1,500 were obtained, were more or less flawed. Some of the tourmalines found later by Mr. Lamb were cut into gems of emerald-green color.

Crystals of light bluish-green beryl also occur rather abundantly, embedded in the solid pegmatite. One hexagonal beryl found about 1898 is reported by J. S. Towne to have been 4 feet in diameter and 20 feet in length, but the majority do not exceed 1 foot in length and a few inches in diameter. Near the gigantic beryl mentioned occurred several pockets bearing the finest crystals of herderite ever found on Mount Apatite; the form and composition of these have been described by Penfield.[b]

Apatite occurs occasionally in crystals of fine luster and transparency, the colors being light pink, purple, light blue, and blue

a Clarke, F. W., The lepidolites of Maine: Bull. U. S. Geol. Survey No. 42, 1887, pp. 15–17.
b Penfield, S. L., Herderite from Auburn, Me.: Am. Jour. Sci., 3d ser., vol. 47, 1894, p. 336.

green. The crystals occur singly or in groups and vary in size from 1 mm. to 15 mm. long and from 1 to 20 mm. wide.

Other minerals reported [a] from Mount Apatite are allanite, amblygonite, autunite, cassiterite, columbite, cookeite, damourite, gummite, magnetite, molybdenite, triplite, and zircon.

Neither the exact form nor the area of the pegmatite body could be determined, but it occupies practically the whole top of Mount Apatite, and it is probable that further stripping of the soil in the neighborhood of the present workings will disclose considerable amounts of commercially valuable feldspar and possibly portions valuable enough to be worked for their gem minerals. The presence in the pegmatite of one of the northern pits of a 2-foot band of epidotized altered quartzite which is nearly flat lying and is regarded as a remnant of the sediments into which the pegmatite was intruded, and the presence in other pits of this quarry and in the neighboring quarries of nearly flat-lying bands particularly rich in small garnets, both indicate that the general attitude of the whole pegmatite mass is rather flat lying.

On the floor of one of the pits is exposed an instructive cross section of a dike of pegmatite cutting the main pegmatite mass. This dike is a foot in width and cuts graphic granite whose usual variations of texture are wholly unaffected, although the two rocks show crystallographic continuity along the immediate contact. The dike at its borders is mainly feldspar, the separate more or less blade-shaped crystals being disposed at right angles to the walls. The center of the dike is an irregular band of light-gray quartz. The dike was probably intruded soon after the partial or complete solidification of the main mass of pegmatite under conditions favoring more segregation of the quartz and feldspar than usually took place. Only one other dike of similar character was observed by the writer in the course of two months' field study. Their rarity argues for the essential contemporaneity of most of the pegmatite intrusions.

Pockets are of rather rare and irregular occurrence and are found only in the coarser portions of the deposit. Very few were observed by the writer. Most of them are said to be under 1 foot in diameter, but one about 4 by 6 by 5 feet in size is said to have been found. Clear crystalline quartz is the commonest mineral found in the pockets, though some tourmalines and beryls of gem quality and crystals of herderite occur. Here, as at other localities, the clevelandite variety of albite is common near the pockets.

Several dikes of typical fine-grained diabase, whose minerals under the microscope show only slight alteration, cut the pegmatite. One observed was 20 feet in width and another 6 feet in width.

[a] Kunz, G. F., On the tourmalines and associated minerals of Auburn, Me.: Am. Jour. Sci., 3d ser., vol. 27, 1884, pp. 303-305.

The topographic situation of this deposit on the crest of the hill favors the ready disposition of the waste from the quarries and also provides a down-hill haul most of the way from the quarry to the mill. The excavating is accomplished by steam drilling and blasting, the material then being broken up with sledges and picked over by hand. It is hauled 2 miles by teams to the mill at Littlefield station. The usual force consists of a foreman and 10 laborers.

The feldspar quarried at Mount Apatite is ground at a mill located at the side of the Grand Trunk Railway at Littlefield station. The ground spar is loaded directly into cars at the mill and shipped in bulk mainly to potters at Trenton, N. J., and East Liverpool, Ohio. The equipment consists of one chaser mill, in which each stone weighs about 3½ tons, and a ball mill, which is larger than that used at most feldspar mills, grinding 3 tons at a load; the capacity of the plant is about 15 tons in twenty-four hours. Eight men and a foreman are employed. The power is supplied by a 75-horsepower Westinghouse motor, the current coming from a power plant on Androscoggin River.

Turner feldspar quarries.—Three small pits on the southern part of the summit of Mount Apatite have been worked intermittently during the past ten years by E. Y. Turner, of Auburn, the product being ground principally at the mill of the Maine Feldspar Company. The quarries were idle at the time of the writer's visits in 1906 and 1907, but had been worked more or less at other times during these years. The total amount of material which has been taken out is small.

The westernmost pit is a nearly circular opening 25 feet in diameter and about 10 feet in maximum depth. Most of the rock is crowded with blades of biotite and is therefore commercially valueless, though a small amount of feldspar free from iron-bearing minerals is exposed on the floor of the pit. Some black tourmaline occurs, and rosette-shaped graphic intergrowths of quartz and muscovite are common.

The easternmost pit is about 75 feet long by 30 feet wide and 10 feet in maximum depth. At this pit two distinct bands, rich in small, dark-red, opaque garnets, run through the pegmatite; they are from 1 to 6 feet apart and dip about 15° NW. Another zone about 1 foot thick lying just above the garnetiferous zone is particularly rich in black tourmaline, and above this is a 4-foot zone which shows an unusual profusion of muscovite and biotite crystals. The 5 feet of pegmatite below the garnetiferous bands contains much feldspar of good commercial quality, iron-bearing minerals being rare. None of the upper layers at this quarry will yield feldspar suitable for pottery purposes, and the expense of removing the upper layers would probably render it unprofitable to work the layer of better quality at the bottom of the pit.

A third small pit, 40 by 40 feet and 8 feet in average depth, just north of the one described, shows some feldspar of commercial grade, as does also a small prospect pit on the southeastern slope of the hill. In the unopened natural exposures near these quarries practically all the rock is too fine grained or too rich in muscovite or iron-bearing minerals to be valuable for pottery purposes. As far, therefore, as can be judged from the present exposures these quarries show little prospect of yielding much feldspar of pottery grade. The material may ultimately prove of value for poultry grit, fertilizer, or other uses where iron-bearing minerals are not detrimental.

The pegmatite of these quarries, though of poorer quality commercially than that at the quarries of the Maine Feldspar Company, appears to form a part of the same large pegmatite mass. The excavating has been in part by hand drilling and blasting and in part by steam drilling. The equipment includes a small derrick.

Towne feldspar and gem quarry.—In April, 1907, a quarry was opened by J. S. Towne, of Brunswick, Me., on the Pulsifer farm about one-half mile northwest of the Maine Feldspar Company's quarries on Mount Apatite. This quarry is operated by the Maine Feldspar Company for feldspar, the gems found being handled by Mr. Towne.

The workings were visited by the writer in October, 1907, at which time they consisted of three very small pits all on the same half acre. All are in pegmatite but only two expose the pockety or gem-bearing zone. The third pit is higher on the hill slope, and has not yet got down to the pocket-bearing layer; in the lower pits it has penetrated it for 4 feet but has not yet reached its base. The gem-bearing layer, though grading gradually into the other pegmatite, is distinguishable from it not only by the presence of pockets but by being somewhat coarser than other portions of the pegmatite. It is characterized by the presence of clevelandite, lepidolite, and green tourmaline embedded in the solid pegmatite, the usual "indicators" of proximity to gem tourmalines. The pocket-bearing layer appears to dip about 10° E. The bordering schists are not exposed in the vicinity of this quarry.

The feldspar obtained from these pits is similar to that mined at the Maine Feldspar Company's quarry, and of equal value. Black tourmaline is abundant near many of the pockets, as is also green tourmaline in semitransparent crystals up to one-eighth inch in diameter, penetrating or interleaved with muscovite. As at most localities where gem tourmalines are found, biotite is almost entirely absent. Garnets are not abundant in the pocket-bearing layer, though fairly abundant in the bordering phases of the pegmatite. Lepidolite occurs both in granular aggregates of small scales and prisms and in large curved crystals with rounded botryoidal surfaces one-half inch to 1½ inches across; many of its curved crystals are interlaminated with the bladelike crystals of snow-white clevelandite or are partly embedded in light-gray, more or less transparent quartz. Amblygonite occurs in the solid pegmatite in irregular masses, some of them 6 to 8 inches across. Some small crystals of columbite, cassiterite, and rhodochrosite occur, but their crystal faces are usually only imperfectly developed. One crystal of zinc spinel of perfect form, five-eighths inch in diameter, was found embedded in the feldspar. At the time of the writer's visit only two gem-bearing pockets had been found. One of these bore dark grass-green tourmalines and the other light-green tourmalines tipped with opaque pink. The largest of the dark-green tourmalines was about three-fourths inch in diameter and 1½ inches long but was badly flawed. A number of other pockets bore only crystals of transparent quartz. Some fine specimens of herderite have also been found at this locality. This mineral occurs in short prisms, few of them over one-fourth inch long, commonly as an incrustation on the quartz crystals of the pockets. One short stout crystal attached to muscovite was as large as the end of one's thumb. This mode of occurrence is similar to that observed at Stoneham, where it was first discovered, and there can be little doubt that it was formed through gaseous or aqueous deposition after the solidification of the main pegmatite mass.

The feldspar obtained at this locality is hauled 2 miles for grinding to the mill of the Maine Feldspar Company. The gem tourmalines are cut and sold, principally in Maine, by Mr. Towne.

Wade and Pulsifer gem quarries.—A pegmatite mass located on the farm of P. P. Pulsifer, within 100 yards of the Towne quarry, was opened up in 1901 and was worked intermittently until 1904 for its gems and other rare minerals.

The quarry was visited by the writer in August, 1906. The original pit, opened by Mr. Pulsifer in 1901, is about 25 by 25 feet and 8 feet deep; it connects with another pit about 75 by 30 feet, with a maximum depth of 8 feet. The mineral rights at this second pit were acquired from Mr. Pulsifer by the Maine Tourmaline Company, and were worked in the summers of 1904 and 1905.[a] The two pits constitute virtually a single quarry.

The rock at this locality is practically bare, so that little or no stripping is necessary in working the deposit. The pegmatite is similar in general character to most of the gem-bearing pegmatites of the State. The main mass of the rock is a graphic intergrowth of quartz with orthoclase and microcline, showing abrupt variations in coarseness. The deposit as a whole seems to be rather flat lying, as is shown by the presence near its base of a nearly horizontal

a Wade, W. R., The gem-bearing pegmatites of western Maine: Eng. and Min. Jour., vol. 87, 1909, pp. 1127-1129.

garnetiferous layer, with more or less wavy upper surface, which could be traced continuously for over 50 feet. The garnetiferous band itself is nowhere over 1½ inches wide and is a rather finely granular crystallization of quartz, feldspar, and garnet, the crystals of garnet constituting about half of the band, but few of them exceeding one-fourth inch in diameter. In places the main garnet layer is paralleled below at a distance of 1 to 2 inches by another similar band less rich in garnets. Outside these bands garnet occurs in the pegmatite in graphic intergrowth with quartz and in small irregular masses between the other minerals. The pegmatite shows very different characters below and above these garnetiferous layers. The rock just above is much coarser, does not show graphic texture, and does show albite, in part massive and in part of the clevelandite variety, as its dominant feldspar, though it contains also some orthoclase in graphic intergrowth with quartz. Muscovite in brush-shaped and rosette-shaped intergrowths with quartz is also more abundant above than below the garnet layer, and black tourmaline is common in places in graphic intergrowth with quartz. The pegmatite just below the garnetiferous band is a rather fine-grained graphic intergrowth of quartz and orthoclase showing a more or less radial structure trending about at right angles to the garnetiferous layer.

Only small portions of the feldspar are of commercial grade for pottery purposes, both muscovite and biotite being quite abundant.

Quartz is mainly present in intergrowth with other minerals or as crystals developed on the walls of the pockets. Most of it is white or light gray, but some small amounts of rose quartz are found.

The muscovite commonly occurs with quartz in brush-shaped or rosette-shaped intergrowths averaging 4 to 5 inches in diameter and disposed with utter irregularity throughout the pegmatite mass. Some of these grade at their outer borders into spearhead-shaped bundles of muscovite penetrating the neighboring quartz masses, the latter being apparently continuous with the quartz of the fine muscovite intergrowths. No plate mica occurs, and the only possible utilization of the mineral is as scrap mica.

Biotite is abundant, though much less so than the muscovite. It occurs in small lath-shaped crystals, oriented in every direction in the pegmatite mass. A few are a foot long and 2 inches wide, but the majority do not average more than 2 inches long and 1 inch in width. A central "stalk" of biotite with smaller lath-shaped crystals radiating from it is not uncommon.

Lepidolite is abundant near the pockets in irregular aggregates of small plates or prisms one-sixteenth to one-eighth of an inch across, and in larger more or less curved crystals. In many places it forms narrow borders about hexagonal muscovite plates, the two varieties of mica being crystallographically continuous. Mr. Wade reports one

diamond-shaped book of muscovite a foot across with a border zone
of lepidolite 4 inches wide.   As in the other Maine quarries in which
gem tourmalines occur, the presence of the lithium mica is considered
a favorable indication of the near presence of gem-bearing pockets.

Black tourmaline, as already stated, occurs in the pocket-bearing
zone of the pegmatite above the garnetiferous layers.   It is never
found in the pockets, where all the tourmalines are colored either
pink, blue green, or occasionally emerald green.   Most pockets contain tourmalines of only a single color, but in some both pink and
green varieties are found, and, indeed, the two colors frequently occur
in the same crystal.   Colored tourmalines, most of them partly or
wholly opaque, also occur in the solid pegmatite near the pockets in
association with lepidolite, clevelandite, and quartz, and some of these
crystals are curved through angles as great as 60° or even 90°.   Green
tourmalines also occur intergrown parallel to the plates in the muscovite books.

The hydromica cookeite occurs principally in the pockets with
quartz as a coating on lepidolite, quartz, feldspar, and tourmaline.

The tourmalines, lepidolite, and clevelandite are beyond doubt
crystallizations from the original pegmatite magma.   The cookeite,
purple apatite crystals, and certain opaque white outer coatings of
quartz on the clearer crystals of gray quartz, are believed to be later
crystallizations from gaseous or aqueous solutions.

All of the pockets thus far encountered in this pegmatite have
been in the portion lying above the garnetiferous bands.   The portion
below it seems to be wholly devoid of pockets and hence of gem
minerals.   No pockets were exposed at the time of the writer's visit,
but those which have been encountered are said to range from a few
inches to several feet in diameter.   Though occurring apparently
only within a nearly flat-lying pocket-bearing zone their horizontal
distribution seems to be totally irregular.   Their walls usually consist mainly of clevelandite, lepidolite, and quartz, but have in most
cases been much weathered and shattered by frost.

The early excavations at the original Pulsifer pit disclosed a number
of pockets containing beautiful and very perfect crystals of purple
apatite.   The form of these crystals and their mode of occurrence
have been described by Wolff and Palache;[a] most of them are now
in the mineralogical museum of Harvard College.   The largest
pocket yielded over 2 pounds of loose crystals and a dozen large
groups of crystals in the matrix.   Most of them occurred on or
embedded in layers of the opaque white quartz which coat many of
the crystals of transparent quartz in the pockets.

The distribution of the cavities is exceedingly irregular, and no
prediction can be made as to the success which will attend further

a Wolff, J. E., and Palache, C., Apatite from Minot [should be Auburn], Me.: Proc. Am. Acad. Arts and Sci., vol. 37, No. 18, 1902, p. 515.

mining. The relations shown in the present pit seem to indicate that the trend of the garnetiferous layer above described may be taken as an indicator of the trend of the pocket-bearing portion lying just above it. Further excavation in this zone is fairly certain to disclose gem-bearing pockets, but excavation below the garnet-bearing layer has not been fruitful. Great care should be used in drilling and blasting, for injudicious placing of the drill holes and heavy blasting with dynamite are likely to shatter valuable material.

The pegmatite at this locality is cut by a dike, $2\frac{1}{2}$ feet wide, of fine-grained altered diabase.

The precise value of the gems and museum specimens taken from this locality can not be determined, but so far as known to the writer, no gems of over 6 or 8 carats have been obtained. Mr. Pulsifer estimates the value of the materials taken from the pit operated by him at about $2,000.

MINOT.

In the southeastern part of the town of Minot, near the Auburn line, some pegmatite which appears to be of commercial grade occurs on the farm of Edward Hackett, where masses of practically pure feldspar, $2\frac{1}{2}$ to 3 feet across, are associated with masses of pure quartz of similar dimensions. Almost no biotite, garnet, or black tourmaline was seen. The pegmatite seems to underlie a mass of finely pegmatitic granite. There is no doubt of its commercial quality, but as the present outcrops cover an area only about 100 feet or so square, it is uncertain whether the quantity would warrant mining. The locality is, however, worth prospecting.

POLAND.

A quarry located just across Androscoggin River from Mount Apatite, about 3 miles from Littlefield station, on the Lewiston branch of the Grand Trunk Railway, in the town of Poland, is operated for feldspar and occasional gem minerals by A. R. Berry, R. D. No. 7, Auburn, Maine.

The quarry was opened in 1900 and has been worked intermittently on a small scale ever since. It was visited by the writer in August, 1906. The openings, which are very irregular and cover an area of about 2 acres, are shallow open pits, none of them more than 18 or 20 feet in maximum depth.

The general character of the pegmatite is similar to that at the Maine Feldspar Company's quarries at Mount Apatite. The rock is mainly a graphic intergrowth of quartz with buff-colored microcline and some orthoclase. Some albite in irregular crystals a few inches across is encountered.

Muscovite occurs, as at the Wade and Pulsifer quarries, in brush-like and rosette-like intergrowths with quartz. No plate mica occurs, and no attempt has been made to market the material as scrap mica.

Biotite is locally very abundant, occurring as irregularly disposed blades or bundle-like masses in which thin layers of feldspar or quartz occur between the blades. Such biotitic bundles occur in association with the coarser phases of the pegmatite, and render valueless for pottery purposes much feldspar which could otherwise be used.

The lithium mica, lepidolite, occurs in the pockets and near them in the usual forms, similar to those described from the Wade and Pulsifer quarries. (See pp. 57–58.)

Black tourmaline is abundant in certain parts of the pegmatite, usually in intergrowth with quartz, one mass of intergrown quartz and black tourmaline being 10 to 12 inches across. One black tourmaline crystal observed was 5 by 12 inches in size. In the pockets no black tourmaline is found, but some emerald-green, blue-green, and pink transparent varieties occur, usually embedded in a mass of kaolin, cookeite, etc., at the bottoms of the pockets. The largest colored tourmaline obtained at this quarry was a pale-green crystal about 1½ inches in diameter. Only an inch of the base was found and it was too much flawed to cut any gems. Many of the smaller, colored tourmalines are hollow and can be strung like beads.[a] Slender flattened prisms of opaque to transparent green tourmaline occur, penetrating and interleaved with muscovite plates.

A few fine crystals of purple apatite similar to those found at the Wade and Pulsifer quarries have been obtained from some pockets. In some of the finer-grained portions of the pegmatite the writer observed numerous small vugs, rarely more than a cubic centimeter or two in volume. These were generally surrounded by albite in small bladelike crystals. Attached to or embedded in the albite at their base or along their flanks, but otherwise free, occur hexagonal prisms, from one-sixteenth to one-fourth inch in diameter, of pale greenish blue to pale lavender apatite. These plainly were among the last of the pegmatite constituents to crystallize, being in part contemporaneous with the albite and in part later. Blue-gray apatite in flat, bladelike prisms one-fourth to one-half inch across also occurs. Beryl and amblygonite occur as constituents of the solid pegmatite, as in most of the pegmatites bearing gem tourmaline. Herderite in crystals up to one-half inch in length is found in some pockets.

The distribution of pockets at this quarry is very irregular, and the writer saw no structures which indicated even in a general way the attitude of the deposit. There is unquestionably a considerable

---

[a] In the summer of 1910, since the above account was written, several pockets containing fine gem tourmalines were discovered by Mr. F. S. Havey in the western part of the quarry near a diabase dike. Mr. Havey was working the quarry for feldspar for the Maine Feldspar Company.

amount of commercial feldspar of pottery grade still available at the locality.

The feldspar is excavated by hand drilling and blasting, and after hand sorting is hauled by wagons 3 miles to Littlefield station, where it is sold to the Maine Feldspar Company and ground at that company's mill. Gem tourmalines and minerals of value as cabinet specimens are not encountered so frequently that it is profitable to work the deposit for them alone. In 1906 the quarry force consisted of three men. The gems and other valuable minerals obtained are marketed irregularly through local collectors, and no estimate of their value is obtainable. The feldspar output is a few hundred tons a year.

CUMBERLAND COUNTY.

BRUNSWICK.

The relations between the granite and pegmatite in the town of Brunswick is well shown at the Woodside quarry, about $2\frac{1}{2}$ miles southeast of Hillside station. This is an old quarry, where granite for flagging and underpinning has been obtained. The sheeting of the granite here is very perfect and nearly horizontal.

On the south wall of this quarry much pegmatite is associated with the granite. Many of the pegmatite masses of lenticular or extremely irregular form grade into the granite in the most gradual and complete manner and are characterized by identical minerals. They differ from the granite only in texture, and there can be no question that the two rocks solidified practically contemporaneously from the same magma. Other pegmatite dikes, however, distinctly cut the granite with sharp contacts. The entire mineralogic similarity of this second type to the pegmatite which grades into the granite leads to the belief that the two types are genetically connected and that the intrusion of the pegmatite masses that show sharp boundaries followed quickly on the solidification of the granite which they cut.

Very similar relations were observed at the Grant quarry, about $1\frac{1}{2}$ miles east of Hillside and 3 miles west of Brunswick. This quarry has been described by Dale.[a]

The relations between the pegmatite and foliated rocks, which are probably of igneous origin, is well exhibited in Brunswick village at a quarry for road materials near the Lewiston branch of the Maine Central Railroad. The folia in the rocks are in many places very straight and regular for considerable distances. Much of the rock is a light-gray schist which has the mineral composition of a hornblende granite.

The slide of this rock examined shows an interlocking granular texture in which most of the grains range from 0.15 to 0.60 milli-

---

[a] Dale, T. N., The granites of Maine: Bull. U. S. Geol. Survey No. 313, 1907, p. 76.

meter. It is composed of about two-fifths quartz, two-fifths feldspar, and one-fifth hornblende, with subordinate titanite and biotite. Some of the hornblende crystals are 1.2 millimeters in length. Their tendency to parallel elongation and to greater abundance in some layers than in others gives the rock its schistose character. Biotite is also most abundant in the layers that are most hornblendic. The feldspar is principally orthoclase with a little microcline and plagioclase near andesine. Many of the quartz grains show strain shadows, but there is no other evidence of dynamic action.

Alternating with this rock are bands of very dark gray to nearly black hornblende-biotite schist with lustrous cleavage faces. An intermediate phase is a dark-gray hornblende schist with a few narrow quartz bands up to about one-eighth inch across.

Under the microscope this rock is seen to consist of quartz, plagioclase, and hornblende. The plagioclase is andesine and is about equal to hornblende in abundance. Quartz is slightly less abundant than either. Titanite is subordinate. Occasional narrow bands are more coarsely crystalline and are largely quartz, with some feldspar. Their grains interlock intimately with those of the finer portions of the rock. The schistosity, as in the more acidic bands, is due to the concentration of hornblende along certain planes and of quartz along certain others and to parallel elongation of many of the hornblende crystals.

If these schists represent original sediments their recrystallization has been so complete as to obliterate all traces of such an origin. The abundance of feldspar, on the other hand, especially in the more basic bands, renders it much more probable that they are primary or flow schists.

The pegmatite in some cases is in sharp contact with the gneiss, and the contacts may parallel or cut across the foliation. In other cases the pegmatite seems to grade into the gneiss with such completeness as to indicate either that portions of the gneiss were not yet completely solidified when the pegmatite was intruded or that the pegmatite produced locally very complete recrystallization in the schist. The pegmatite is a typical biotite pegmatite showing much graphic granite and a few crystals of pure feldspar 4 or 5 inches across.

WESTBROOK.

A quartz deposit which was worked to a small extent many years ago is located about 1 mile northwest of the village of Cumberland Mills. The quartz forms part of a pegmatite dike intruding mica schist and granodiorite. The width of the dike varies from 2 to 10 feet, and its trend is nearly north and south. Most of the mass is typical granite-pegmatite of moderate coarseness, but with this is associated a body of nearly pure white quartz, which in places seems intrusive in the pegmatite, though elsewhere passing gradually into it. The quartz quarried was taken to Portland and there ground for use in pottery and filters.

HANCOCK COUNTY.

Pegmatite is present only in relatively minor amounts in association with the granites of Hancock County. The occurrence of molybdenite with pegmatite at Catherine Hill, near Tunk Pond, has been described by Emmons.[a]

LINCOLN COUNTY.

EDGECOMB.

The rocks of the town of Edgecomb are mainly quartz-mica schists of sedimentary origin which have been intruded by pegmatite, granite, and minor amounts of granite gneiss. The pegmatites have been exploited for feldspar at one locality near the center of the town.

Edgecomb feldspar quarry.—A feldspar quarry, long since abandoned, is situated 2½ miles south of the village of Newcastle and about one-half mile south of the road extending from North Edgecomb to Briar Cove, on Damariscotta River. It is within the Boothbay quadrangle of the United States Geological Survey.

The locality was visited by the writer in August, 1906. The excavations consist of two open pits, one 150 feet long and 50 feet wide, filled with water at the time of the writer's visit; the other 50 feet long, 25 feet wide, and 15 feet deep. The soil overburden is slight. The pegmatite resembles in its mineral character that quarried at Topsham, in Sagadahoc County, but contains less feldspar of commercial grade.

The quartz is not abundant enough to be of commercial importance. The largest masses observed are between the two pits and are 3 feet across. The color varies from white to dark gray.

The feldspar is buff to cream-colored orthoclase and microcline, occurring principally in graphic intergrowth with quartz. At the northwest end of the larger pit some masses of nearly pure feldspar are 3 feet across, but such size is quite exceptional.

Biotite in the usual lath-shaped crystals, in places attaining a length of 3 feet, is very abundant and is the most injurious of the mineral constituents, black tourmaline being wholly absent so far as observed.

Pink opaque garnets occur locally but are not abundant. Many of them are inclosed by muscovite.

As far as could be observed, very little feldspar of a quality suitable for the pottery trade remains at this locality, the prevalence of

---

a Emmons, W. H., Ore deposits of Maine and the Milan mine, New Hampshire: Bull. U. S. Geol. Survey No. 432, 1910, p. 42.

biotite rendering most of the material worthless for that purpose. The water in the larger pit of course prevented its thorough examination. An examination of the vicinity yielded no information as to the trend or extent of the deposit, and showed no other masses of commercially valuable feldspar. No gem minerals have been reported, and there are no indications, such as the occurrence of pockets, lepidolite, black tourmaline, etc., that any are likely to be found. Under present commercial conditions, the deposit may be regarded as worked out. It may in the future be of value if some commercially practical method of separating the mica can be devised, or it may be used for purposes where the presence of black mica (biotite) is not detrimental, such as for fertilizing, poultry grit, ready roofing, etc.

Geologic relations.—About half a mile north of the Edgecomb feldspar quarry, on the north side of the road, the predominant rock is a medium-grained granite of slightly varying texture, which along certain bands and in some irregular patches is pegmatitic. The constituents of the granite are identical with those of the pegmatite and there can be no question that the two rocks solidified from the same parent magma at about the same time. Muscovite is almost entirely absent from this granite, as it is from the pegmatite of the above-described feldspar quarry, biotite being the dominant mica. West of these granite outcrops extensive ledges of pegmatite intrude quartz-mica schists in a very irregular manner, at many places cutting sharply across their foliation.

Typical structural relations between the pegmatite and the schists are well shown along the north shore of the narrow gurnet known as the Oven Mouth. Here the schists are traversed by numerous small pegmatite intrusions, most of which are parallel to the schist folia or cut them at low angles only.

The smaller pegmatite intrusions commonly assume the form of a series of connecting lenticles or show periodic swellings along their lengths. The schists are dark gray to purplish and show quartz, biotite, and hornblende as their dominant constituents, with muscovite and garnet as accessories. Feldspar was not observed and if present at all is very meager in amount. The schists are almost certainly of sedimentary origin.

BOOTHBAY HARBOR.

Character and relations of the pegmatite.—The rocks of the town of Boothbay Harbor are largely quartz-mica schists which are intruded and in many places intimately injected by granite and pegmatite. Two occurrences of the very unusual rock prowersose were also observed. Very excellent and instructive exposures occur along the irregular shore line of this region, and although none of the pegmatites have proved commercially valuable their geologic relations at a number of points are of much scientific interest.

Excellent exposures on the first point west of Boothbay Harbor village show the intrusive pegmatite and the intruded quartz-biotite schists locally very much contorted, much as if the two had been stirred up together with a gigantic spoon. In most places, however, the schist is of fairly uniform trend over considerable areas. Other exposures just west of these show a number of schist fragments inclosed by the pegmatite. The fragments are subangular, but at their extremities tail out somewhat into the pegmatite. The fragments as a whole appear therefore to have maintained their rigidity but to have yielded somewhat about their borders to the deforming action of the intrusive pegmatite.

On the shore of McKown Point about one-fourth mile south of the United States fish hatcheries pegmatite and granite are intrusive into quartz-mica schists. The contact between the schist and the igneous rocks is sharp, neither rock showing any notable changes in grain or texture as the contact is approached. The transition from pegmatite to granite is also abrupt, although crystallographic continuity is preserved. It is impossible to say which is the intruded and which the intrusive rock, and their association is extremely irregular. The granite shows distinct flow lines parallel in a general way to the schist walls and particularly well developed next the pegmatite. The latter also shows a tendency toward the development of faint flow lines next the granite, these being defined by a concentration of biotite plates along certain planes.

The granite gneiss is dark buff to gray and shows a rather faint foliation due to the aggregation of the biotite along certain planes or lenses few of which are continuous for more than one-half or three-fourths of an inch. The interspaces are largely quartz and feldspar. Under the microscope the mineral constituents in order of abundance are seen to be quartz > orthoclase and microcline > or = oligoclase > biotite > muscovite. Orthoclase is greatly in excess of microcline and occurs in larger grains. The average size of grain is about 1 millimeter, though a few feldspars are 2 millimeters across. The rock is very fresh, though some of the feldspars show a slight clouding with decomposition products. No parallel structure is observable under the microscope. There is complete interlocking of the grains, which show no important amount of fracturing, no crushed borders, nor any other evidence of dynamic action. The foliation appears to be an original feature developed by flowage before complete solidification.

The pegmatite associated with the gneiss shows light-gray quartz and gray to buff feldspars in nearly equal amounts, with biotite the dominant mica, as in the gneissic granite. The texture is wholly irregular and typically pegmatitic because of the great range in size exhibited by crystal grains of the same mineral species. Quartz is the most abundant mineral with microcline > oligoclase > biotite > or = orthoclase > muscovite. The rock differs from the associated gneissic granite mainly in its texture and in the fact that microcline dominates over orthoclase instead of bearing the reverse relation to it.

The close association of the granite and pegmatite and the fact that the same minerals are present in the same order of abundance in both rocks is highly suggestive of a genetic connection between the two.

At a point on the east shore of Boothbay Harbor the fine-grained pegmatite was observed to be traversed by a vein of white quartz 2 to 3 inches in width. The borders of this vein are not sharp; feldspar crystals of the bordering pegmatite project into it, and in some instances their inner borders (next the quartz) show well-developed crystal faces. Isolated crystals of feldspar up to 3 inches in length also occur, apparently wholly surrounded by the quartz of the vein. The feldspathic character of this vein and the absence of a sharp or straight boundary between it and the pegmatite indicate that it was not deposited as a fissure filling along a fracture plane traversing solid pegmatite, but rather that it was genetically a part of the pegmatite magma and was formed before the complete solidification of its host. Apparently it represents an end product of the pegmatite crystallization. The sheetlike form of the vein indicates presumably that the pegmatite was sufficiently rigid to permit the formation of a rift of some sort along which the more quartzose magma could penetrate, but that coarsely interlocking crystallization between vein and wall was still possible. Similar relationships have been observed by the writer on a larger scale in some of the feldspar quarries of Connecticut. (See Pl. XVI, B, p. 18.) They are of importance as showing without much question that many at least of the quartz veins associated with the pegmatites may be regarded as an end product of the crystallization of the pegmatite magma.

Southward along the east shore of Boothbay Harbor to Spruce Point abundant dikes of pegmatite are found traversing the schists; they vary from one-fourth to one-half an inch to 10 feet or even 50 feet across. Nearly all of the dikes and particularly the smaller ones assume the form of a succession of connecting lenses, indicating a very uneven penetration of the pegmatite magma between the schist folia. The schists usually exhibit a thickening of their laminæ opposite the "nodes" of these irregularly bulging dikes, indicating a crystallographic rearrangement of the schist constituents as an accompaniment of the pegmatite intrusion.

It is significant that numerous dikes of granite also exposed along this shore never exhibit such irregular swelling and thinning, but are nearly parallel-walled even where intruded parallel to the foliation of the bordering schists.

On the point due north of Cabbage Island the rocks are almost entirely granite and pegmatite associated in a very irregular manner. The pegmatite forms dikes of varying width and irregular boundaries in the granite and also forms narrow stringers and wholly irregular patches. In general the change from one rock to the other is rather abrupt, although characterized by complete crystallographic continuity. In the places where the association is most intimate and irregular it is difficult to see how the granite could have been wholly solidified at the time of the pegmatite crystallization.

The granite is gray to pinkish, with a faint local foliation. The average size of grains is about one-half to three-fourths of a millimeter. The texture is typically granitic with quartz > orthoclase and microcline > oligoclase > biotite > muscovite. The quartz shows undulatory extinctions. Some of the smaller quartz crystals are inclosed by orthoclase or oligoclase and show rounded outlines. Some of the quartz also crystallized earlier than or contemporaneously with the biotite crystallization. The bulk of the quartz, characterized by more irregular outlines and larger grains, is a later crystallization than the biotite and appears to be about contemporaneous with the feldspars. Among the feldspars orthoclase is present in greater abundance and larger grains than microcline. Oligoclase is almost equal to the potash feldspar in abundance. Many of the feldspar crystals inclose small crystals of muscovite, which are apparently original. Some micrographic intergrowths of feldspar and quartz occur.

The pegmatite is characterized by the same minerals as the granite. Quartz is the dominant constituent, with orthoclase and microcline second and oligoclase third. Biotite dominates over muscovite, but is less abundant than in the granite. The quartz exhibits little or no undulatory extinction. Some of the grains exhibit crystal outlines on certain sides, but the outlines of others are very irregular. The feldspars exhibit only slight decomposition.

It is notable that both rocks carry the same minerals in the same order of abundance.

In general the pegmatite characteristic of the Boothbay Harbor region shows considerable uniformity in mineralogical make-up. Characteristically it shows irregular crystals of orthoclase-microcline, ranging in diameter up to 6 inches, surrounded by a less coarsely crystalline association of potash feldspar, white to gray or amber-colored quartz in masses sometimes several inches across, small amounts of nearly white plagioclase, and varying proportions of muscovite and biotite in crystals seldom over an inch across, usually more or less aggregated in bunches. Red garnets are present in varying but small numbers and are rarely over one-fourth inch in diameter. Small amounts of a white sugary matrix are not uncommon and consist largely of a fine graphic intergrowth of quartz and feldspar.

Schist associated with pegmatites.—A specimen of schist collected along the shore near the United States fish hatcheries on McKown Point illustrates the indeterminate character of some of the foliates associated with the pegmatite. The rock is dark-gray, millimeter grained, with a fairly perfect foliation due mainly to parallel orientation of the mineral grains but accentuated by quartz laminæ 1 to 2 millimeters across.

Under the microscope the texture is seen to be interlocking granular, the constituents being quartz > hornblende > labradorite, with biotite, titanite, calcite, and apatite subordinate. Mineralogically the rock is therefore a quartz-rich diorite. Many of the quartzes extinguish abruptly, though some show slight undulatory extinction. The green hornblende grains are very irregular, but show a tendency towards elongation in a parallel direction. This elongate character, together with the tendency toward aggregation of the quartz grains along certain lines, produces the foliated structure. Titanite is very abundant in irregular grains and also in grains showing elongate rhombic outlines. The hornblende shows no alteration whatever. The feldspar is in part perfectly fresh but some of the grains show saussuritization.

Calcite, which is present in moderate amounts, is in contact with quartz, titanite, or unaltered feldspar or hornblende, the contacts being as sharp as between any others of the rock constituents. Its abundance is scarcely explainable by the very slight alteration characteristic of most of the rock, and it is necessary to assume either that it completely replaced certain grains or portions of grains of other minerals, without any of the mottling and irregular penetration usually characteristic of such replacement, or else to assume that it crystallized at the same period as the quartz, feldspar, hornblende, etc., with which it is in contact. Such an association could readily be explained as the result of contact or regional metamorphism of a slightly calcareous arkose. The texture and mineral composition and even the presence of calcite is not, however, incompatible with an igneous rather than a metamorphic-sedimentary origin.

We are accustomed to reason by analogy from the phenomenon of calcining observed when carbonates are heated under ordinary surface conditions to the postulate that carbonates, if they existed in igneous rocks, would undergo the same changes, and thence to conclude that carbonates can not exist as such in igneous rocks.

The reasoning is obviously weak, because in the one case the conditions are those of low pressure and ready escape of gases, whereas in the case of a magma cooling to form a granular rock of moderate coarseness they are probably those of relatively high pressure and much greater ability to retain components which under surface conditions would be freed in a gaseous form. The microscopic evidence of the original character of the carbonate in this case is regarded as suggestive rather than conclusive, but there appears to be no a priori reason why it should not be original.

The schist described lies between two intrusions of pegmatite, one 5 to 6 feet wide and the other 4 to 5 feet. The field and microscopic evidence is insufficient to determine whether it is igneous or metamorphic-sedimentary in origin, and because of the abundance of plagioclase it is doubtful whether a chemical analysis would furnish conclusive evidence.

Schists of the Boothbay Harbor region which she believes to be of metamorphic-sedimentary origin have been described and analyses given by Dr. Ida H. Ogilvie.[a]

Syenite porphyry.—In 1906 the writer described[b] a rock of peculiar appearance and unusual composition from the town of Appleton in Knox County. The rock is a porphyry showing blue-gray phenocrysts of potash feldspar up to $1\frac{1}{2}$ inches in length in a dark-green groundmass composed mainly of biotite and hornblende with minor amounts of titanite, apatite, quartz, magnetite, and albite. Chemically it is unusual because of the great dominance of potash over soda in a rock so femic and so high in lime.

Rocks which in the field are indistinguishable from prowersose from the Appleton locality and which on chemical analysis fall in very closely related divisions of the quantitative system of rock classification, from several localities in the Boothbay Harbor region, have been described by Dr. Ida H. Ogilvie.[c]

A number of Dr. Ogilvie's localities were visited by the writer before he became familiar with her published descriptions. A locality not specifically mentioned by her is the shore of Linekin Bay, southeast of Mount Pisgah. At this locality and on Spruce Point the syenite is intruded by dikes of pegmatite and of fine-grained granite. Many central portions of the syenite intrusions show little or no foliation and a very heterogeneous orientation of the phenocrysts, but in the narrower masses or near the borders of the larger masses foliation is well developed, and is found to be due to crushing and shearing movements, probably accompanying

a Ogilvie, I. H., A contribution to the geology of southern Maine: Ann. New York Acad. Sci., vol. 17, pt. 2, 1907, pp. 526–527.

b Bastin, E. S., Some unusual rocks from Maine: Jour. Geology, vol. 14, 1906, pp. 173–180.

c Ogilvie, I. H., A contribution to the geology of southern Maine: Ann. New York Acad. Sci., vol. 17, pt. 2, 1907, pp. 536–541.

dynamic metamorphism. On Spruce Point many of the feldspar phenocrysts are nearly black on account of the abundance of minute inclusions.

OXFORD COUNTY.

ALBANY.

The rocks of most of the town of Albany are quartz-mica schists of probable sedimentary origin which have been intensely injected by pegmatite and intruded by dikes of fine-grained granite. In all observed places where the granite and pegmatite were associated, the former was the older rock. Along the road running nearly parallel to Crooked River, near the center of the town, diorite or quartz diabase is of abundant occurrence and is intruded by dikes of fine diabase, fine-grained granite containing few dark-colored minerals, and pegmatite. In the northwestern part of the town a gray granite gneiss forms the country rock over large areas.

French Mountain beryl locality.—In the eastern part of the town of Albany a pegmatite mass very rich in quartz has yielded some beryls of fine gem quality. The locality is in the woods in a sag between two knobs of the hill crest and is difficult to discover without a guide. Only a few blasts have been made in the ledge. Much of the quartz is very clear and some is of a fine rose tint. The locality is of interest to the mineral collector but is not of commercial importance.

Bennett mica prospect.—A small mass of pegmatite which has been prospected for mica by W. S. Robinson is situated in the western part of the town of Albany on the farm of F. H. Bennett, about 5 miles west of Hunt Corners. The pegmatite dike has an exposed thickness of 10 feet and is intrusive in granite gneiss similar to that occurring farther west. The pegmatite is a coarse association of quartz, muscovite, orthoclase, and black tourmaline. The muscovite occurs in graphic intergrowth with quartz and also in "books" up to 6 inches across, though mostly under 3 inches. Nearly all is of the wedge variety and shows twinning. Feldspar is too intimately mixed with black tourmaline to be of any value. Neither the quantity nor the quality of the materials here seem to warrant further development.

Pingree mica prospect.—Another pegmatite mass, situated on the farm of C. P. Pingree, in the extreme western part of the town of Albany, was worked to a slight extent for mica in 1878–79, and was opened again in 1900 by W. S. Robinson; no shipments, however, except of samples, have ever been made. The ledge has yielded some beryls of gem quality. In the absence of the owner of this property the writer was unable to visit it. Bethel, the nearest station, is about 8 miles distant on the Grand Trunk Railway.

ANDOVER.

F. G. Hillman, of New Bedford, Mass., has reported his discovery in pegmatite in Andover of lilac-colored spodumene, or kunzite, as well as of some with a greenish color. A cleavage specimen sent to the Survey measured about 12 by 10 by 3½ millimeters and had a very pretty clear pink color. It was not entirely without cleavage cracks, however. The greenish material was a pale aquamarine, nearly clear, though rather badly fractured. This spodumene was obtained near the surface, and excavating to a greater depth has disclosed no material of gem quality.

BUCKFIELD.

The rocks of the town of Buckfield are largely quartz-mica schists which have been injected by pegmatite. The pegmatites have not been extensively worked in any part of the town but have at a few places yielded golden beryl, aquamarine, and cæsium beryl. A fine twinned crystal of chrysoberyl from this town in the museum of the Sheffield Scientific School of Yale University is 2 inches long and one-half inch thick. This same collection also contains very perfect diamond-shaped crystals of muscovite from Buckfield.

GREENWOOD.

So far as known the rocks of the southern part of the town of Greenwood are schists which have been intruded by granite and pegmatite. In the northern part of the town granite is believed to become more abundant.

A small abandoned mine which has yielded many interesting mineral specimens and some gem tourmalines is situated about three-fourths of a mile east of Hicks Pond in the southern part of the town. The pit, which is 15 feet in width and about 25 feet long, is located on the western slope of a steep forested hillside, near its summit. It was visited by the writer in September, 1906.

The rock is a coarse pegmatite made up largely of quartz, muscovite, albite of the clevelandite variety, and some orthoclase-microcline. The feldspar does not occur in commercial amounts. Some of the muscovite books are 14 inches across the plates and a foot in thickness, but all except a few show twinning and wedge structure, which render them useless as a source of plate mica. In places mica constitutes half of the rock. Black tourmaline is present but is not abundant.

Pockets are numerous, most of those observed being under 1 foot in diameter. One gigantic one was 7 feet wide and 10 feet long, with a depth of at least 4 feet, the floor being buried under a considerable thickness of detritus; numerous small lobes add irregularity to its form. Wherever the walls of this pocket have not "shelled off" by the action of frost, etc., they are covered with a coating of minute crystals of quartz. In some places the minerals which have been coated in this way have subsequently decayed, leaving only their quartz covering. As these quartz crystals are transparent and usually show hexagonal forms they probably crystallized below 575° C., presumably as a deposition from meteoric waters. Where this secondary quartz has been deposited on original quartz crystals it has grown in perfect crystal continuity with them but is distinguished by being opaque white rather than transparent. It is interesting to note that this growth of secondary quartz has been most rapid at the apices of the quartz crystals, the coating here being much thicker than on the sides of the crystals.

The precise form and extent of the pegmatite deposit could not be ascertained, but it appears to be irregular. The coarse pegmatite is traceable for about 25 feet north of the present pit, beyond which it is concealed by soil. The southern wall of the pit is composed of schists, which strike N. 50° W. and dip nearly vertical.

The locality has yielded a considerable number of tourmalines of gem quality, but very few have been marketed, much of the material being still in the hands of George Noyes, of Fryeburg, who developed the property. Other minerals occurring here are apatite in small, opaque, olive-green crystals (present in great abundance in some of the fine-grained parts of the pegmatite), opaque, pale lilac-colored spodumene, cassiterite, beryl, herderite,[a] zircon, and phenacite.

The locality, though affording many interesting mineral specimens, can not be regarded as of much commercial importance.

HEBRON.

The rocks of the town of Hebron are principally quartz-mica schists, extensively intruded and injected by pegmatite, which shows great variations in coarseness. The coarser phases have proved of economic importance for feldspar at Number Four Hill in the western part of the town and on the Hibbs farm north of Hebron village, and gem tourmalines and various mineral specimens have been obtained at Mount Rubellite, about 2 miles northeast of Hebron village.

Hibbs feldspar and mica mine.—A small feldspar and mica mine was opened in 1906, about 1½ miles north of Hebron village near the Buckfield road. It is located on the farm of Alton Hibbs and was operated during 1906 by J. A. Gerry, of Mechanic Falls, and W. Scott Robinson. It was abandoned in 1907. The property was visited by the writer in August, 1906, after considerable stripping and prospecting had been done. The ledge was exposed for a distance of 300 to 350 feet along the southwest side of a small creek valley, the

---

a Described by S. L. Penfield, Am. Jour. Sci., 3d ser., vol. 47, 1894, p. 337.

average width of outcrop being about 30 feet, though increasing to 50 feet at at least one point; only shallow excavations had been made. The exposures show numerous masses of pure orthoclase-microcline feldspar 2 to 3 feet across, associated with much graphic granite. The spar is mottled buff to blue-gray. Small amounts of the soda feldspar, albite, are found. The principal iron-bearing impurity is black tourmaline, so aggregated that it can be readily separated in the mining. It was estimated that feldspar of commercial grade for pottery purposes formed about 60 per cent of the rock mined. Biotite is present in the usual lath-shaped crystals up to 1 foot wide and 3 feet long but is not at all abundant.

Muscovite is found in most parts of the pegmatite in small books up to 2 to 3 inches across; but it occurs in abundance and in larger plates only at the southwestern border of the mass, where in a zone averaging 3 to 4 feet in width the mica books average 5 inches in diameter and one reaches 30 inches; this specimen, however, was imperfect. It is estimated that in this zone muscovite constitutes on the average at least 10 per cent and sometimes 20 per cent of the rock. Of this it was estimated that fully 60 per cent could be trimmed into plates, the remainder being usable only as scrap mica. Wedge structure and ruling are the common de-

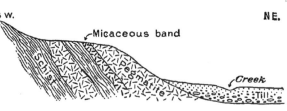

FIGURE 6.—Relations of pegmatite and wall rock at Hibbs feldspar and mica mine, Hebron.

fects. Plates as large as 5 by 6 inches could be trimmed from a few of the mica books.

Exposures are not numerous enough to reveal the full form or extent of the pegmatite mass. On its southwest side it is bounded by quartz-mica schists, which trend from N. 30° W. to N. 50° W., averaging about N. 45° W., and apparently dip about 45° NE. The northeast border of the deposit is wholly obscured by drift. The mica-rich band which follows the southwest margin of the pegmatite mass can be traced for 300 to 350 feet—nearly the whole distance through which the pegmatite mass itself is exposed. The apparent relations of the pegmatite and schist are shown in figure 6.

From the exposures at the time of the writer's visit this property was regarded as a promising one for both feldspar and mica mining. It seems probable that further stripping will show that the deposit extends northwest and southeast of the present exposures, and since it seems to be steeply inclined there is no reason why it should not persist in good quality to considerable depth. The development work was suspended for reasons wholly aside from the quality of the deposit. All output must be hauled by teams 3 miles to Hebron station, on the Rangeley division of the Maine Central Railroad.

Mount Rubellite.—A hill known as Mount Rubellite, situated about 2 miles northeast of Hebron village, was formerly worked to a slight extent for its gems and rarer minerals by Augustus Hamlin, of Bangor, and Loren B. Merrill, of Paris. The writer's visit was made in August, 1906.

The small opening exposes a face of rock about 5 feet high and 35 feet long on a southwestward sloping hillside. The pegmatite resembles in a general way that at Mount Mica (p. 86), but has yielded few pockets, Mr. Merrill reporting the occurrence of only three or four, one of which was about 3 feet wide, 6 feet long, and 18 inches deep. Buff-colored orthoclase-microcline feldspar is in many places so penetrated by black tourmaline, the principal iron-bearing impurity, as to be useless for pottery purposes, but a few pure masses 5 feet across indicate that the locality may be worth working. At one place books of mica, some of them 5 to 6 inches across, but mostly smaller, show on the surface of the unopened ledge above the pit, but they do not seem to form a definite vein. Probably some of this mica could be marketed in connection with the feldspar; but the indications do not warrant development for the mica alone.

Colored tourmalines have been found at this locality, but for the most part in the solid pegmatite rather than in pockets, so that their excavation without shattering was not practicable. As may be inferred from the name given to the locality, the pink or rubellite variety was of common occurrence.

Other minerals from this locality are ambylgonite, apatite in small opaque green crystals, arsenopyrite, beryl, cassiterite inclosed in clevelandite, childrenite, cookeite, damourite (an alteration product of tourmaline), halloysite, herderite,[a] lepidolite,[b] pollucite[c] (embedded in the "sand" at the bottom of two pockets), and vesuvianite.

The trend or extent of the coarse pegmatite could not be determined.

It is possible that it would pay to work this locality for its feldspar, mica, and occasional gems, but it would probably be unprofitable to work it for any one of these alone. The haul to Hebron station, on the Rangeley branch of the Maine Central Railroad, is about 3 miles.

Streaked Mountain.—Streaked Mountain, in the extreme northwest corner of the town of Hebron, shows in a striking way the large size which some of the masses of coarse pegmatite may assume. The

---

a Wells, H. L., and Penfield, S. L., Am. Jour. Sci., 3d ser., vol. 44, pp. 114–116, 1892, also 3d ser., vol. 47, p. 333, 1894.

b Clarke, F. W., Bull. U. S. Geol. Survey No. 42, 1887, p. 14.

c Wells, H. L., On the composition of pollucite and its occurrence at Hebron, Me.: Am. Jour. Sci., 3d ser., vol. 41, 1891, pp. 213–220.

crest of this mountain trends in a northwest-southeast direction and was examined for over half a mile of its length. The width of outcrop examined from southwest to northeast across the trend of the ridge was also about half a mile. The whole area traversed and the remainder of the mountain so far as it could be seen was underlain almost exclusively by coarse pegmatite, the mountain being essentially a "boss" of this material. Near the highest part a few patches of schist a few square yards in surface are entirely surrounded by pegmatite. Another schist mass was 40 to 50 feet wide and 100 feet long. It was bordered on three sides by pegmatite, its fourth contact being obscured by vegetation. These masses appear to be entirely unconnected with any large schist areas.

The pegmatite is of the usual type, being an association, often in graphic intergrowth, of quartz, orthoclase-microcline, muscovite, black tourmaline, and subordinate amounts of biotite. In a few places, as on the highest part of the mountain, it is coarse enough to yield feldspar of suitable quality for pottery purposes, some masses of pure potash feldspar being 2 to 3 feet across and rather coarse graphic granite being abundant. Its inaccessible location would, however, render its working impracticable under present conditions. Certain portions of this pegmatite consist almost wholly of graphic granite, intersected by blades of muscovite, but these areas grade into others characterized by a granular-pegmatitic texture and containing the same minerals, but also much black tourmaline and some garnet.

It is difficult to conceive of a mass of this size and general uniformity crystallizing under anything like vein conditions. With high gaseous content and hence high mobility it would be natural to expect more differentiation both in texture and composition. Although the composition of the pegmatite magma was probably slightly different from the normal granite magma, it seems probable that the rigidity of the mass was not greatly less than that which would characterize a granite boss of similar dimensions.

Mills feldspar quarry.—A small abandoned feldspar quarry, situated on Number Four Hill, near the Paris–Hebron line, was visited by the writer in August, 1906. The quarry was worked by the Mount Marie Mining Company in 1901 but was soon abandoned.

The principal pit is about 75 feet long by 30 feet wide and 10 feet in maximum depth. A second pit close by is about 30 by 30 feet and 10 feet deep.

The bulk of the feldspar belongs to the potash varieties, orthoclase, and microcline, though some albite of the clevelandite variety occurs in the coarser-grained portions. In the northwestern part of the larger pit some masses of pure spar are 3 to 4 feet across. The bare ledge to the north of the smaller pit for a length of 40 or 50 feet and a width of about 30 feet shows feldspar in crystals 2 to 4 feet across but containing numerous small crystals of black tourmaline. In the larger pit there is a small amount of feldspar of commercial grade at its northwest end, but in the smaller pit and in the unopened ledge near the pits black tourmaline is so intimately and abundantly associated with the feldspar as to render most of the latter valueless for pottery purposes under present commercial conditions. The coarsest and most highly feldspathic portion of the deposit as exposed in the larger pit contains some clevelandite and granular lepidolite and a few colored tourmalines of pink and green tints, which are translucent to opaque. A few small pockets occur and several less than a foot in diameter were exposed at the time of the writer's visit. In some of the pockets a few transparent tourmalines of gem quality were found during the mining operations. South of the workings the ledge shows very little feldspar of pottery grade and within 200 feet there begins to be some admixture of schist with the pegmatite.

Muscovite has been saved during the mining, but most of it is what is known as wedge mica and would be valueless except as a source of ground mica. Biotite or black mica is very rare, black tourmaline being the principal iron-bearing impurity.

The trend and exact limits of this deposit could not be determined, but there is every indication that the supply of feldspar suitable for use in the pottery trade is very small, most of the material showing too great an abundance of black tourmaline. An examination of the whole coast of the hill south of the pits showed no spar or other minerals of commercial grade. Even if the mica and tourmalines were marketed as accessories it is probable the deposit could not be made to pay.

No mining machinery was installed at this locality. The feldspar was hauled 5 miles, mostly down grade, to South Paris, on the Grand Trunk Railway. Only a few tons of it was shipped, and much spar now lies in stock piles at the quarry.

NEWRY.

The rocks of Newry were studied only in the extreme northeast corner of the town at a quarry formerly operated for gem tourmalines.

The Dunton tourmaline mine is situated near the summit of a considerable hill that rises back of the farm of Joshua Abbott, about 1 to 1½ miles west of the wagon road between North Rumford and South Andover. It was operated in the summers of 1903 and 1904 by H. C. Dunton, of Rumford Falls.

. The pegmatite mass appears to be sill-like in form, with an average thickness of about 20 feet and a dip of about 40° SE. The wall rock has been intensely altered, but whether this is largely due to contact metamorphism by the pegmatite is uncertain. It is a light-green rock, exceedingly tough, and is composed largely of muscovite, actinolite, and quartz, with a little acidic plagioclase. The mineral grains interlock with no trace of schistose structure.

The higher slopes of the mountain between the mine and the wagon road show much pegmatite, but the lower slopes near the road are principally a quartz-mica schist, which is shown by locally recognizable bedding planes to be of sedimentary origin.

The pegmatite mass is of exceedingly coarse texture, and the principal minerals are quartz, orthoclase-microcline, muscovite, bladed albite (clevelandite), spodumene, lepidolite, and tourmaline, with beryl, columbite, and autunite as minor constituents.

The quartz and orthoclase-microcline are commonly in graphic intergrowth, as are also quartz and muscovite. Orthoclase is the dominant feldspar in most parts of the pegmatite mass. The muscovite is not of commercial quality, defects of twinning, wedge structure, and A structure being common. Many muscovite plates inclose crystals of transparent green tourmaline, some of those observed being one-fourth inch wide and 2 to 3 inches long. None are large enough or perfect enough to yield gems.

The central 5 or 6 feet of the sill-like

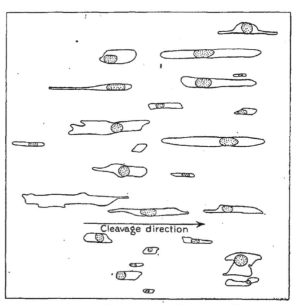

FIGURE 7.—Fluidal cavities in spodumene from Newry.

mass of pegmatite constitutes the gem-bearing zone and is characterized by a different mineral association. Quartz, orthoclase-microcline, and muscovite occur, but clevelandite is locally more abundant than potash feldspar; some of its bladelike crystals are 10 to 12 inches in length. With it is closely associated lepidolite, usually in small aggregates, but occasionally in large masses; one mass measured 6 by 2 by 3 feet but inclosed some clevelandite and pink tourmaline. The lepidolite, as at most of the gem localities, forms granular aggregates of minute plates and prisms. Spodumene occurs in flat crystals, some of which are 2½ feet in length; it is opaque and mostly white, though pale pink tints are sometimes found. Elongate fluid inclusions, nearly all of which are elongate parallel to the principal cleavage and contain vacuoles, are abundant in this spodumene; their size and shape are shown in figure 7.

Most of the tourmaline is an opaque dark blue-green, though some is nearly black. Association of this variety with the clevelandite is particularly common. Other tourmalines of lighter color are also abundant, particularly varieties characterized by pink centers surrounded by borders of light grass green. Some of these crystals are transparent in part and have yielded gem material, but they are inclosed in the solid pegmatite and are difficult to remove without shattering. Some of the pink and green tourmalines are of large size, one being reported as 4 to 5 inches across and about 2 feet long; the larger ones, however, are not of gem transparency. So far as known no pockets have been encountered.

Beryl was not seen in place, but a small loose crystal, though flawed, was perfectly transparent and almost deep enough in color to be classed as emerald. Autunite occurs in crystals, few of them over one-sixteenth of an inch across, embedded in or lying between plates of clevelandite. Most of it has wholly decomposed, leaving a small cavity and a canary-yellow stain in the surrounding feldspar.

The locality was abandoned because the tourmalines could not for the most part be removed from the ledge without being shattered so much as to destroy their gem value. If further excavation should reveal the presence of pockets in this pegmatite, some of these would almost certainly contain gem tourmalines which could be excavated by careful mining. In view of the fact that no pockets have yet been found it seems rather doubtful if further excavation will reveal any.

NORWAY.

The rocks of the town of Norway are largely quartz-mica schists intimately injected by pegmatite. No commercially important pegmatite deposits are known to occur, but some localities are of interest to the mineral collector.

At Tubbs Ledge, 2 miles northwest of Norway village, a pegmatite mass which has been blasted at several localities in a pasture shows orthoclase, white quartz, rose quartz, clevelandite, black and green tourmalines, and lepidolite, the latter a granular aggregate of unusually small plates. The presence of lepidolite, colored tourmalines, and clevelandite shows that the locality is a favorable one for further prospecting for gem tourmalines.

In the northeast corner of the town near Cobble Hill and near the road corners due southwest of West Paris a pegmatite ledge opened by George Howe, of Norway, has yielded small but perfect crystals of chrysoberyl, zinc spinel, and zircon. The pegmatite containing these minerals shows distinct evidence in a somewhat schistose structure and slickensided talcose surfaces of some movement since solidification. The chrysoberyl is clearly an original constituent, but the minute zircons one-sixteenth to one-eighth inch in length lie upon the talcose slickensided surfaces and were probably formed during the shearing process.

Two dikes, cutting pegmatite of moderate coarseness in a roadside exposure in the eastern part of Norway, are instructive. One dike, ranging from 6 inches to 3 feet in width, is a coarse aggregate of quartz (some rose colored), feldspar, muscovite, and black tourmaline; it is not separated from the wall rock by sharp boundaries. The other dike is similar in texture and mineral composition, but has quite sharply defined walls, next to which the texture is less coarse. At one end, however, this dike grades imperceptibly into the same pegmatite wall rock which it elsewhere intrudes sharply. These are plainly examples of contemporaneous pegmatite dikes.

PARIS.

The writer's observations extend over only those portions of the town of Paris lying between South Paris and Paris and from there northeastward to the Buckfield line. The rocks are quartz-mica schists intruded by pegmatite, quartz veins, and occasional small trap dikes. The schists reveal their original sedimentary character in the preservation here and there, as at the Crocker Hill mine near Paris Hill, of distinct bedding planes due to an alternation of highly quartzose layers with others that are more argillaceous. In a few localities small beds of crystalline limestone occur in the schists.

The collection of the Sheffield Scientific School of Yale University contains some fine diamond-shaped crystals of muscovite from the northern part of the town of Paris.

The only locality in the town where the pegmatites have proved of economic importance is Mount Mica, near Paris Hill.

HILL NORTH OF CROCKER HILL.

Certain relations observed on the next large hill north of Crocker Hill, about 2½ miles from Paris village, bear on the origin of the pegmatite and their physical characters at the time they were intruded.

Nearly the whole hilltop is bare, and fully three-quarters of the rock is a quartz-orthoclase-muscovite-black tourmaline pegmatite, which has been broken into at one place in a search for beryl of gem quality. At this opening the feldspar is sufficiently free from black tourmaline and occurs in large enough crystals to be of commercial grade for pottery purposes, but its total quantity is very small, most of the pegmatite of the hill being too quartzose and too intimately shot through with black tourmaline to be of commercial value under present conditions. The rock associated with the pegmatite is a schist or gneiss similar to that at Mount Mica, but more intensely injected by quartz and feldspar and more highly garnetiferous. It almost certainly represents a schist of sedimentary origin subsequently injected by pegmatitic material. Garnets are very abundant in this gneiss and some are $1\frac{1}{2}$ inches in diameter. There are also some knots or lenticles made up entirely of quartz and garnet in irregular association. Most of these are under 1 foot in greatest dimension, but one observed was 8 feet long and $1\frac{1}{2}$ feet in greatest width. A band 2 to 3 feet in width in the gneiss and traceable for about 25 feet is fully three-quarters garnets up to $1\frac{1}{2}$ inches in diameter, the interspaces being occupied by quartz and some feldspar. In all probability this profusion of garnets is a contact-metamorphic effect of the pegmatite intrusion. The prevailing strike of the gneiss is about N. 45° W.

The boundaries of the larger masses of pegmatite may parallel the banding of the gneiss or break directly across it. Considerable differences exist in the trend of the gneiss, even in outcrops only 20 feet apart; this is not due to gradual curving of the folia, the changes being abrupt and due to bodily displacements of blocks of the schist during the intrusion of the pegmatite. The absence of any great amount of softening of the schist consequent on the intrusion of the pegmatite is also well illustrated by Plate X, A, in which is shown a pegmatite mass 2 to 3 feet across and a number of smaller masses, all intrusive in the gneiss. The gneiss folia do not in general conform to the outline of the pegmatite mass, as they would if any considerable amount of softening of the schist had occurred, and only in a zone an inch or two wide along the contact of the gneiss and pegmatite do they show distortion. Any considerable softening, therefore, seems to have been confined to a zone 1 to 2 inches wide. The bending of the gneiss folia in a manner such as is shown in the figure also indicates that the pegmatite when intruded behaved to a certain extent like a solid body, and was capable of exerting differential thrust on its inclosing walls of gneiss. In a body behaving essentially like a liquid, pressure would become equalized in all directions, and it is difficult to see how such bending could have been produced.

The pegmatite of the hill is cut by a number of quartz veins or dikes mostly under 6 inches wide and mostly subparallel in trend. Most of them parallel the rather poorly defined system of joints in the pegmatite. Some of the quartz veins possess sharp boundaries; others are rather vaguely delimited from the bordering pegmatite. Quartz veins of the latter type are particularly likely to contain some feldspar (orthoclase-microcline, some of the crystals 3 inches across) and some muscovite and black tourmaline. Black tourmaline is also found frequently in veins which otherwise are composed wholly of quartz; in some of the narrower veins it may be even more abundant than the quartz. The two often show interpenetration. At one place the relations shown in figure 3 (p. 19) were observed within a space 3 or 4 feet square. The pegmatite is in sharp contact with the gneiss, into which it sends off a tapering apophysis. The latter for a short distance from the main pegmatite mass is true pegmatite, but beyond this becomes rapidly more quartzose. Most of this branch vein consists wholly of quartz.

The inferences to be drawn from the relations described may be summarized as follows:

(1) The relations shown in Plate X, A, and the fact that the changes in trend of the schists are abrupt and due to displacement of schist blocks en masse indicate that the pegmatite intrusions produced no extensive softening of the schists. Such softening, when present at all, was confined to a zone an inch or two wide immediately adjacent to the pegmatite. (2) The bending of gneiss folia next the pegmatite (see Pl. X, A) suggests that the dike, even before its border portions had entirely solidified, behaved essentially as a rigid body capable of transmitting differential thrust and not as a liquid.

The relations shown in figure 3, the fact that feldspar, muscovite, and black tourmaline occur in many of the quartz veins, and the fact that these veins are in some places not sharply differentiated from the inclosing pegmatite, indicate that at least many of the quartz veins are to be regarded as end crystallizations from the pegmatite magma.

MOUNT MICA.

History.—Mount Mica, a small hill situated about $1\frac{1}{2}$ miles east of the village of Paris at an elevation of approximately 900 feet, is one of the most famous mineral localities in the United States, and is known to mineralogists all over the world because of the size and beauty of its tourmaline crystals.

The discovery of its mineral wealth dates back to the year 1820,[a] when two students, Elijah S. Hamlin and Ezekiel Holmes, the former a resident of the town of Paris, becoming interested in the study of mineralogy, spent much time in searching for minerals in the exposed ledges and the mountains around the village. In returning from one of their expeditions in the autumn of 1820, Hamlin's eye was caught by a gleam of green from an object caught in the roots of a tree upturned by the wind. The object proved to be a fragment of a transparent green crystal lying loose upon the earth which was still attached to the roots of the tree. This was the first colored tourmaline taken from the locality which afterwards yielded them so prolifically, but its character was not recognized until somewhat

---

[a] Hamlin, A. C., The history of Mount Mica, Bangor, Me., 1895.

later, when the same students sent similar crystals for identification
to Professor Silliman, of Yale.

The winter's snows setting in the night after the discovery prevented further exploration until the following spring, when the two
students searched the bare ledge and the overlying soil and were
rewarded with thirty or more crystals of tourmaline of remarkable
beauty and transparency, with which were associated masses of purplish red to pink lepidolite and splendid crystal groups of white and
of smoky quartz.

Subsequent examination indicated that the ledge was perforated with cavities in
which the tourmalines and other minerals had been deposited and that the crystals
that had been gathered by the students had been set free from their cavities by the
disintegration of the surface of the ledge. Parts of the ledge were fairly honeycombed
with small cavities and soft spots where the decomposing feldspar was crumbling
away. In these cavities and decayed places other tourmalines were obtained by
breaking away the edges of the cavities or removing the decomposed material.[a]

The finding of the first of the large pockets is described by Mr.
Hamlin[b] as follows:

Two years after the discovery (1822), the two younger brothers of the discoverer,
Cyrus and Hannibal Hamlin, although scarcely in their teens, resolved to make a
more complete exploration of the ledge. Having borrowed some blasting tools in
the village, they proceeded to the hill and managed in a rough way to drill several
holes in the ledge and blast them out. These operations, though of trivial magnitude, were attended with unlooked-for results, for the explosions threw out, to the
astonishment of the boys, large quantities of bright-colored lepidolite, broad sheets
of mica, and masses of quartz crystals of a variety of hues. The last blast exposed a
decayed place in the ledge, which yielded readily to the thrusts of a sharpened stick
or the point of the iron drills. As the surface was removed, great numbers of minute
tourmalines were discovered in the decomposed feldspar and lepidolite. The rock
became softer and softer as the boys proceeded in their work of excavation, and soon
they reached a large cavity of two or more bushels capacity. This hollow place, or
rotten place, appeared to be filled with a substance resembling sand, loosely packed.
Amongst this sand or disintegrated rock, crystals of tourmaline of extraordinary size
and beauty were found scattered here and there in the soft matrix. Scratching away
with renewed energy, the boys soon emptied the pocket of its contents, and found
that they had obtained more than twenty crystals of various forms and hues. One of
these was a magnificent tourmaline of a rich green color and a remarkable transparency. It was more than 2½ inches in length by nearly 2 inches in diameter, and both
of its terminations were finely formed and perfect.

Several others possessed extraordinary beauty, and some of them were quite 3
inches in length and an inch in diameter. The colors of these tourmalines were quite
varied, but were chiefly red and green. * * * The exact number of the crystals
obtained by the boys is not known, but when collected together with the fragments
of others they filled a basket of nearly two quarts capacity. Besides the tourmalines,
the quantity of lepidolite, mica, and other choice minerals thrown out by the blasts
or found in the sides of the cavity was so great that the boys were obliged to seek for
an ox team to transport them home.

From 1822 until 1864 the locality was visited by many minerals-
gists, geologists, and mineral collectors, who excavated to some extent

---

a Op. cit., p. 10.   b Op. cit., pp. 11–12.

U. S. GEOLOGICAL SURVEY

GENERAL VIEW OF THE TOURMALINE QUARRY AT MOUNT MICA IN NOVEMBER, 1908. LOOKING WEST.

The upper layers of rock in the middle ground are the schist capping. In the foreground is the gigantic pocket shown in Plate XIII. The rock at the right is waste, piled in the worked-out portions of the pit.

and secured a number of valuable and beautiful tourmalines, though no systematic working was attempted. Observations were made by Professor Shepard, of Amherst College, between 1825 and 1830.[a]

In 1864 Samuel R. Carter, of Paris, commenced work in front of the pit made by former explorers and started a cut in the ledge 40 or 50 feet to the west, intending to strike the mineral belt at a depth greater than had before been reached, but after removing many tons of rock and finding no sign of the deposit he stopped work. Shortly after the close of the civil war A. C. Hamlin, the discoverer of the deposit, made a few test blasts and discovered a small pocket showing green tourmalines touched at the base with pink. In 1871 he renewed his work and after some excavation disclosed a pocket containing one of the finest crystals of white tourmaline (achroite) that has ever been found. This was 4½ inches in length and 1½ inches in diameter, white at the top, but changing to a smoky hue toward the base, and tipped at both ends with green. It is now in the mineralogical museum of Harvard College. About 1873 Mount Mica was worked for muscovite by a party of explorers and the contents of several fine pockets which they opened were scattered or destroyed. About 1880, in order to continue the work for gem minerals, Dr. Hamlin formed the Mount Mica Company and continued to operate intermittently and with varying degrees of success until about 1886, when work was suspended owing to the belief that the deposit did not extend farther to the east. In 1890 Loren B. Merrill, who had been engaged to some extent in gem mining at Mount Apatite, and L. Kimball Stone, both of Paris, purchased the rights to operate the property and have worked it successfully to the present time.

Mount Mica was visited by the writer in August, 1906, and again in October, 1907, and November, 1908. In 1908 the pit was about 150 feet long from northeast to southwest and from 50 to 100 feet wide. The maximum depth was about 20 feet. W. H. Emmons, who visited the mine in July, 1910, reports that the pit was then 300 feet long and 35 feet in maximum depth. These dimensions do not mark the total area which has been worked over, for most of the quarry waste has been piled in the abandoned workings. Plate XI gives a general view of the quarry.

Gem-bearing zone.—As at most of the Maine quarries where pegmatite deposits are worked the relations between the pegmatite and the wall rock and between pegmatite of various degrees of coarseness are very irregular. The general position of the gem-bearing zone and its relation to the bordering schists is, however, rather clear. Figure 8 represents a section through the mine from northwest to southeast,

---

[a] Shepard, C. U., Mineralogical journey in the northern parts of New England: Am. Jour. Sci., 1st ser., vol. 18, 1830, pp. 293–303.

the portions excavated previous to 1908 being inclosed in a dotted line. As shown in this diagram, the Mount Mica pegmatite mass dips gently 20° to 30° SE., being intruded in general parallel to the trend of quartz-mica schists, which at the quarry strike N. 50° to 60° E. and dip 20° to 30° SE. The significance of certain schist fragments inclosed in the pegmatite is discussed on page 135.

The schists are unquestionably of sedimentary origin but are locally so much injected by narrow sheetlike offshoots from the larger pegmatite masses that they resemble igneous gneisses. The contact of the pegmatite on the schist is generally very sharp and there is no indication of any absorption of the schist, though the abundance of garnets near the contact indicates some contact metamorphism.

The whole pegmatite mass is not productive (see fig. 8), the gem and pocket bearing portion constituting a zone ranging from a few inches to 6 or 7 feet in thickness lying immediately below the schist capping. The productive layer originally outcropped at the surface, a relation to which was due its discovery and the ease with which it was worked in the early days. At present the southeastern wall of

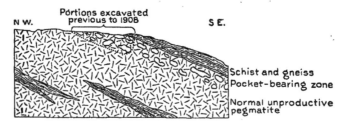

FIGURE 8.—Diagram showing geologic structure at Mount Mica tourmaline mine, Paris.

the quarry is capped by about 10 to 15 feet of schist which must be stripped off before the pocket-bearing zone is reached. According to present indications increasingly great thicknesses of schist must be removed as the workings are extended to the southeast, though the pegmatite may show irregularities the nature of which can not be predicted. If the work is extended far to the southeast tunneling may be found to be cheaper than stripping. There is very little question, however, that further lateral excavation to the southwest and northeast of the present workings, in prolongation of the original line of outcrop of the pocket-bearing zone, would disclose a continuation of the productive layer. Prospecting at least along these lines should be undertaken before the excavations are carried to any great depths in a southeast direction along the dip of the deposit.

The gem-bearing zone is not very sharply differentiated from the pegmatite below it, but is in general somewhat coarser and is separated from the underlying unproductive pegmatite by a narrow layer very rich in small garnets. This layer is similar to the garnetiferous bands observed at the Wade and Pulsifer quarry in Auburn,

REPRODUCTION OF AN OLD PHOTOGRAPH OF THE MOUNT MICA TOURMALINE MINE AT THE TIME WHEN THE POCKET-BEARING ZONE WAS CLOSE TO THE SURFACE.

The position of each pocket is marked by a stick with a white card attached. (From a negative in the possession of Mr. T. F. Lamp, of Portland.)

and it was clearly recognized by A. C. Hamlin as marking the line between the productive and unproductive rock. Out of the 80 pockets known to him previous to 1895, not one was found below this garnetiferous layer, nor have later excavations revealed any. The pocket-bearing zone is further differentiated from the rest of the pegmatite by the abundance of clevelandite, lepidolite, and some other minerals not found elsewhere.

Pockets.—An idea of the abundance of pockets may be gained from Plate XII, a reproduction of an old photograph showing the workings at a time when the pocket-bearing zone could be reached by very shallow excavation. In this picture the position of each pocket is shown by a small stick with a white card attached. The abundance of pockets differs greatly in different parts of the mineral zone, as does also their richness in tourmalines, so that certain portions of the productive zone have proved much more valuable than others. Most of the pockets are more or less spherical in outline, but some are very irregular, many consisting of several connected cavities. Few of them are angular in form. One that may be regarded as of average shape, though somewhat above the average in size, is shown in Plate IX, *B*, and is 3 feet in diameter. In size they vary from those having a capacity of only about a pint to one which was 20 feet long, 12 feet wide, and 7 feet high and contained three connecting chambers. This largest known pocket is shown in Plate XIII. One pocket 6 feet below the surface of the ledge, found in 1868, was scarcely larger than the hand and contained nothing but one transparent tourmaline crystal 3 inches long and 1 inch in diameter.[a] The total number of pockets found up to October, 1907, was estimated at 430, of which 350 have been found by Merrill & Stone, the present operators. Only a small proportion, however, yielded any gem material; out of 60 opened by Merrill & Stone in one autumn, only five or six yielded anything of value, and out of the entire 350 opened by them only about 50 were worth much.

According to Dr. Hamlin,[b] "The cavities generally were roofed with albite, whilst the sides were composed of limpid or smoky quartz mixed with lepidolite, crystals of tin (cassiterite), spodumene, amblygonite, and other rare minerals."

Few pockets were observable at the time of the writer's visit, but Hamlin's description is probably essentially correct, although albite was not observed to be any more abundant above the pockets than below them or at their sides.

The action of frost and percolating water has in most places produced much disintegration in the walls of the cavities, and their floors are generally formed of a sandy or clayey mass consisting of partly decomposed fragments of clevelandite and lepidolite associated in

[a] Hamlin, A. C., The history of Mount Mica, p. 63 and Pl. XV.   [b] Idem, p. 49.

greater or less abundance with kaolin and the hydromica cookeite. In this mass of decomposed material the tourmalines are embedded. There can be no doubt that they were once attached to the walls of the cavities, but they have been loosened from their original position, many being fractured in the process, and now lie in every conceivable position in the material forming the floor of the cavity. Many of the groups of quartz crystals which adorned the walls have been loosened in a similar way, some of them now lying embedded in the materials of the floor with the apices of the crystals downward just as they fell from the roof of the cavity. In some of the cavities the amount of kaolinic material is very large, about a ton of the pink kaolin montmorillonite having been taken from the large one shown in Plate IX, B.

Minerals.—The bulk of the pegmatite found at this quarry is in general similar to that at other pegmatite workings in Maine but differs from these in the relative scarcity of graphic intergrowths of quartz and potash feldspar. The principal constituent minerals are quartz, orthoclase and microcline, muscovite, biotite, and black tourmaline, and their association seems to be wholly irregular. Even in the pocket-bearing layer these are the principal minerals, though here the clevelandite variety of albite, lepidolite, and colored tourmalines are also found.

Quartz is present in the solid pegmatite, principally in small irregular opaque masses which are white to slightly smoky in color. Rarely it is graphically intergrown with feldspar. In the pockets it occurs as groups of very perfectly developed transparent colorless crystals. Where these have become detached from the walls they may lie embedded in kaolin and cookeite in the bottom of the pockets.

The principal feldspar is buff-colored orthoclase and microcline, occurring mainly in small, irregular masses intergrown with the other common pegmatite minerals. A very few masses of pure feldspar as much as 2½ feet across were observed. The dump is now (1910) being picked over by the Maine Feldspar Company, of Auburn, to obtain spar for pottery purposes, but before this the feldspar was not utilized in any way. In the pocket-bearing zone pure white albite of the clevelandite variety is abundant, associated particularly with lepidolite, muscovite, and quartz.

Muscovite occurs in graphic intergrowth with quartz and also in books, many of which are 5 to 6 inches across. One seen on the waste pile was 12 by 14 inches in size, and another was 1 foot long and 7 to 8 inches wide. A few of the books inclose long, slender crystals of opaque green tourmaline, the largest observed being 4 inches long and one-fourth inch in diameter. The finest muscovite crystal from this locality known to the writer is in the public

LARGEST POCKET EVER FOUND AT MOUNT MICA.

This pocket measures 20 by 12 by 7 feet and contains three connecting chambers. Mr. Merrill at the right.

library at Paris and is a clear, perfect piece of roughly hexagonal outline, measuring about 8 by 2½ inches. Good specimens of plumose mica, produced by close-spaced ruling, are also to be found in the collections at Paris. Where not too intimately mixed with other minerals, the mica is saved in the quarrying process and has brought $25 per ton as taken from the quarry. At another time 12½ cents per pound was offered for the thumb-trimmed product. The largest perfect plates of cut mica obtained from this material would probably not exceed 3 by 4 inches in size. Much is defective owing to wedge structure and ruling and is valuable only as scrap mica.

Biotite is not abundant, but it occurs in a few places in its usual form of long, narrow, and very thin crystals, the largest seen being 10 inches long and one-half inch wide.

Lepidolite or lithium mica is of common occurrence in the pocket-bearing portions of the pegmatite. The largest mass found, though impure, is reported as weighing 10 tons, and it is not difficult to obtain fairly pure masses 8 or 10 inches across. The mineral occurs mostly in the granular forms, though some curved and globular crystals have been found. The color varies from lavender to peach-blossom pink. The granular varieties commonly show some admixture of quartz, muscovite, and clevelandite and not uncommonly contain interbedded crystals of opaque pink and more rarely green tourmaline; some specimens which have been sawed into small blocks and polished make handsome paperweights. Lepidolite from this locality has been described by Clarke, who also gives analyses.[a]

Black tourmaline or schorl, which is the most abundant iron-bearing mineral present at the quarry, occurs in prismatic crystals, mostly compound, many of which are a foot in length and 4 to 5 inches in diameter. A few having a length of 2½ feet were seen by the writer, and one 4 feet in length is described by Hamlin. A few large compound prisms of black tourmaline separate at their ends into a brushlike aggregate of small prisms, the interspaces being filled with quartz and an aggregate of minute muscovite scales. The black tourmalines occur in the solid pegmatite, penetrating it in all directions; except for a few small crystals, they have never been found in pockets. Some colored tourmalines occur in the solid pegmatite near the pockets, associated usually with clevelandite, muscovite, lepidolite, and quartz; a few of these are curved through considerable angles. Most of these colored crystals are opaque, though a few small, delicate, transparent ones are interleaved with muscovite. Fine specimens of these latter are found in the Carter collection in the public library at Paris; other specimens are much larger, some containing interleaved tourmalines 3 or 4 inches in length and one-fourth inch or so in thickness. In a few instances tourmalines

a Clarke, F. W., Lepidolite of Maine: Bull. U. S. Geol. Survey No. 42, 1887, p. 13.

cross each other with mutual penetration about at right angles, but most commonly several crystals diverge from single points, forming fan-shaped aggregates extending through 60°, 90°, or even 100°.

None of the above-described tourmalines are of gem value.

Amblygonite is the only other mineral occurring at all abundantly in the pegmatite. It is found only as a constituent of the solid pegmatite in irregular masses often 4 to 8 inches across. One mass is estimated to have weighed nearly 800 pounds. The mineral usually occurs near the pockets and is regarded as an indicator of their proximity.

Spodumene occurs in opaque gray flat crystals, usually associated with lepidolite. One crystal measured 2 feet long, 7 inches wide, and 2 inches thick. Portions of a few of the crystals are a transparent pale blue or pink. According to Mr. Merrill, an abundance of beryl or spodumene about a pocket generally signifies that the latter contains few if any tourmalines. A white spodumene crystal in the Hamlin collection at Paris is 7 inches long and 4 inches thick and is split by a wedge-shaped mass of granular lepidolite tapering from 1 inch to one-half inch in thickness.

Apatite occurs in the solid pegmatite in irregular opaque green masses, some few of which weigh a couple of pounds. A small deep-blue bipyramidal crystal one-fourth inch in length with crystal faces developed in remarkable perfection has been described and figured by Prof. E. S. Dana.[a]

Cassiterite occurs rarely, usually associated with clevelandite near the pockets. Some crystals are found embedded in the sandlike materials at the bottom of the pockets.

Columbite is rare and usually occurs in irregular bladelike crystals.

Arsenopyrite was observed in veinlike masses, mostly one-eighth to one-fourth inch in width and 2 or 3 inches in length, flanked by irregular borders of quartz, which in turn are irregularly bordered by orthoclase and microcline. The arsenopyrite therefore virtually forms the central portion of small contemporaneous quartz veins or lenses in the pegmatite.

Triphyllite occurs mostly in aggregates, many of which weigh from 10 to 20 pounds and a few as much as 50 pounds.

Zircons occur mostly associated with triphyllite, few crystals being over one-eighth inch in diameter.

Kaolin occurs in considerable amounts in the bottoms of some of the pockets as a decomposition product of feldspar. In the giant pocket shown in Plate XIV over a ton of the pink kaolin montmorillonite was aggregated at one end of the pocket.

Other minerals found at Mount Mica are autunite, brookite, childrenite, damourite, halloysite, löllingite, petalite, pyrite, sphalerite,

a Am. Jour. Sci., 3d ser., vol. 27, 1884, p. 480.

LARGEST CRYSTAL OF TOURMALINE EVER FOUND AT MOUNT MICA.

Length, 15$\frac{1}{2}$ inches; maximum width, 7 inches; weight, 31$\frac{1}{2}$ pounds.

yttrocerite, and zircon. Cookeite from Mount Mica has been described in detail by Penfield.[a]

Gems.—The gem tourmalines of this locality show remarkable variety in form, size, and color. Those of value occur without exception in the pockets, usually but not invariably detached from their original position on the walls and lying at the bottom in a sandlike matrix of kaolin and cookeite. Most of them range in color from olive green through emerald green to blue green; some are nearly colorless, some show beautiful pink tints, and the central portions of some are a deep ruby red when viewed along the main crystal axis; a few are the color of amber and of port wine; and some are a purplish red. Many show a zonal distribution of colors. A polished cross section of a crystal about three-fourths of an inch in diameter, preserved in the Cambridge Museum of Natural History, shows a blue-green center about one-half inch across, surrounded by a transparent pink border one-eighth inch wide, outside of which is a pale transparent olive-green border about one-sixteenth inch wide. Crystals with pink centers and olive-green borders are not uncommon. One shade commonly predominates in a pocket, but some pockets contain gems of different colors. Some single crystals shade from white at one termination to emerald green, then to light green and pink, and finally to colorless at the other termination. Green crystals tipped with pink are especially common. Generally these transitions of color are very gradual, but in some specimens the colors are not mingled in the least, and the crystals, though crystallographically continuous throughout, seem to be composed of several distinct sections.

In some pockets the tourmalines when first disclosed lie in apparent perfection of form and color in their clayey matrix, but crumble away as soon as touched. In others certain portions only of the crystals crumble away, leaving a smooth nodule of perfectly fresh tourmaline, usually beautifully transparent and in form resembling somewhat the nodules produced by the etching of quartz crystals with hydrofluoric acid. Some of the finest gems have been cut from such nodules. Some hollow crystals of tourmaline are found, commonly of small diameter, but including some as much as an inch in length; they were probably produced through disintegration of the core of the crystal. Some tourmalines have not only suffered disintegration, but have been partly or entirely removed, leaving only their impressions in the kaolin which formed the matrix.

In size the colored tourmaline crystals differ greatly, ranging from those of needle-like dimensions to the large ones described below. Many of the largest are compound.

Anything like a complete descriptive list, even of the larger and finer tourmalines found at Mount Mica, is impracticable in this report, but a few of the most remarkable will be briefly described.

---

[a] Penfield, S. F., On cookeite from Paris and Hebron, Me.: Am. Jour. Sci., 3d ser., vol. 45, pp. 393–396.

The largest tourmaline ever found at Mount Mica came from the pocket shown in Plate IX, B, and is itself figured in Plate XIV. It is now in the Paris library, to which it has been loaned by Edward Hamlin, of Boston. It is 15½ inches long, 7 inches in maximum breadth, weighs 31½ pounds, and is valued at not less than $400. As shown in the plate, the base is fractured so that the crystal is now in three segments. The crystal is transparent to translucent grass green at the tip, where, too, the prism faces are best developed. The middle and lower flanks of the terminal segment are made up of a mass of small colorless to pale-pink or brownish prisms between one-eighth and one-fourth inch in diameter, many of them set at all sorts of angles to the main axis of the compound crystal. A small crystal of white quartz about 2 inches long is attached to the side of this segment. The basal segments, which are about 4 inches across, show an alternation of small translucent to opaque pink and green prisms, the colors grading into one another parallel to the prism axes and also across them.

The same pocket contained another compound tourmaline crystal, somewhat similar to that just described in its general form and very similar in coloring, but smaller. Its length is about 10 inches, its maximum width 3½ inches, and its weight 6½ pounds. It is now in the possession of Mr. Merrill.

Besides these two compound crystals the pocket yielded two simple crystals, one of which is shown in Plate XV in natural size. The upper segment of this is in Mr. Merrill's possession, the lower having been cut into gems. The companion crystal, which was slightly smaller, is the property of the Hamlin estate. Both crystals are green in the upper part and pink and red at the base. They are transparent to translucent, and the segment which is in Mr. Merrill's possession may contain some gem material in its upper portion. The same pocket also yielded many small crystals of green and red, which furnished about 75 carats of cut gems, mostly red and pink, but some green. Three nodules of colorless tourmaline were also found, one of which would cut an 8-carat stone. Some of these were remarkably limpid and brilliant when cut. In all, there were about 75 pounds of tourmaline crystals in this pocket. The two largest tourmaline groups and most of the others lay loose in the disintegrated clevelandite and cookeite in the bottom of the pocket. No kaolin was present. Lepidolite occurred around the walls and across the bottom. Many quartz crystals lay loose in the bottom of the pocket, the upper ones having the apices of the crystals downward, showing that they had fallen from the roof.

A large tourmaline, consisting of a bundle of prisms diverging slightly toward the apex of the crystal, is now in the Cambridge Museum of Natural History. It is 7 inches long, 3½ inches wide near

1 Inch

LARGE SINGLE CRYSTAL OF TOURMALINE FROM MOUNT MICA. NATURAL SIZE.

From the same pocket as the giant tourmaline shown in Plate XIV.

the apex, and 2½ inches wide at the base. Most of the crystal is a deep grass green, but at the base the outer green layers have shelled off, revealing a cone of deep pink, which, however, does not appear to penetrate far. The base, a nearly straight surface inclined about 70° to the main prism axis, appears to be a fracture surface and is conchoidal. It is partly coated with cookeite, as are the lower flanks of the prism, showing that the crystal had become detached from its original position on the wall of the pocket before the cookeite was deposited. The summit terminations are not crystal faces, but are fracture planes standing nearly at right angles to the main axis. The sides are closely and beautifully striated. The crystal is transparent to translucent and does not appear to contain any gem material. This tourmaline was the largest found in the giant pocket shown in Plate XIII. It lay loose in the bottom in a mass of kaolin and of cookeite sand. A few other smaller tourmalines were found, but none were of gem quality, and in proportion to its great size the pocket was remarkably unproductive. The pocket contained large amounts of massive and crystal quartz plugged full of small opaque tourmaline crystals. In one end there was about a ton of the pink kaolin montmorillonite.

The largest transparent crystal of green tourmaline found at Mount Mica was discovered by Samuel R. Carter in 1886 and is now in the Cambridge Museum of Natural History. It is 10 inches in length, 2¼ inches in diameter, and weighs 41 ounces. Both terminations have been preserved, but they are not at all perfect.[a] Although broken into four pieces, the parts have been easily joined by cement. Its middle portion would probably yield some fine gems. This crystal came from an unusually large pocket 4 feet in diameter, along whose sides and at whose bottom, embedded in a sand of decomposed cookeite, lepidolite, etc., were found fragments of certainly 50 well-defined tourmaline crystals.

The most remarkable crystal of white tourmaline or achroite found at this locality is also in the Cambridge Museum of Natural History. It was obtained in 1869 from a large pocket which yielded several other crystals of smaller size. This crystal is transparent, but when viewed in light transmitted at right angles to its axis appears smoky toward the base; when viewed along the axis its hue is crimson. Both ends are tipped with green, but its terminal faces are not preserved. Its length is about 4 inches and its width 1½ inches.

The finest crystal of blue tourmaline or indicolite found at Mount Mica is in the Hamlin cabinet. It is transparent throughout its entire shaft, although broken into five parts. Both terminations are preserved. The color, when viewed at right angles to the prism

---

[a] Hamlin, A. C., The history of Mount Mica, Pl. XXX and pp. 39–40.

length, is a beautiful sapphire blue, changing at the top into a delicate green. It is about 4 inches long and one-half inch in diameter. It is illustrated in color in "The history of Mount Mica," Plate XXVI.

A remarkable curved crystal of gray to green tourmaline, transparent to translucent in places, was found in 1891, and is now in the Carter collection in the public library at Paris. It is about 5 inches long and three-fourths to 1 inch in diameter, and is curved through an angle of about 20°.

The largest flawless gem ever cut from tourmaline from Mount Mica weighs 69¼ carats and is now in the Tiffany collection. It was part of a crystal found in November, 1893, and was sold by Merrill & Stone for $1,000. The crystal from which it came is described and figured in "The history of Mount Mica," page 71 and Plate XLIII. It yielded a number of other fine gems, one of which, a pink one, weighed 18 carats.

What is probably the largest flawless piece of transparent tourmaline known is in the possession of L. B. Merrill, its finder, the present operator of the Mount Mica mine. In its uncut condition it weighs 411 carats. It formed the tip of a crystal 8 inches long and 1 inch in diameter, much of which was greatly disintegrated.

Beryl occurs principally in the solid pegmatite, though occasionally found in the pockets. The varieties found in the solid pegmatite are mainly pale blue-green and opaque or translucent. Certain small portions of the crystals may be transparent, and from these some small aquamarines of good quality have been cut. One beryl 6 inches across, observed by the writer, inclosed both muscovite and black tourmaline. The beryl found in the pockets is mostly colorless to pale pink cæsium beryl; it cuts into gems which in artificial light have almost the beauty of diamonds. It is apt to occur in short, button-shaped prisms, many with both terminations complete. Two fine specimens of cæsium beryl are in the Hamlin collection at the Paris public library. One is about 6 inches in diameter and 1 inch high and has three sides of the hexagonal prism perfect. The other is about 6 inches high, shows a good basal plane, four prism faces quite perfect for most of their length, and two pyramid faces. These crystals are only in small part transparent and are much flawed and iron stained along fractures.

Production and method of mining.—It is impossible accurately to estimate the amount and value of material for gems and museum specimens which Mount Mica has yielded, but Hamlin in his history of Mount Mica estimated that up to 1895 the locality had yielded more than 100 tourmaline crystals which would be considered unusually fine specimens of the mineral, besides many thousand smaller crystals. The total value of the gems and cabinet specimens which have been taken from the locality up to the present day probably exceeds $50,000.

The mine is worked by Merrill & Stone, the drilling being done by hand and the blasting with black powder, so as to run as little risk as possible of shattering valuable gem material. A derrick operated by a horse windlass is used in transferring the waste rock to the dump. At present it is necessary to remove a considerable thickness of schist overlying the pocket-bearing layer. It is probable that the thickness of the cover rock increases southward, and that in the near future tunneling will be found the most economical method of working.

PERU.

The pegmatites of Peru were studied at only one locality, an old mica prospect on the farm of J. P. York near the central part of the town. The mine is located near the summit of the southwest slope of a steep hill and was worked only in the summer of 1902.

The whole pegmatite mass is hardly over 150 feet wide on the level of the principal openings and appears to have the form of an irregular lens elongate in a general east-west direction. The bordering rock is a granite gneiss locally very rich in biotite. The openings are below the crest of the hill, and as the pegmatite mass is traced eastward toward the summit it is found to be associated with larger and larger amounts of granite gneiss. The lowermost exposures on the hill slope also show much granite gneiss associated with the pegmatite; the latter therefore appears to pinch out rather rapidly both above and below, and consequently to be of rather small extent. The trend of the granite gneiss where it borders the pegmatite on the north is about N. 70° E.; its folia dip steeply to the northwest.

The pegmatite varies greatly in coarseness from point to point. Its dominant components are orthoclase-microcline, quartz, muscovite, and biotite. A few feldspar crystals are 3 feet across, but for the most part this mineral is so intimately mixed with biotite as to be commercially valueless. Locally the biotite forms blades 4 to 5 feet long and 2 to 3 inches wide. Some crystals show muscovite surrounding biotite in parallel growth. No muscovite books more than 3 to 4 inches across were seen either in the solid pegmatite or in the dump piles of the mine, and specimens preserved at a neighboring farmhouse and said to be as good as any of the mica obtained would none of them cut pieces of clear mica measuring more than 2 by 3 inches. There is no distinct vein particularly rich in muscovite and the property can not be regarded as a commercial proposition for mica mining.

RUMFORD.

The town of Rumford is occupied by quartz-mica schists, intruded and in some places intimately injected by granite and pegmatite. The relations at a number of localities throw light on the genesis of the rock concerned.

Vicinity of Rumford Falls.—The exposures examined were on the east shore of Androscoggin River at the falls, a mile or so above Rumford Falls village. The schists are dark gray to purplish on the fresh surfaces and purplish to rusty brown on the weathered surfaces. They are garnetiferous quartz-mica schists and strike N. 30° to 40° W., with dips of 20° to 30° NE. The schists are intruded by sills and dikes of fine-grained gray granite, by pegmatite, and by small quartz veins.

An instructive contact between the schist and pegmatite is shown in Plate X, *B*, and has already been described on pages 34.

Another intrusive mass in the schists is of irregular sill-like form, and consists partly of biotite granite and partly of pegmatite. It is interesting because of gradual and complete gradation between granite and pegmatite. The biotite granite is gray in color with an average size of grain of not over 1 millimeter. The pegmatite in addition to quartz and feldspar shows muscovite, but very little biotite.

A number of small dikes of fine-grained granite intrude the schists at this locality, both parallel to and transverse to the trend of the latter. All of these are characterized by sharp parallel walls and are in great contrast to the pegmatite dikes which traverse the same schists but are characterized by wavy and irregular forms, the two sides of the dike or sill in few places being parallel. The intrusion of the schist by the fine-grained granite in the railroad cut opposite the falls is so intimate that a dike network results.

Microscopic comparisons were made between the medium-grained granite of this locality and the pegmatite of an irregular dike cutting the granite. The dike is exposed for 20 feet and is 1 foot wide at its base, but broadens upward within 2 feet to a width of 4 feet, thence narrowing again within a few feet to a width of 1 foot. There is complete crystallographic continuity between the two rocks at their contact, but the transition from one to the other is usually complete in a space of one-fourth to one-half inch. The minerals characteristic of the two rocks are identical.

The granite shows considerable and irregular variations in color, due to differences in the abundance of biotite. Few of its mineral grains exceed one-eighth inch, and their average size is about one-sixteenth. Its dominant minerals are quartz, orthoclase and microcline, oligoclase (extinction angles up to 13°; refractive index about equal to balsam), and biotite. Garnet and muscovite are subordinate accessories. Oligoclase appears to be only slightly less abundant than the potash feldspars. Small quartzes of rounded cross section and a few with hexagonal outlines (some with corners rounded) are inclosed by orthoclase, microcline, or other quartz. A few small biotite laths are wholly inclosed by oligoclase, and a few rounded crystals of oligoclase are inclosed by orthoclase. These relations point to the existence in the magma of small crystals of quartz, biotite, and oligoclase not long before the bulk of the rock crystallized. A few small areas show an intergrowth, more or less graphic in pattern, of quartz with oligoclase or microcline.

The minerals of the pegmatite are identical with those of the granite, but form much larger crystals and exhibit markedly greater diversity in the size of the mineral grains. Microcline is the dominant feldspar, and much of it is perthitically intergrown with plagioclase, which appears to be albite-oligoclase in composition. The same plagioclase also forms separate crystal grains, usually much smaller than those of microcline. Biotite is abundant and has altered somewhat to chlorite. In a few places quartz is micrographically intergrown with the plagioclase. Many small quartzes of rounded outline or showing hexagonal forms with rounded corners are inclosed by the microcline. Muscovite is rare.

The mineralogical similarity of these two rocks even as regards the composition of the plagioclase, and the presence in both of small quartzes of an earlier crystallization inclosed by later feldspar, taken in connection with their close field association, suggest their derivation from the same magmatic source.

Black Mountain mica mine.—A mine which has been operated for scrap mica by Oliver Gildersleeve, of Gildersleeve, Conn., is located on Black Mountain in the northern part of the town of Rumford. The two quarry pits are hillside excavations about two-thirds of the way up the mountain on its western slope and are about three-fourths of a mile from the road between North Rumford and Roxbury Notch. The upper pit is about 200 feet long, 50 feet wide, and 25 feet in greatest depth. Another just below it on the slope is about 100 feet wide, 100 feet long, and 35 feet in maximum depth.

The rock at these pits is an exceedingly coarse pegmatite which is intrusive in an irregular manner in metamorphosed sediments trending N. 30° to 40° W. and dipping 70° to 80° NE. The latter are slightly contorted but reveal their sedimentary origin through an alternation of quartzitic and more shaly beds.

The pegmatite here shows some characters which differentiate it from any of the other deposits studied, though in general its characters approach more closely to the pegmatite of the gem-tourmaline localities than to that of the other mica prospects in the State. Potash feldspar is almost entirely absent, the dominant feldspar being albite of the bladed clevelandite variety. Muscovite is the mineral next in abundance, constituting about 30 to 40 per cent of the whole deposit. Locally, however, it forms three-fourths of the pegmatite mass. The largest crystal of mica seen by the writer was 1½ feet wide and 3 feet long, but blade-shaped or spearhead-shaped crystals, 1 to 2 feet long, are very common. Some masses weighing half a ton are almost purely mica. All of the mica shows one or more of the defects known as twinning, wedge structure, and ruling. None of it will yield any plate mica. Several of the mica books observed were 1 foot thick (at right angles to the cleavage). Near the walls of the pegmatite mass the mica books tend to orient themselves with their long axes perpendicular to the contact, though only within 6 inches or so of the wall is there any noticeable decrease in the coarseness of the pegmatite. The quartz of this pegmatite is mostly opaque but is pure white. Spodumene is unusually abundant in long flat crystals, some of them 2½ feet long and 3 to 4 inches thick. The color is light gray to white. Some of the spodumene is intimately intergrown with quartz.

A remarkable feature of this deposit is the presence in the pegmatite of irregular masses of medium-grained granite, which in some parts consists of muscovite, quartz, and plagioclase, and along certain bands or irregular bunches is one-third to one-half bright pink tourmaline, producing a stone of considerable beauty. Under the microscope the principal minerals are seen to be quartz, muscovite, pink tourmaline, and basic oligoclase (extinction angles up to 17°; refractive index near balsam). In the thin section only very faint pleochroism is seen in the tourmaline. Tourmaline constitutes the largest crystals in the rock and shows a tendency toward the development of radiate bundles, one-eighth to one-fourth inch across, made up of small prisms. The average size of grain, exclusive of the tourmaline crystals, is from 0.3 to 0.6 millimeter. This granite is plainly a crystallization from the pegmatite magma and, like the pegmatite, numbers quartz, muscovite, and pink tourmaline among its chief constituents. Many large spodumene crystals are embedded in this tourmaline granite. Its quantity and uniformity are not sufficient to give it any commercial importance.

In the pegmatite, greenish-black tourmaline occurs in crystals averaging one-half inch to 1½ inches in diameter and 4 to 8 inches in length. They are commonly associated with quartz or clevelandite and only rarely are in contact with muscovite, being rare in the more micaceous parts of the pegmatite. Pink to gray opaque tourmaline also occurs, generally surrounded by quartz. One aggregate exposed in a loose quartz fragment is 7 inches long. It is a brush-shaped aggregate of tourmaline crystals and enlarges from a diameter of about 2½ inches at the base to about 4 inches at the top, the cross section being nearly circular.

Most of the schist exposed near this mine is somewhat weathered. Noticeable contact metamorphism, though confined to the immediate vicinity of the pegmatite, has been more severe than along most of the pegmatite contacts studied. It has resulted in the abundant development of prisms of cinnamon-brown tourmaline from one-fourth to one-half inch long and one-sixteenth to one-eighth inch in diameter in certain of the more muscovitic layers. More biotitic portions present a mottled appearance, due to the occurrence of the biotite in irregular aggregates one-eighth to one-fourth inch in diameter. Under the microscope this mottled rock is seen to consist of brown biotite, light-green hornblende, quartz, labradorite, titanite, magnetite, and apatite, the latter in small hexagonal prisms filled with a cloud of very minute inclusions. The tendency to aggregation of the biotite, hornblende, titanite, and magnetite gives the mottled appearance, the white intervening areas being largely quartz and labradorite. The mineral grains of this rock are interlocking and the texture granular and indistinguishable from that of an igneous rock. Field relations show, however, that the rock is a phase of the sedimentary schist wall rock which has undergone complete recrystallization.

It is notable that neither of the metamorphosed phases of the wall rock described above contains any minerals except the common ones, quartz and muscovite, that are characteristic of the neighboring pegmatite. The tourmaline of the schist is brown and wholly dissimilar from any found in this or any other pegmatite of the State. Additions, if any, received by the wall rock from the pegmatite during the complete recrystallization of the former were ionic in their character, the minerals characteristic of the pegmatite, with the possible exception of quartz, not being added as such to the intruded rock.

The quarry was opened in about 1901 by Oliver Gildersleeve and has been worked for four seasons. About 250 tons of mica is reported to have been mined in 1905. The quarry was idle throughout 1906, in which year the writer visited it, and so far as is known has not reopened since. Steam drills were employed and sheds built for hand picking the mica, which was packed in 100-pound bags and hauled by team 7 miles to Frye, on the Rangeley division of the Maine Central Railroad. From Frye it was shipped to a grinding mill at Gildersleeve, Conn. About 1,000 tons in all are reported to have been shipped. The quantity of scrap mica still available at this quarry is large, but there is no plate mica, nor is it probable that further excavation will disclose any. It is doubtful if at present the property can be profitably exploited for scrap mica in view of the fact that the refuse cuttings from plate mica properties appear able to meet entirely the present demand for scrap mica.

STANDISH.

The rocks of Standish were studied only in the western part of the town, in the Spence Hills, which lie about 5 miles north-northeast of Paris village. The rocks are schists of the same metamorphic-sedimentary type observed in the town of Paris, and are rather flat lying. As in Paris, they are intruded by granite and pegmatite, but these rocks are much less abundant than at most places in Paris, and large masses of the schist are wholly free from granitic material of any kind.

The collection of the Sheffield Scientific School of Yale University contains several fine crystals of columbite from the pegmatites of this town.

STONEHAM.

GEOLOGY.

The rocks of the town of Stoneham are almost exclusively gneisses intruded by pegmatite and granite, the igneous rocks being on the whole more abundant than in most of the towns to the east.

Excellent exposures on the south shore of Keewaydin Lake (Lower Stone Pond), near the village of East Stoneham, show rather fine-grained pegmatite intruding a purplish-gray gneiss, indistinguishable in the field from certain gneisses exposed at the Auburn reservoir site on Goff Hill. This rock is a quartz-feldspar-muscovite-biotite schist whose origin can not be definitely stated. It closely resembles many phases of the sedimentary schists which have been intensely injected by pegmatite and may be of similar origin. Both schist and pegmatite are intruded at "Striped ledge," on this lake, by a remarkable dike network of fine-grained diabase. (See Pl. XVI, A.)

Granite found a few miles west of Keewaydin Lake, in the bed of a creek flowing into Upper Kezar Lake, is a millimeter-grained, light-gray rock, in which a faint gneissic habit is recognizable, due to the occurrence of biotite in slightly greater abundance along certain vaguely defined bands than along others. The microscope shows its minerals to be quartz, albite, biotite (partly altered to chlorite), and a little muscovite. The rock differs from most of the granites of Maine in being a soda granite, potash feldspar being apparently wholly absent. The microscopic texture is typically granitic.

GEM LOCALITIES.

Pegmatites have not been systematically worked at any place in this town but have yielded to prospectors and mineral collectors a large number of beryls, some of which are among the finest of their kind, and also fine specimens of topaz, amethyst, beryllonite, and other minerals. Some of the finest of these specimens have been obtained from localities which can not now be identified.

A.   NETWORK OF DIABASE DIKES CUTTING PEGMATITE AND ASSOCIATED GNEISS AT
KEEWAYDIN LAKE, IN STONEHAM.

B.   QUARTZ DIKE CUTTING PEGMATITE AT HOWE QUARRY, SOUTH GLASTONBURY, CONN.

Showing light-colored feldspar crystals with well-developed crystal faces projecting into the quartz of the
dike.   The quartz appears dark in the photograph.

Sugar Hill.—Two fine aquamarines, found near Sugar Hill, in the western part of Stoneham, are described as follows by Kunz: [a]

The writer obtained at Stoneham, Oxford County, Me., two beryls, exceptional for the United States. These were found in 1881, several miles apart and several miles from the topaz region, by farmers who were traversing pastures in the township. The first was found in two pieces, as if it had been roughly used, and broken, and discarded as worthless, or else broken in taking from the rock and then rejected, its value not being known. This crystal measured $4\frac{3}{4}$ inches (120 millimeters) long and $2\frac{1}{10}$ inches (54 millimeters) wide, and was originally about 5 inches (130 millimeters) long and 3 inches (75 millimeters) wide. The color was rich sea green viewed in the direction of the longer axis of the prism, and sea blue of a very deep tint through the side of the crystal. In color and material this is the finest specimen that has been found at any North American locality, and the crystals, unbroken, would equal the finest foreign crystals known. It furnished the finest aquamarine ever found in the United States, measuring $1\frac{3}{8}$ inches (35 millimeters) by $1\frac{3}{8}$ inches (35 millimeters) by three-fourths inch (20 millimeters). It was cut as a brilliant and weighs $133\frac{3}{4}$ carats. The color is bluish green, and, with the exception of a few hair-like internal striations, is perfect. In addition to this remarkable gem, the same crystal furnished over 300 carats of fine stones.

The other crystal is doubly terminated, being $1\frac{3}{8}$ inches (41 millimeters) long and $\frac{3}{8}$ inch (15 millimeters) in diameter. Half of it is transparent, with a faint green color; the remainder is of a milky green and only translucent.

The large 133-carat gem cut from the first of these two crystals is now in the possession of the Field Museum of Natural History at Chicago.

Fine crystals of golden beryl have been obtained at Edgecomb Mountain in Stoneham.

On the south flank of Sugar Hill a ledge of coarse pegmatite has yielded a number of fine transparent beryls. The pegmatite mass here appears to be rather flat lying and, as exposed in a near-by vertical face, is at least 15 feet in thickness; it can be followed for 100 feet or so along the hillside. The buff-colored potash feldspar of this ledge forms large enough crystals and is sufficiently free from iron-bearing minerals to be of commercial grade for pottery purposes, but its distance from the railroad would render its exploitation unprofitable at the present time.

Crystals of beryllonite, a phosphate of beryllium and sodium, have been found in western Stoneham on the farm of Eldin McAllister, on the south side of Sugar Hill, a few rods below the beryl locality just described. When visited by the writer, in September, 1906, the only opening consisted of a small pit dug in the talus and glacial drift near the foot of the hill. The soil in which the beryllonite crystals were found contains also fragments of quartz, feldspar, and mica, and a few of apatite, beryl, cassiterite, columbite, and triplite. Some of the beryllonite crystals themselves are attached to apatite and some retain what appear to be the impressions of muscovite crystals. There can be little doubt therefore that the beryllonite occurred

---

[a] Kunz, G. F., Gems and precious stones, pp. 92–93.

as a constituent of a pegmatite mass, and it probably occurred in pockets. The minerals were probably dislodged, by the action of glacial ice, from a decomposed pegmatite ledge somewhere on the flanks of Sugar Hill and were subsequently deposited in their present position at the base of the hill. Prospecting on the hill northwest of the beryllonite locality may eventually disclose the source.

The locality was first worked by E. D. Andrews, of Albany, who, in searching for smoky quartz, found an unknown mineral, which was later identified by E. S. Dana in 1888 as a new species and called beryllonite. Its mineral characters have been fully described by Dana and Wells.[a]

Harndon Hill.—A well-known topaz locality is located on the summit of Harndon Hill, in the southwestern corner of the town of Stoneham, within one-fourth mile of the Stow line. It was opened in the early eighties by Nathan H. Perry, of South Paris, and worked intermittently for a number of years, but at the time of the writer's visit in September, 1906, had been practically idle for over ten years. The workings consist of several openings close together, a few feet across and 2 or 3 feet in depth, in the coarse pegmatite which caps the hill at this point.

The locality has been visited by George F. Kunz, of New York, and its minerals described by him.[b] He describes the character and mode of occurrence of the topaz as follows:

This locality is the first in New England that has furnished good, clear, and distinct crystals of topaz, and thus far it has produced the best crystals found in the United States. Of these crystals, nearly all the finest were found in one pocket in clevelandite (lamellar albite) at its junction with a vein of margarodite (hydromica) and one was entirely surrounded by clevelandite. The finest crystals vary in size from 10 millimeters to the largest, which measures transversely 60 by 65 millimeters and vertically 56 millimeters. They are transparent in parts, and contain cavities of fluids, the nature of which has not yet been determined. A few small perfect gems have been cut from the fragments of a large crystal that was broken.

The finest crystals are colorless or faintly tinted with green or blue. Some opaque crystals are as much as 300 millimeters across the largest part and weigh from 10 to 20 kilograms each. They are not perfect in form, the faces are rough, and generally they were broken before they were taken from the rock. The color in these rough crystals is more decided than in the finer ones and is a light shade of either green, yellow, or blue. The specific gravity of the transparent material is 3.54, and the hardness the same as that of the yellow topaz from Ouro Preto (formerly Villa Rica), Brazil.

The properties of this topaz have been further discussed by Penfield and Minor;[c] its chemical composition has been studied and its alteration to damourite has been described by Clarke and Diller.[d] No topaz was visible at the time of the writer's visit.

[a] Dana, E. S., and Wells, H. L., Am. Jour. Sci., 3d ser., vol. 37, 1889, pp. 23-32.

[b] Kunz, G. F., Topaz and associated minerals at Stoneham, Me.: Am. Jour. Sci., 3d ser., vol. 27, 1884, pp. 212-216.

[c] Penfield, S. I., and Minor, J. C., jr., On the chemical composition and related physical properties of topaz: Am. Jour. Sci., 3d ser., vol. 47, 1894, p. 390.

[d] Clarke, F. W., and Diller, J. S., Topaz from Stoneham, Me.: Am. Jour. Sci., 3d ser., vol. 29, 1885, pp. 378-384.

Other constituents of the pegmatite at this locality are the following, the descriptions being partly those of Kunz:

1. Apatite occurs in the cavities as small doubly-terminated crystals and in the solid pegmatite as opaque vitreous-green masses weighing up to 2 pounds.

2. Beryl occurs in large colorless to pale-green crystals embedded in the solid pegmatite. Most of them are opaque to translucent with small colorless transparent portions. Kunz reports that one band unusually rich in beryl was traced for nearly 40 feet. Some of the crystals in this band were about a yard long and over a foot across.

3. Clevelandite in white plates is very abundant, as in most of the gem-bearing pegmatites. It occurs in particular abundance and perfection of crystal form on the walls of the pockets.

4. Columbite is usually associated with clevelandite, lying either on crystals of the latter in cavities or else between the plates of it. Its crystals vary in length from 1 to 10 millimeters and are not very perfect. One pocket afforded over 40 pounds of pure material, and one mass which seemed to have belonged to a single crystal group weighed over 17 pounds.

5. Fluorite fills small cavities in the clevelandite. The masses are rarely over 10 millimeters across and the color is very deep purple. A number of very minute octahedra resembling blue topaz have been found.

6. The pink kaolin montmorillonite occurs, according to Kunz, in masses that range in color from a very delicate pink to tints closely approximating red, filling the cavities and interstices in the clevelandite. It also occurs in botryoidal masses resembling rhodochrosite, on crystals of clevelandite.

7. Triplite is scattered irregularly through the solid pegmatite in masses usually under 2 pounds in weight, though one mass broken out in the blasting furnished over 100 pounds of rather pure material.

8. Herderite, in short prisms from 1 millimeter to 1 centimeter long, occurs in the topaz-bearing pockets and has been described by Hidden and Mackintosh [a] and further discussed by Dana [b] and Penfield. [c]

9. Bertrandite occurs in the pockets with herderite and topaz. It has been described by Penfield. [d]

10. A single occurrence of hamlinite has been noted at this locality. The mineral formed minute rhombohedral crystals attached to herderite, margarodite, muscovite, and feldspar, and associated with ber-

[a] Hidden, W. E., On the probable occurrence of herderite in Maine: Am. Jour. Sci., 3d ser., vol. 27, 1884, p. 73. Hidden, W. E., and Mackintosh, J. B., On herderite, a glucinum calcium phosphate and fluoride from Oxford County, Me.: Idem, pp. 135-138.

[b] Dana, E. S., On the crystalline form of the supposed herderite from Stoneham, Me.: Idem, pp. 229-232.

[c] Penfield, S. L., On the crystallization of herderite: Am. Jour. Sci., 3d ser., vol. 47, 1894, pp. 333-336.

[d] Penfield, S. L., Crystallized bertrandite from Stoneham, Me., and Mount Antero, Colorado: Am. Jour. Sci., 3d ser., vol. 37, 1889, pp. 213-215; Note concerning bertrandite crystals from Oxford County, Me.: Idem, 4th ser., vol. 4, 1897, p. 316.

trandite.   It was named in honor of A. C. Hamlin, of Bangor, who for many years developed the famous tourmaline mine at Mount Mica. The mineral has been described by Hidden and Penfield.[a]

Other minerals from this locality are autunite, biotite, gehlenite, garnet, muscovite, quartz, triphylite, and zircon.

STOW.

The rocks of the town of Stow, so far as seen by the writer, are all granitic; they include pegmatite, normal granite, and granite gneiss.

Amethystine quartz has been obtained on Deer Hill near the New Hampshire line.   When visited by the writer in September, 1906, the only openings observed were a number of shallow pits dug in the soil on the southeastern slope of the hill.   The amethyst crystals occur loose in this soil or attached to loose fragments of feldspar. ·The small pieces found by the writer were all of a very pale lavender tint and in most of them the color was very unevenly distributed.   The amethyst was probably derived from pockets in the pegmatite, but so far as known the ledge has not been opened.   The whole summit of the hill is composed of pegmatite of the type usual in western Maine. Certain portions are coarse enough and sufficiently free from iron-bearing minerals to be of commercial grade for pottery purposes, but their quantity is small.

The characters of the rocks are well shown in the bed of Great River near the road bridge just southwest of Deer Hill, where the principal rock is a rather fine-grained biotite-muscovite granite, in part massive, but mostly of gneissic texture.   This is crossed by an irregular band of muscovite-biotite pegmatite, which ranges from 6 inches to 2 feet in width; it is without sharp walls and grades imperceptibly into the granite gneiss.   The mineralogic similarity and the gradation from one rock into the other indicate a common magmatic source. The pegmatite appears to have been intruded before the complete solidification of the granite.

From Deer Hill southward to Stow village the rocks are pegmatite and fine-grained granite.   From Stow village to Lovell village the bed rock near the roads is obscured by extensive glacial outwash deposits of sand.

WATERFORD.

The rocks of Waterford, so far as seen by the writer, are largely granites and associated pegmatite, though some schist of probable sedimentary origin is found in the eastern part of the town.   The pegmatite at two localities has in the past been worked for mica.

[a] Hidden, W. E., and Penfield, S. L., On hamlinite, a new rhombohedral mineral from the herderite locality at Stoneham, Me.: Am. Jour. Sci., 3d ser., vol. 39, 1890, pp. 511–513. Penfield, S. L., On the chemical composition of hamlinite and its occurrence with bertrandite at Oxford County, Me.: Am. Jour. Sci., 4th ser., vol. 4, 1897, pp. 313–316.

South Waterford mica prospect.—An old mica mine located in the southwestern part of the town near the Sweden line was visited by the writer in September, 1906. It consists of a single pit about 40 feet long, 15 feet wide, and 15 feet in depth, located on an eastern hillside. The predominant rock at this locality is a gray muscovite-biotite granite varying somewhat in texture but mostly fine grained. It differs in shade from point to point, owing mainly to variations in the amount of biotite it contains.

Under the microscope the texture is seen to be typically granitic and nearly equigranular. The rock is very fresh and consists in order of abundance of quartz, microcline, biotite, plagioclase feldspar, and muscovite. The plagioclase appears to have the composition of oligoclase (refractive index > microcline and > = < Canada balsam; extinction angles low). Much of the quartz shows rounded outlines and is inclosed by microcline. This quartz appears to represent the earliest crystallization, even the biotite plates conforming to its rounded outlines. Microcline and other quartz are plainly later crystallizations.

Locally aggregations of biotite in the granite form flat lenticles, many of irregular form and variously oriented. Biotitic aggregations are also present in the finer portions of the pegmatite.

The pegmatite penetrates the granite in an exceedingly irregular manner, locally with the most gradual transition. The pegmatite shows great variation in coarseness, the coarsest portions containing crystals of orthoclase $1\frac{1}{2}$ to 2 feet across. Its mineral constituents appear to be identical with those of the granite, though present perhaps in somewhat different proportions. The dominant feldspar is microcline (with some orthoclase); oligoclase is present in subordinate amounts (refractive index > microcline and about = balsam; extinction angles up to 12° and 13°).

In texture and mineral composition the granite of this quarry is very similar to that at Rumford Falls (pp. 94–95). Both granite masses are of relatively small extent and exhibit within short distances differences in composition more marked than is characteristic of the normal granites of the large granite areas of the State. In the granite of Waterford the tendency toward segregation is further shown by the presence of the biotite nodules already mentioned. In both localities granite is so similar in mineral composition to the associated pegmatite and the gradation from one rock to the other is in many places so gradual and irregular that it seems necessary to conclude that granite and pegmatite crystallized fron the same magmatic source at nearly the same time. Some of the pegmatite shows megascopic evidence, in the presence of thin irregular skins of muscovite and other secondary foliated minerals along certain planes through the rock, of very slight internal movements subsequent to its solidification. Microscopically the effects of these movements are recognizable in local granulation within certain quartz and feldspar individuals and marked strain in others.

The coarsest portions of the pegmatite have been worked for mica. A few of the muscovite books are as much as 1 foot across, but the majority are under 4 inches. The larger plates are only in part clear, being injured by ruling and twinning. The writer saw no plates that would cut clear pieces larger than 2 by 3 inches, and even such as would were rare. Most of the material could be utilized only for scrap mica. The property hardly appears to merit further development.

Beech Hill mica mine.—Another mica mine, located a few miles north of the first, on the farm of George L. Kimball, on Beech Hill, represents the most serious attempt at mica mining that has been made in the State. The mica occurs as a constituent of a sill-like mass of coarse pegmatite, which dips to the east at about 30°. Its thickness is at least 12 feet, the base not being exposed. Commercial mica is confined to a zone about 5 feet thick in the lowest part of the pegmatite layer as now exposed. Within this 5-foot zone muscovite is estimated to form from 10 to 20 per cent of the material of the pegmatite.

Some of the masses of pure orthoclase feldspar associated with the mica are 5 feet across, but the total quantity present is not sufficient to make it of commercial importance. Intergrowths of quartz and muscovite are common.

The pegmatite contains no biotite and no black tourmaline. The associated rock is a granite gneiss, and both gneiss and pegmatite are intruded by a dike of diabase.

Some of the muscovite books are 1 foot across, but most of them are under 5 inches. The larger plates are invariably cut up by ruling planes into a number of smaller pieces. Much of the mica is worthless for anything but scrap because of the prevalence of ruling, wedge structure, and twinning. Most of the thumb-trimmed material seen by the writer was in pieces 2 or 3 by 3 inches in size. The mine was not being worked at the time of the writer's visit in September, 1906, and although several tons of mica lay in the trimming sheds, the best of the output was reported to have been sold. It was therefore impossible to make a wholly fair estimate of the average value of the mica mined, but the quality of the material is superior to that from any other known locality in Maine and appears to warrant further development.

The property was opened in 1900 and was also worked in 1902 by the Beech Hill Mining Company, who subsequently sold the property to New York persons. About a ton of thumb-trimmed mica was marketed at prices ranging from 8 cents to $1 a pound, and about 10 tons of scrap mica was sold. The remainder of the material quarried was still in the mine buildings at the time of the writer's visit. The equipment includes a steam drill and boiler and a shed where the trimming was done. .

SAGADAHOC COUNTY.

GEORGETOWN.

The rocks of Georgetown are mostly sedimentary schists and intruded masses of pegmatite, normal granite, and flow gneiss. The only pegmatite deposit now worked is on the east side of Kennebec River, near its mouth, where feldspar is quarried by Golding's Sons Company, of Trenton, N. J.

Georgetown Center.—The relations between the pegmatite and schists on Bay Point Peninsula (see below) are repeated in good exposures at the four corners west of Georgetown Center. Here a mass of pegmatite 10 feet in maximum width intrudes the schists irregularly, sending off into them an apophysis 1 foot in width at its base, but tapering out within 6 feet. This branch shows the same irregular pegmatitic texture as the larger dike but becomes finer grained as it tapers. The bordering schist contains numerous quartz stringers, some of which are distinctly traceable into the pegmatite and near the latter carry a few mica plates.

On the hill east of the gurnet at Georgetown Center a number of prospect pits for feldspar were opened by J. S. Berry. Black tourmaline and biotite are so abundant in most of the pegmatite as to render it useless for pottery purposes.

Hinckleys Landing.—On the shore, about one-half mile south of Hinckleys Landing, a pegmatite mass in the schist gives off a branch dike 3 to 6 inches wide, which very near where it leaves the parent mass becomes fine grained and typically granitic in texture.

Golding's feldspar quarry.—One of the most productive feldspar quarries in Maine, and one that has been worked intermittently for over thirty years, is located near the east shore of Todds Bay near the mouth of Kennebec River and is now owned and operated by Golding's Sons Company, of Trenton, N. J. It may be reached by a drive of 11 miles from Woolwich or by steamer from Bath to Bay Point Landing, which is only about 1½ miles from the quarry. The Bath quadrangle of the United States Geological Survey includes this area. The property was visited by the writer in July, 1906, and again in November, 1908.

The excavations cover an area of about 3 acres and consist of three open pits. The southernmost pit, which is the oldest and largest, had been abandoned for many years at the time of the writer's visit in 1906, but in 1908 the quarry waste which had been dumped in it was being removed and new excavating had revealed considerable amounts of excellent feldspar. It is significant that much of the waste material dumped into this pit in the early mining is of good commercial grade according to present standards and is being saved. In the early days graphic granite was mostly discarded and only practically pure feldspar utilized. This pit is now about 100 feet in depth. The northernmost pit, from which large amounts of spar have recently been taken, is 200 feet long in a direction N. 25° E., 40 to 75 feet wide, and 20 to 30 feet deep.

In this quarry the commercially valuable rock is mainly a coarse graphic intergrowth of feldspar and quartz, which is estimated to comprise about one-half the total material excavated, the other half being waste which is highly quartzose or contains muscovite or iron-bearing minerals. (See Plate XVIII).

The quartz of this quarry is mostly gray and semiopaque, and in many places has a granular appearance. In a few places it is slightly pinkish in hue. Masses of pure quartz are usually small, the largest observed by the writer being a mass 6 feet across in the northern-most pit. It is not utilized commercially.

Most of the feldspar is orthoclase or microcline with small amounts of albite. The following analysis by the Pittsburg testing laboratory of the United States Geological Survey is of the best grade of buff-colored feldspar:

Analyses of feldspar from Golding's Sons Company quarry.

Silica (SiO_2)	65. 23
Alumina (Al_2O_3)	20. 09
Iron oxide (Fe_2O_3)	. 71
Lime (CaO)	None.
Magnesia (MgO)	None.
Potash (K_2O)	11. 60
Soda (Na_2O)	2. 00
Loss on ignition	. 36
	99. 99

Very few large masses of pure feldspar are exposed in the present quarry openings, but it is said that in the past single blasts have loosened 100 tons of almost pure material. In the southern pit a number of masses of pure feldspar several feet across were exposed in 1908, but most of the rock here and practically all exposed in the middle and northern pits is an intergrowth of quartz and feldspar. Most of this intergrowth, however, is of excellent quality for pottery uses, since injurious minerals such as muscovite and black tourmaline are usually confined to certain portions of the mass and can be readily separated from the rest of the rock in mining. Although the graphic form of quartz and feldspar intergrowth is the most common, very perfect dendritic penetrations of feldspar by quartz are also present.

Muscovite is not present in sufficient amounts to be of any commercial importance. All the larger books are of the wedge variety. Graphic intergrowths of quartz and muscovite are also found locally, as are rounded aggregates made up almost entirely of small muscovite crystals and similar to those observed at the G. D. Willes quarry in Topsham.

Biotite is almost entirely absent, but in its stead occurs black tourmaline. The latter is locally very abundant in prismatic crystals, some of which are $2\frac{1}{2}$ to 3 inches in diameter and a foot or more in length. The tourmaline is not evenly distributed through the pegmatite but is confined almost entirely to certain irregular zones which may be avoided or discarded in the quarrying process. It is more abundantly associated with the quartz than with the feldspar.

Garnet occurs in deep flesh-colored crystals, usually small and associated with quartz and muscovite. Some light-green opaque beryl is found, one mass penetrating quartz being 14 inches long and 4 inches in diameter.

The contact of the pegmatite with other rocks is not exposed in any of the quarry openings, but is fairly well shown a few rods northeast of the quarry near the highest part of the same hill, where the bordering rocks are schists which strike slightly east of north and dip nearly vertical. The contact nearly parallels the trend of the schists and the pegmatite is plainly intrusive, locally cutting across the foliation of the schists and sending off broad apophyses into them. A noteworthy feature of this contact is the complete absence of any change in texture or coarseness in the pegmatite as the schist is approached. A coarse aggregate of black tourmaline crystals, some of which are $1\frac{3}{4}$ inches in diameter, occurs within 2 feet of the contact; and graphic granite of the same coarseness as in the central parts of the pegmatite mass occurs along its border. The schist is a quartz-biotite rock, in many places highly garnetiferous and containing abundant stringers of white to brownish quartz, which, at this point at least, have no traceable connection with the associated pegmatite and are no larger nor more numerous near the contact than some distance away. The schist folia in many places show numerous minor contortions.

The present excavations cover almost the whole area of outcrop of the pegmatite body. Future work will probably consist largely in deepening the present pit, but there is reason to expect that the deposit will continue of good quality and of about the same dimensions to a considerable depth. A number of other dikes of pegmatite of similar size and shape occur in the vicinity and some of them have been worked to a slight extent. None of these, so far as seen, show any large amounts of feldspar of commercial grade.

The rock is excavated by steam drilling and dynamite blasting and in the largest pit is hoisted by derrick and hoisting engine. It is broken up and sorted by hand and hauled by wagon one-fourth mile to the shore, where it is transferred to small sailing barges, which convey it either to vessels for shipment to Trenton by water or up Kennebec River 10 miles to Bath for shipment by rail. About fifteen men are usually employed in this quarry.

Small Point feldspar quarry.—A small feldspar quarry, now abandoned and partly filled with water, is located one-half mile east of the Golding quarry, near the head of Sagadahoc Bay and east of the highway. It is a single pit about 75 feet long, 35 feet wide, and probably 30 to 40 feet in depth, though only 25 feet of wall shows above the water level. The rock is similar in nearly ever respect to that quarried at the Golding quarry, but the area of the deposit seems to be very small, schist occurring within a hundred feet or so north, west, and south of the pit.

Schist-pegmatite contacts on Bay Point Peninsula.—The contacts between the pegmatites and the schists are well exposed at a number of points along the shores of Bay Point Peninsula. A few rods north of the steamboat landing at Bay Point the pegmatite cuts directly across the schist folia, sending off quartz stringers into the schist. The pegmatite shows no noticeable change in texture or composition to a point within about 10 inches of the contact, but from there on tends to become finer grained and less feldspathic, the rock close to the contact being an aggregate of quartz and muscovite. Muscovite also occurs in some of the quartz stringers near their point of departure from the main pegmatite mass. The schist near the pegmatite is rich in dark-brown tourmaline crystals, some of which are one-half inch long and one-eighth inch in diameter; they are probably the results of contact metamorphism.

Although the quartz stringers described above are traceable into the pegmatite, in many other places the pegmatite cuts distinctly across both the folia and quartz stringers of the schist. In such places, although the quartz stringers may not be offshoots of the pegmatite mass immediately associated with them, the absence of genetic connection with other pegmatite of the vicinity is not proved. Such a connection is rendered probable by the presence of some feldspar in a number of the larger quartz lenses. Near the north end of Bay Point Peninsula one quartz lens bearing some feldspar is 1½ feet in greatest width and 3 to 4 feet in length.

The conversion of certain of the schists into injection gneisses through their penetration by pegmatite and quartz stringers proceeding from a larger pegmatite mass is well shown in Plate IV, *B*, reproduced from a photograph taken along the wagon road near the center of Bay Point Peninsula. The large pegmatite mass shown in this picture is quite quartzose, with masses of pure quartz 4 to 5 feet across. The feldspar is in small crystals intergrown with quartz and mica and does not occur in large crystals comparable to the quartz masses. The quartz stringers of the schist are traceable in many instances with perfect continuity into the quartz of the schist, and a number of the quartz stringers contain muscovite crystals. Within $1\frac{1}{2}$ feet of the main pegmatite mass the schist becomes darker colored through the abundant development in it of dark-brown tourmaline.

On the east shore of Kennebec Point, about half a mile northeast of the extreme southern tip, schists are intruded by pegmatitic granite similar in mineral composition to the coarse pegmatite at the Golding quarry, its principal constituents being quartz, potash feldspar, muscovite, and black tourmaline. The average size of grain in this granite is not over one-fourth inch, although some of the feldspars are 3 inches long. None of the black tourmaline crystals are over one-fourth inch and they average only about one-eighth inch in width. It is significant that the minerals, especially the black tourmaline, show a noticeable amount of parallel orientation in certain parts of the ledge, indicating a certain amount of flowing movement during crystallization. The rock becomes finer grained within 8 or 10 inches of the schist contact. This rock gives every indication of being intermediate in its character between normal granite and the typical coarse pegmatite of this region.

TOPSHAM.

The rocks of the town of Topsham are quartz-mica schists which have been intruded by pegmatite, by flow gneisses of granitic composition, and to some extent by granite. Exposures showing the characters and relationships of these rocks are plentiful and excellent.

Distribution of the quarries.—The pegmatites of the town are now worked for feldspar at several points and were once worked at a number of others now abandoned. The quarries all lie within a belt about a mile in width, extending from Mount Ararat, near Topsham village, in a northeasterly direction nearly to the Topsham-Bowdoinham line. Within this belt are eight quarries, only three of which are now active, and a number of prospect pits. It is significant that the line of distribution of these quarries corresponds closely with the trend of the metamorphosed sedimentary schists into which the pegmatites were intruded. Because of the soil covering it is impossible to determine the exact limits of the coarse pegmatite bodies exposed at each of these eight quarries, but it is evident from a study of the rocks between the various quarries that the pegmatite bodies which are worked are not all of them parts of a single pegmatite mass but are more or less detached intrusions in a region where the

rocks are mainly schists. Within the belt, however, the pegmatitic
intrusions are more numerous and are some of them of coarser texture than in the surrounding country. If we may use the form of
the smaller and finer-grained pegmatite masses as an index to that
of the larger and coarser ones (which are commercially valuable),
the latter are probably, for the most part, somewhat elongate in a
direction slightly east of north, parallel to the general trend of the
inclosing schists and gneisses.

Products of the quarries.—Feldspar is the only mineral of much
commercial importance at any of these quarries. Quartz of excellent quality is present in considerable amounts and is often saved in
the quarrying process, though at present finding but slight market.
At some of the quarries tourmalines and aquamarines of gem quality
are now and then obtained. A description of the quarries in the
order of their distribution from southwest to northeast is given below.

Mount Ararat feldspar quarries.—A quarry from which feldspar
and quartz have been obtained is situated on the east slope of Mount
Ararat, about 1 mile north of Topsham village. The deeper part of
the excavation is about 40 feet long from east to west, 10 feet wide,
and 12 feet in maximum depth. A shallow excavation adjacent to
the northwest part of the deeper pit covers an area of about 20 by 30
feet. The quarry has not been operated for several years.

The lower pit exposes considerable amounts of clean, white, gray,
and nearly black semiopaque quartz but shows few masses of pure
feldspar more than 3 or 4 inches in diameter. Though feldspar was
the principal mineral sought, the quartz was saved in the quarrying
process and tons of it are now piled near the pit. The feldspar is
cream colored to nearly white and is shown by microscopic examination to be principally microcline, with occasional very small amounts
of the white soda feldspar, albite. In the upper and shallower
portion of the quarry the amount of pure quartz is less and the amount
of pure feldspar is greater than in the lower portion. Some of the
masses of pure feldspar there are 3 to 4 feet across. They grade into
a coarse graphic intergrowth of quartz and feldspar and the latter
into extremely fine graphic granite. Only the pure feldspar and the
coarse graphic granite were used commercially. Of the iron-bearing
minerals which would injure the quality of the feldspar for pottery
purposes, black tourmaline is almost entirely absent and black mica
(biotite) is rare. Garnet is rather an abundant constituent, but is
associated mainly with the muscovite and with the finer-grained
portions of the pegmatite, and only rarely with the more feldspathic
parts that are commercially available. Magnetite occurs rarely in
small irregular octahedra.

Muscovite or white mica is also an abundant constituent of the
pegmatite as exposed in the upper pit. It is pale green to nearly

colorless and occurs in books, some of which are 8 to 10 inches in diameter. The great bulk of the muscovite is of the wedge variety and shows twinning; it could be utilized commercially only as scrap mica. A small amount is plate mica and splits readily into sheets, which when trimmed may measure 4 by 5 inches, though mostly smaller. Most of this plate mica incloses between its lamellæ thin branching crystals of magnetite. A few small masses of columbite, generally exhibiting very imperfect crystal forms, are found in the quartz-feldspar masses.

The wall rock of schist or gneiss is nowhere exposed at this quarry, and the soil covering makes it impossible to trace the exact limits of the deposit. If one may judge from neighboring masses of pegmatite whose boundaries are exposed, this mass is probably more or less irregular in outline and somewhat elongate in a direction parallel to the trend of the neighboring schists—that is, somewhat east of north. The deposit does not appear to be very extensive, but the quality is good, and there seems to be warrant for further development work on a small scale.

A second small feldspar quarry, on the northern slope of Mount Ararat, consists of a single hillside pit about 150 feet long, 30 feet in average width, and 20 feet in greatest depth. It was last worked in 1905. The rock is a wholly irregular association of quartz, feldspar, muscovite, biotite, and garnet, with smaller amounts of rarer minerals. The quartz is prevailingly dark gray in color and semiopaque, but in some places is white and in a few nearly black. A number of the pure quartz masses are 3 to 4 feet across; one, flat lying and exposed at the base of one of the quarry walls, is 5 feet in maximum width and 25 feet in length, with very irregular boundaries.

Most of the feldspar is pale pink in color, but certain portions are cream colored, and others decidedly red. Microscopic examination shows that the feldspar belongs mainly to the potash varieties orthoclase and microcline, the former greatly predominating. With these are associated small amounts of the soda feldspar, albite, which is frequently intergrown microscopically with the orthoclase or microcline. Throughout most of the quarry the masses of pure feldspar are not over 4 to 5 inches across, though a few crystals measure 2 to 3 feet. The bulk of the material quarried for pottery use is a graphic intergrowth of feldspar and quartz, most of it coarser than that found at the quarry on the eastern slope of Mount Ararat. The quartz thus intergrown with the feldspar commonly assumes branching or dendritic forms, a characteristic not observed in most of the pegmatite deposits.

Muscovite of the wedge variety occurs sparingly in books up to 6 inches in greatest diameter. No clear plate mica was observed. Of very common occurrence are graphic intergrowths of muscovite

and quartz, many single crystals of muscovite with roughly hexagonal outline grading outward into a fringe of graphically intergrown
muscovite and quartz. In some places muscovite and feldspar are
graphically intergrown. The quartz of these muscovite intergrowths
is in many places continuous with quartz intergrown with feldspar.

Biotite is much more abundant than at the quarry on the eastern
side of Mount Ararat and dominates over muscovite. It occurs in
the characteristic lath-shaped crystals, many of which have a length
of 2 feet, a width of 4 to 5 inches, and a thickness of one-half inch to
1 inch. The largest biotite crystal observed was $3\frac{1}{2}$ feet long, $2\frac{1}{2}$
feet wide, and 1 to 2 inches thick. These crystals penetrate the pegmatite mass in every conceivable direction.

Garnet is rather abundant and is generally dark red and submetallic in appearance. In some places it is intergrown with quartz and
in others with both quartz and muscovite. One garnet crystal was
$2\frac{1}{2}$ inches across. It is most abundant in the finer grained portion
of the pegmatite and in those portions rich in muscovite and is rare
in the parts which are used commercially. Magnetite occurs only
rarely in imperfect octahedra showing step structure.

Schists and gneisses are nowhere exposed in this quarry and near-by
outcrops are not numerous, so that it is impossible to determine the
form or area of the pegmatite. On the north wall of the quarry a
small mass of fine-grained granite showing locally a somewhat
gneissic structure is exposed and is intruded by the pegmatite, the
latter cutting across the banding of the granite gneiss, though there
is crystallographic continuity between the two.

The amount of feldspar of commercial quality now exposed is not
large, and the abundance of biotite and garnet render much of the
material valueless for pottery uses. The extent of the deposit can
not be accurately predicted, but is probably not very great. Further
development on a small scale could probably be profitably undertaken and might reveal some good spar not now exposed. The
deposit is located 2 miles from the Maine Central Railroad station
at Topsham. The nearest point on the railroad is only three-fourths
of a mile southeast of this quarry and the one previously described,
but there is no wagon road available in this direction.

Fisher's feldspar quarry.—A small quarry not now worked is situated $1\frac{1}{4}$ miles west-northwest of Cathance station along the northern
valley slope of Cathance River. This quarry, which was formerly
operated for feldspar by J. A. Fisher, consists of a single pit about
150 feet long from north to south, 20 feet or so in average width,
and about 18 feet in maximum depth. It is located on a southern
hill slope.

As in most of the other feldspar quarries, there is no regularity
in the arrangement of the constituent minerals with the single

exception of muscovite, which occurs principally along certain zones which have, however, no definite trend with respect to the general outlines of the deposit.

The quartz is white to gray in color, but no very large masses are exposed.

The feldspar is cream colored and is shown by microscopic examination to be mainly microcline with some orthoclase. Small amounts of the soda feldspar, albite, probably occur as in the other quarries in this vicinity, though none was observed by the writer. One mass of pure feldspar, 3 to 4 feet wide and 10 feet high, exposed on the west wall of the quarry, passes by perfect gradations into a coarse graphic intergrowth with quartz and this in turn into a much finer graphic intergrowth. As in most of the feldspar quarries, the coarse graphic granite forms the bulk of the material mined for pottery purposes. The chemical composition of graphic granites from this quarry is discussed on pages 40, 124, and their appearance is shown in Plate XVIII.

The muscovite, so far as present exposures show, is all of the wedge variety and is mainly confined to certain zones which penetrate the pegmatite irregularly (see Pl. IX, A, and p. 26); being localized in this manner, it does not seriously interfere with the feldspar mining. The muscovite books are nearly all characterized by twinning and wedge structure. No plate mica was observed. Graphic intergrowths of quartz and muscovite are common. In some parts of the pegmatite biotite dominates over muscovite; it is usually most abundant in the finer-grained portions.

An examination by Wright and Larsen of the white quartz of the larger quartz areas at this quarry showed that it probably crystallized under low-temperature conditions. Quartz from the coarser phases of the graphic granite was also examined and though the results were not conclusive they indicated that the quartz may have crystallized under high-temperature conditions. Since the areas of pure quartz are closely adjacent to those of graphic granite and indeed grade into them most irregularly, these results suggest that the crystallization temperatures of the pegmatite mass as a whole were not far from the inversion point of quartz (about 575° C.); however, the imperfect character of the data must be borne in mind. This matter is discussed in more detail on pages 36–39.

Outcrops are not numerous enough in the immediate vicinity to determine the extent or form of the pegmatite body. The materials exposed in the present excavation seem to indicate that a considerable supply of spar is still available and seem to warrant further development.

William Willes feldspar quarry.—A small quarry situated 1½ miles northwest of Cathance station and operated by William Willes for the

Trenton Flint and Spar Company was opened early in 1906. It occupies an area of a little more than 1 acre, and its average depth is about 10 feet. Natural drainage is possible at present depth, but further excavation will necessitate pumping. The rock is a wholly irregular association of quartz, feldspar, mica, and rarer minerals.

The quartz is mainly light gray in color and occurs locally in pure masses 5 or 6 feet in diameter. Many even of the larger quartz masses exhibit crystal faces along their contact with other minerals. Quartz is saved in the quarrying process but finds only a very irregular market.

The feldspar is buff colored and is shown by microscopic examination to be mainly orthoclase and microcline. The soda variety, albite, also occurs but forms only a small percentage of the total mass of feldspar; a few crystals of albite are 4 to 5 inches across. As at most of the Maine feldspar quarries, the great bulk of the material quarried for pottery purposes is a coarse graphic intergrowth of quartz with potash feldspar. In the northern part of the quarry a mass of pure feldspar 10 feet across is exposed on a glaciated surface.

Muscovite occurs in grapihc intergrowth with quartz and also in books, the latter being mostly wedge mica. Some of these books are 10 inches across. The total amount of muscovite present is not sufficient to make it worth while to save it in quarrying.

Biotite is about equally as abundant as muscovite and occurs in characteristic lath-shaped crystals; one of these was 4 feet long, 8 inches wide, and 1 inch thick. Much of the biotite is decomposed to what appears to be chlorite colored with hematite.

Garnet is moderately abundant, usually occurring in compound crystals of dark-red color with submetallic luster.

Beryl is moderately abundant, some hexagonal crystals being 10 inches in diameter. Some of the smaller crystals are partly transparent and have been sold to mineral collectors.

Some columbite is found in small imperfectly developed crystals but is not sufficiently abundant to be of commercial consequence.

In one place in the quarry a small amount of hornblendic granite gneiss occurs. The pegmatite cuts across the foliation of the granite gneiss and is plainly somewhat the younger. Its exact attitude and boundaries could not be determined because of the scarcity of outcrops in the vicinity, but it is probable that further stripping near the present workings will reveal considerable amounts of commercially valuable spar.

At the time of the writer's visit seven laborers were employed in the quarry besides the foreman and the superintendent. The rock is hauled by two 2-horse teams a distance of $1\frac{1}{4}$ miles to the feldspar mill near Cathance station.

Maine Feldspar Company's quarry.—A small feldspar quarry a few rods southeast of the one just described was opened in 1906 by the Maine Feldspar Company, of Auburn, Me. The rock, which is similar in every way to that at the William Willes quarry, is hauled by team about $1\frac{1}{4}$ miles to Cathance station and from there shipped by rail to the Maine Feldspar Company's mill at Littlefield, 3 miles southwest of Auburn.

G. D. Willes feldspar quarry.—A feldspar quarry operated for the Trenton Flint and Spar Company by G. D. Willes, of Brunswick, is situated about 2 miles northwest of Cathance station and is the oldest and by far the largest of the Topsham quarries. Its irregular opening covers several acres and the material is excavated from several levels, the greatest depth being about 50 feet.

Although the great bulk of the commercial spar now taken from this quarry is a coarse graphic intergrowth of feldspar and quartz, masses of pure quartz and of pure feldspar occur which are larger than those seen at any other quarry in the State. A single mass of pure white quartz in the northern part of the quarry is 50 feet long and is exposed for a height of 10 feet. The pegmatite is in general coarser at the northern than at the southern end of the quarry.

The feldspar also occurs here and there in crystals of large size, one in the northern part of the quarry measuring 15 feet across. The bulk of the feldspar, as shown by microscopic study, belongs to the potash varieties orthoclase and microcline, but some small masses, not many of them more than a few inches across, are of the white soda feldspar, albite.

On the wall at the extreme southern end of the quarry certain portions of the pegmatite up to a foot or so in width are a micrographic granite and exhibit the peculiar structure described on page 123.

Muscovite is concentrated along certain belts traversing the pegmatite mass in various directions. Their general form is similar to that shown in Plate IX, *A*. The central portions for a width of a few inches consist of an aggregate of heterogeneously disposed muscovite plates, few of them over one-fourth inch in diameter. From this finer-grained portion spearhead-shaped books of muscovite, some of them a foot in length, showing wedge structure, project in a direction nearly at right angles to the general plane of the mica belt. In the southern part of the quarry muscovite occurs also in nearly equidimensional aggregates, in some places 5 feet across, made up of small, heterogeneously arranged plates averaging about one-fourth inch across. From their borders these muscovite aggregates send off spearhead-shaped books of muscovite into the surrounding quartz, feldspar, and graphic granite. Some graphic intergrowths of quartz and muscovite occur, but they are not abundant. Under present conditions it would probably not pay to save as scrap mica the muscovite obtained in the feldspar mining. No plate mica was observed.

Biotite is moderately abundant in certain parts of the pegmatite. It penetrates the feldspar and quartz in lath-shaped masses, the largest of which was 2 yards long by 3 inches wide and one-fourth inch thick.

'As in most other feldspar quarries, small garnets are abundant only in certain portions of the deposit, the coarser graphic granite and the pure feldspar being almost entirely free from them, and they are not seriously injurious to the commercial value of the deposit.

Cavities up to 1 foot in diameter and of various form are rather a constant feature of the coarser portions of the pegmatite in the northern part of the quarry. They may occur within the areas of pure quartz or feldspar, on the border between quartz and feldspar masses, or more rarely in the coarse graphic granite. Usually they contain groups of somewhat smoky semitransparent quartz crystals, some of which make handsome cabinet specimens. In a few, transparent green tourmalines and aquamarines (beryl) of gem quality have been found.

The schists and gneisses which border the pegmatite are exposed at the southern end of the quarry, where they show evidence of much softening as a result of the pegmatite intrusion. In general they are rather flat lying. Probably the pegmatite mass is also in general somewhat flat lying, though very irregular. It is probable that the workable pegmatite does not extend southward much beyond the limits of the present pit, but northward it is known to extend into property said to be controlled by the Maine Feldspar Company. Here it has been worked in the past from a number of small openings and very considerable amounts of commercial spar are still available.

The methods of operation at this quarry are somewhat antiquated for a working of this size, the drilling all being done by hand and the blasting by black powder. A tramway carries the waste to dump piles and the good rock to stock sheds, from which it is loaded into wagons and hauled 1¾ miles to the mill near Cathance station (p. 18).

North Topsham feldspar quarry.—A feldspar quarry in the northern part of the town of Topsham, one-half mile west of Cathance River and 1 mile south of the Topsham-Bowdoinham line, was formerly operated by the Trenton Flint and Spar Company, the rock being hauled by team 2 miles to the mill near Cathance station. The quarry is located on the western valley slope of the river and is an irregular opening extending north and south along the hill slope for about 200 feet and extending into the hill for about 40 feet. There is a complete absence of any regularity in the arrangements of the pegmatite constituents.

The quartz is prevailingly white or light gray, though smoky in some places.

The feldspar is white to cream colored, and is shown by microscopic examination to be mainly orthoclase, with small amounts of albite and microcline. The albite in many places forms a fine microscopic intergrowth (microperthite) with the orthoclase. Some pure feldspar masses measure 4 to 5 feet in diameter, but the bulk of the material quarried for pottery purposes was a graphic intergrowth of quartz and feldspar.

Muscovite, mostly pale green in color, is generally graphically intergrown with quartz, though a few books of clean mica up to 5 or 6 inches in diameter occur. These are all, so far as observed, of the wedge variety, and the quantity is so small that it would be hardly worth while to save them for scrap mica.

Biotite is not very abundant in any part of the quarry and in some parts is wholly absent. Where it occurs it forms thin lath-shaped crystals averaging about 6 inches long, 1 inch wide, and one-fourth inch thick.

Garnet is absent from much of the pegmatite but locally is abundant in the finer-grained portions in crystals from one-sixteenth to one-fourth inch in diameter. Very rarely a crystal measuring 3 inches is found, and in these the garnet is usually graphically intergrown with quartz. The color ranges from pink to deep red, with submetallic luster.

The area and form of this pegmatite body could not be determined because of the scarcity of outcrops in the vicinity of the quarry, but the occurrence at short distances east and west of small masses of pegmatite of commercial grade seems to indicate that the deposit may extend considerably beyond the area now exposed.

The quantity of material in sight and the freedom of most of the material from iron-bearing minerals favors further development.

Mill of the Trenton Flint and Spar Company.—The feldspar mill of the Trenton Flint and Spar Company is located on Cathance River about one-half mile north of Cathance station. During high water it utilizes the water power of this small river, but it is also provided with steam power. Its equipment consists of three chaser mills and four ball mills of the usual types. The grinding process is that described on page 127. The capacity of the mill is about 16 tons in twenty-four hours, the ground spar being hauled by wagons for one-half mile from the mill to Cathance station, on the Maine Central Railroad, where it is loaded for shipment.

Vicinity of Topsham village.—At a small road-metal quarry on the west slope of Mount Ararat the dominant rock type is a hornblende granite schist of regular and well-marked foliation. It strikes, in the main, about N. 35° E. and dips 50°. SE. In both megascopic and microscopic appearance it is practically identical with the lighter phases of the schist from the road-metal quarry in Brunswick village (p. 61). As at that quarry, dominant acidic bands of schist, prevailingly pink or gray in tone, alternate with smaller amounts of dark-gray bands of quartz diorite and other nearly black bands of diorite schist. Under the microscope these schists show no cataclastic structures; they owe their foliated structure to parallel elongation of the hornblende grains and to some extent also of the grains of biotite and quartz. Nothing either in their texture or their composition indicates that they are not primary-flow gneisses.

Both in the lighter and darker phases of the schist, but much more abundantly in the lighter, are coarser bands of pegmatitic texture, consisting mainly of quartz and feldspar, with some biotite and magnetite. Many of these are parallel to the foliation of the schist and are of even width and uniform character for several yards. Others, especially the larger masses, cut distinctly across the schist folia, the contact being sharp and without suggestion of absorption.

An interesting feature of some of the pegmatite bands which parallel the foliation of the schists is the presence in them of a slight foliation parallel to that of the inclosing schist. As in the schist, this foliation is defined by bands richer than the bordering portions in hornblende and biotite. In one place a faint foliation is perceptible in the center of a pegmatite mass 1½ feet wide that cuts across the foliation of the schists. It does not parallel the trend of the dike but does parallel the foliation of the inclosing schist and is defined by the arrangement of the quartz in elongate and somewhat irregular bands. As there is no evidence of appreciable absorption of the schist by the pegmatite magma, and also no evidence of metamorphism subsequent to the intrusion of the pegmatite, such foliation in the pegmatite is strongly suggestive of parallel flowing movements in the schist and in some of the pegmatite. The field and microscopic evidence on the whole favors the conception that the schists are of primary or flow-igneous origin, and that some of the pegmatite was crystallizing before flowage had entirely ceased in the bordering schist, but that other portions of the pegmatite were intruded after the schist had completely solidified. The practical identity in mineral character between the different masses of pegmatite at this quarry suggests that the distinctly intrusive portions were only slightly later crystallizations than their host and that all the pegmatite had the same magmatic source.

One of the largest masses of graphic granite observed was on the west slope of the 180-foot hill in the sharp bend of Androscoggin River just west of Brunswick. The ledge, which is in plain sight from the railroad track, is 150 feet long and averages 25 feet wide.

Practically this whole mass is a graphic intergrowth of quartz, with white to pale pink orthoclase and microcline. Some of the feldspar crystals of this intergrowth are shown by reflections from their cleavage faces to be 2½ feet across. The coarseness varies rapidly from point to point even within the range of a single feldspar individual. At the south end of the outcrop the graphic granite grades into pegmatite of irregular texture, showing some masses of pure feldspar 2 to 3 inches across. Both the graphic granite and this irregular-textured pegmatite inclose scattered biotite laths.

At the south end of this exposure also there is some associated gray gneiss. In one place the pegmatite cuts directly across the folia of the gneiss. In other places graphic granite forms knots or short lenses up to 6 inches in width between the gneiss folia. The mass of graphic granite exposed in this ledge is the largest continuous mass observed by the writer in the State.

ECONOMICALLY IMPORTANT PEGMATITE MINERALS.

FELDSPAR.

The feldspars are compounds of alumina and silica with one or more of the bases potash, soda, and lime; rarely barium is present. They fall into two principal groups, the potash-soda feldspars and the lime-soda feldspars, both of which may be present in the same deposit or even intergrown in the same crystal.

POTASH-SODA FELDSPARS.

The principal representatives of the potash-soda feldspar group are orthoclase and microcline, both of which have the composition $KAlSi_3O_8$ or $K_2O.Al_2O_3.6SiO_2$. These two varieties have also the same crystal form and are similar in most of their physical properties. For commercial purposes they may be regarded as identical, for they can not be distinguished from each other with the unaided eye and are often associated in the same crystal. The theoretical percentage composition of pure orthoclase or microcline is silica (SiO_2), 64.7 per cent; alumina (Al_2O_3), 18.4 per cent; and potash (K_2O), 16.9 per cent. Soda may partly or completely replace potash in these feldspars. If it is more abundant than the potash, the feldspar is called anorthoclase.

The feldspar of the potash-soda group mined in the United States is mostly pale flesh colored to nearly white, though that from Bedford, N. Y., is reddish and that from near Batchellerville, N. Y., is pearl gray. The potash spars from Norway and from Bedford, Ontario, are reddish in color. The cause of the reddish color is not definitely known, but in some feldspars it seems to be due to the presence of small quantities of finely divided iron oxide. The percentage of iron oxide is smaller, however, in many pink feldspars than in those of lighter color. All the pink spars burn perfectly white, and the iron content is too small to be in the least detrimental in pottery manufacture. Fresh feldspar is so hard that only with difficulty can it be scratched with a knife blade.

As found in the quarries, the potash-soda feldspars seldom show true crystal faces, but when undecomposed break readily into angular pieces, bounded in part by smooth cleavage faces. There are three directions of cleavage, intersecting at definite angles, which are practically identical in orthoclase and microcline and are only slightly different in the soda-bearing feldspars of this group. Only two of the cleavages are well defined, and these invariably intersect approximately at right angles. Both of these principal cleavage surfaces show a high luster, comparable to that exhibited by a plate of glass, though one cleavage face is a trifle less brilliant than the other. The hardness and the two lustrous cleavage planes intersecting at right angles are usually sufficient to identify a mineral as belonging to the group of potash-soda feldspars.

Recent experiments have shown that the potash-rich feldspars have no definite melting point, as metals have, for example. Fusion tests made on finely powdered microcline in the geophysical laboratory of the Carnegie Institution [a] showed that at 1,000° C. traces of sintering were evident; at 1,075° the powder had formed a solid cake; at 1,150° this cake had softened somewhat; and at 1,300° it had become a viscous liquid which could be drawn out into glassy threads. In most of the determinations complete fusion has taken place in the dry state at temperatures below Seger cone No. 9, which fuses at 1,310° C., or 2,390° F.

The great bulk of the feldspar quarried in the eastern United States and in Canada belongs to the class described above, being orthoclase or microcline or an intergrowth of the two. In most quarries this is associated with minor quantities of soda feldspar—albite or oligoclase—occurring either in separate crystals or delicately intergrown with the potash feldspar, as shown in Plate XVII. The presence of the soda spar renders the ground product slightly more fusible. The specific gravity of orthoclase and microcline varies from 2.54 to 2.56.

LIME-SODA FELDSPARS OR PLAGIOCLASES.

The lime-soda group of feldspars, the plagioclases, as they are called, form a continuous series ranging from pure soda feldspar, albite, at one end to pure lime feldspar, anorthite, at the other end. The chemical composition of albite is represented by the formula $NaAlSi_3O_8$ (designated Ab) or $Na_2O.Al_2O_3.6SiO_2$, being similar to that

[a] Day, A. L., and Allen, E. T., The isomorphism and thermal properties of the feldspars: Pub. 31 Carnegie Inst. of Washington, 1905, pp. 13–75; also Am. Jour. Sci., 4th ser., vol. 19, 1905, pp. 93–142.

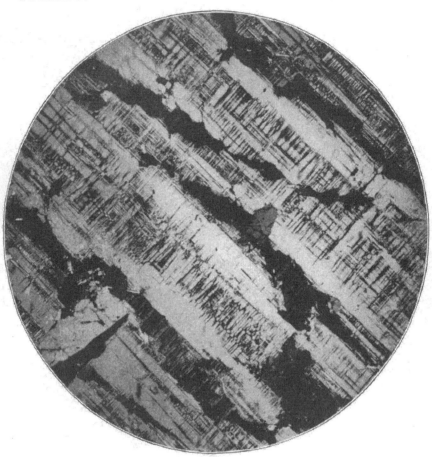

MICROPHOTOGRAPH OF THIN SECTION OF FELDSPAR FROM QUARRY OF GOLDING'S SONS
COMPANY, GEORGETOWN, MAINE. MAGNIFIED ABOUT 40 DIAMETERS.

Showing perthitic intergrowth of potash and soda feldspar characteristic of many commercial feldspars.
The lighter portions with striæ crossing at right angles are potash feldspar (microcline). The darker
portions with striations in only one direction are soda feldspar (albite).

of orthoclase, except that soda is present in place of potash. The composition of anorthite is represented by the formula $CaAl_2Si_2O_8$ (designated An) or $CaO.Al_2O_3.2SiO_2$. The intermediate members of this feldspar series are mixtures in varying proportions of the two molecules Ab and An and have been divided arbitrarily, as shown in the following table:

Lime-soda series of feldspars.

Albite.............	Ab_1An_0 to Ab_6An_1	Labradorite........	Ab_1An_1 to Ab_1An_3
Oligoclase.........	Ab_6An_1 to Ab_3An_1	Bytownite..........	Ab_1An_3 to Ab_1An_6
Andesine...........	Ab_3An_1 to Ab_1An_1	Anorthite..........	Ab_1An_6 to Ab_0An_1

The following table shows the percentages of the various oxides corresponding to each feldspar variety:

Percentage weights of the oxides in the feldspars in the lime-soda series.

	SiO_2.	Al_2O_3.	Na_2O.	CaO.
Albite, Ab_1 An_0............................	68.7	19.5	11.8	0.0
Ab_6 An_1..................................	64.9	22.1	10.0	3.0
Ab_3 An_1..................................	62.0	24.0	8.7	5.3
Ab_1 An_1..................................	55.6	28.3	5.7	10.4
Ab_1 An_3..................................	49.3	32.6	2.8	15.3
Ab_1 An_6..................................	46.6	34.4	1.6	17.4
Anorthite, Ab_0 An_1.......................	43.2	36.7	.0	20.1

The field and microscopic studies made by the writer and the few analyses available indicate that most of the plagioclase present in feldspar deposits worked for pottery purposes belongs to the sodic varieties, albite or oligoclase, though the more calcic varieties are probably also present in minor amounts in a few localities. In color the albite and oligoclase range from pure white to pale green. In their commonest forms they show, as do the feldspars of the potash-soda group, two principal cleavage faces with brilliant luster, but these intersect not at 90°, as in orthoclase and microcline, but at about 86°. This difference in angle is not readily recognizable without careful measurements, and in the field albite and other lime-soda feldspars are most readily distinguished from the potash-soda feldspars by the presence in them of faint, perfectly straight striations on the most brilliant of the cleavage faces. These are the result of repeated twinning of the crystal and are best seen by holding the crystal in the sunlight so as to catch the reflection from the principal cleavage face. By turning the crystal slightly one way or another the striations, if present, are readily recognized.

Pure soda feldspar, or albite ($NaAlSi_3O_8$, designated Ab), like potash feldspar, has no definite melting point but, as shown by Day and Allen,[a] melts at temperatures having a range of 150° C. or more, certain portions of a crystal persisting solid while other portions are

---

[a] Day, A. L., and Allen, E. T., loc. cit.

fluid. Melting in a piece of natural albite was observed to begin below 1,200° C. and was not complete at 1,250°. Complete fusion takes place in albite at a somewhat lower temperature than in orthoclase and microcline. Hence in the manufacture of pottery a glaze prepared with albite will become fluid and will run at a kiln temperature at which a potash-feldspar glaze remains more viscous and yields good results.

The feldspars of this class that contain notable amounts of calcium have fairly well defined melting points. These melting points, as determined by Day and Allen,[a] are given below, with the determinations of their specific gravity:

Melting temperature and specific gravity of lime-soda feldspars.

	Melting temperature (°C.).	Specific gravity of crystalline form.
Albite, $Ab_1 An_0$		2.605
$Ab_3 An_1$	1,340	2.649
$Ab_2 An_1$	1,367	2.660
$Ab_1 An_1$	1,419	2.679
$Ab_1 An_2$	1,463	2.710
$Ab_1 An_3$	1,500	2.733
Anorthite, $Ab_0 An_1$	1,532	2.765

As shown in this table the melting points become progressively higher and the minerals become heavier with increase in the percentage of calcium.

If a melt composed solely of the constituents of pure potash feldspar or pure soda feldspar is allowed to cool the result is invariably a glass; a crystalline product has not yet been obtained in this way. If, however, melts of the lime-rich feldspars are cooled, partial or complete crystallization usually takes place. It is this property of cooling to a glass that renders the potash and soda rich feldspars serviceable for use in making glazes for pottery and enamelware. The crystallization that takes place in the lime-rich feldspars under similar conditions makes them worthless, or at least much less desirable, for these uses.

The following analyses show the chemical characters of typical feldspars that are used commercially. Most of the specimens of crude material analyzed were especially selected for their purity and are not typical of the material in commercial use. Nos. 5 and 6, however, are analyses of specimens of ground "spar" collected by the writer personally from the bins at feldspar mills and represent materials in actual commercial use.

a Day, A. L., and Allen, E. T., loc. cit.

Analyses of feldspars.

	Selected specimens of crude feldspar.				Commercial specimens of ground feldspar.	
	1.	2.	3.	4.	5.	6.
Silica (SiO₂)	64.7	64.98	66.23	65.95	76.37	65.87
Alumina (Al₂O₃)	18.4	19.18	18.77	18.00	a 13.87	a 19.10
Ferric oxide (Fe₂O₃)		.33	Trace.	.12		
Lime (CaO)		Trace.	.31	1.05	.26	.20
Magnesia (MgO)		.25	None.	Trace.	None.	None.
Potash (K₂O)	16.9	12.79	12.09	12.13	5.24	12.24
Soda (Na₂O)		2.32	3.11	2.11	3.74	2.56
Water (H₂O)					.30	.64
Loss on ignition		.48				
	100.0	100.33	100.51	99.36	99.78	100.61

. *a* Includes trace of iron and any TiO₂ and P₂O₅ that may be present.

1. Theoretical composition of pure orthoclase or microcline.
2. Specimen of crude Norwegian potash feldspar, probably with some intergrown soda feldspar (albite). Used at the Royal Porcelain Works at Charlottenburg, Sweden.
3. Crude pink orthoclase-microcline feldspar, evidently intergrown with some soda feldspar (albite). From feldspar quarry of Richardson & Sons, Bedford, Ontario. Analysis by J. B. Cochrane, Royal Military College, Kingston, Ontario.
4. Crude pink potash feldspar; microcline intergrown with small amounts of soda feldspar (albite). From feldspar quarry of P. H. Kinkles's Sons, Bedford, Westchester County, N. Y. Analyses made for John C. Wiarda & Co.
5. Ground commercial feldspar from Kinkles's quarry, Bedford, N. Y.; so-called No. 3 grade; used in glass manufacture but not for pottery. Sample taken by writer from bins at mill of P. H. Kinkles's Sons. Analysis by George Steiger, in laboratory of United States Geological Survey.
6. Ground commercial feldspar from quarry of J. B. Richardson & Sons, Bedford, Ontario, No. 1 grade. Sample taken by writer from bins at mill of Eureka Flint and Spar Company, Trenton, N. J. Analysis by George Steiger, in laboratory of United States Geological Survey.

The approximate mineral composition of the samples of the commercial ground feldspars (Nos. 5 and 6), as computed from the analyses, is as follows:

Approximate mineral composition of feldspars Nos. 5 and 6, above.

	5.	6.
Quartz (SiO₂)	34.37	3.84
Potash feldspar (microcline or orthoclase) (KAlSi₃O₈)	30.58	72.28
Soda feldspar (albite), containing some lime (NaAlSi₃O₈ and CaAl₂Si₂O₄)	32.83	22.59
Moisture (H₂O)	.30	.64
Other constituents	1.63	1.22
	99.72	100.57

Samples Nos. 5 and 6 may be taken to represent, so far as the percentage of quartz is concerned, the two extremes among potash "spars" in commercial use. No. 5 is much richer in quartz and in soda feldspar than the higher grades from this same quarry and is suitable only for use in glass making, for enamel ware, and for like uses. No. 6 is the best grade of Canadian spar, which is almost free from quartz and brings as high a price as any spar on the market. The bulk of the No. 2 grade or standard spar that is on the market is intermediate in its percentage of quartz between samples 5 and 6, the percentage in most of it being between 15 and 25 per cent.

GRAPHIC GRANITE.

Much of the quartz and feldspar of certain pegmatite deposits is regularly intergrown in the form of graphic granite. (See Pl. XVIII and p. 22.) At the majority of feldspar quarries most of the material shipped is graphic granite, though whatever pure feldspar occurs is usually also included and serves to raise the percentage of feldspar in the whole mass. Analyses of four specimens of graphic granite are given below. These analyses were made by George Steiger in the laboratory of the United States Geological Survey.

Analyses of graphic granite.

	1.	2.	3.	4.
SiO_2	73.89	73.92	72.76	71.00
Al_2O_3	13.75	14.26	a 15.47	a 16.31
Fe_2O_3	} .26	.30	....	....
FeO				
MgO	None.	None.	None.	None.
CaO	None.	None.	.19	.22
Na_2O	2.10	2.06	2.35	3.44
K_2O	9.00	8.99	9.28	8.66
H_2O	.24	.11	.15	.12
	99.24	99.64	100.20	99.75

a Includes trace of iron and any TiO_2 and P_2O_5 that may be present.

1. Coarse graphic granite from Fisher's feldspar quarry (abandoned), Topsham, Me. Trace of P_2O_5. The quartz layers in this specimen average about 0.1 inch and the feldspar layers 0.4 inch across. The feldspar is cream-colored potash feldspar (microcline), finely (perthitically) intergrown with smaller amounts of soda feldspar (albite).

2. Moderately coarse graphic granite from Fisher's feldspar quarry (abandoned), Topsham, Me. Grades into No. 1. Trace of P_2O_5. The quartz layers in this specimen average about 0.05 inch across and the feldspar layers about 0.15 inch across. The feldspars are of the same character as in No. 1.

3. Fine-grained graphic granite from Kinkles' feldspar quarry, Bedford, Westchester County, N. Y. The quartz layers in this specimen average about 0.03 inch across and the feldspar layers about 0.08 inch across. The feldspars are pale pink microcline finely intergrown with smaller amounts of soda feldspar (albite), containing a little lime.

4. Graphic granite from Andrews quarry, Portland, Conn., varying in coarseness, but all extremely fine grained. The quartz layers in this specimen average not more than 0.02 of an inch across and the feldspar layers not more than 0.05 inch across. Some small areas of pure feldspar were associated with the graphic granite in this specimen, so that the silica percentage shown in the analysis is lower than it would be for graphic granite alone of this fineness. The feldspars are white potash feldspar (microcline), intergrown with smaller amounts of soda feldspar (albite), containing a little lime.

If allowance is made for the water present and the proportion of quartz to feldspars calculated from the above analyses, the results are as follows:

Proportions of quartz and feldspar in graphic granites Nos. 1 to 4 above.

	1.	2.	3.	4.
Quartz (SiO_2)	27.13	26.26	22.94	17.65
Potash feldspar (microcline) ($KAlSi_3O_8$)	54.42	55.22	54.95	51.37
Soda feldspar (albite) with small amounts of lime feldspar in Nos. 3 and 4 ($NaAlSi_3O_8, CaAl_2Si_2O_8$)	18.45	18.52	20.99	30.05
Other constituents	Trace.	Trace.	1.12	.92
	100.00	100.00	100.00	99.99

NOTE.—Nos. 1 and 2, representing graphic granite from Fisher's quarry in Topsham, Me., show practically identical proportions between the quartz and the feldspar, although No. 2 is more than twice as coarse as No. 1. In No. 3, from Bedford, N. Y., soda-lime feldspar is more abundant than in Nos. 1 and 2, and the proportion of quartz is slightly less. In No. 4 some pure feldspar is associated with the graphic intergrowth of feldspar and quartz, so that the proportion of quartz in the whole specimen is lower than in any of the other samples.

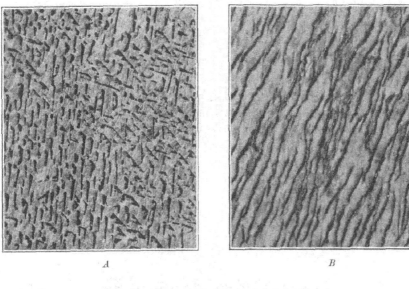

A
B

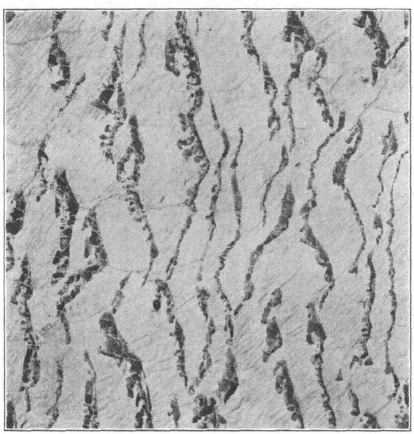

C

INTERGROWTHS OF FELDSPAR AND QUARTZ. SHOWING CHARACTERISTIC GRAPHIC
GRANITE STRUCTURE. NATURAL SIZE.

A, Graphic granite from Bedford, N. Y. *B*, Fine graphic granite from Topsham, Maine. *C*, Coarse
graphic granite from Topsham, Maine.

A graphic intergrowth of potash feldspar and quartz from Elfkarleö, Sweden, which was so fine grained that the graphic structure could be seen only under the microscope, showed on analysis about 79.2 per cent of feldspar and 20.8 per cent of quartz. From the analyses given above and from numerous others which have been published the conclusion seems justified that the proportion of feldspar to quartz in graphic granites, though varying somewhat according to the composition of the feldspars, is nevertheless fairly constant and is not dependent on coarseness of grain. This fact is of practical importance, for a large proportion of the commercial "spar" produced is graphic granite, and it has been the practice at some quarries to discard the finer-grained varieties on the supposition that they contained a larger percentage of quartz than the coarser kinds. Such mining practice is unwarranted, the fine graphic granite being as desirable as the coarse, though both should be mixed with a certain amount of pure feldspar in order to reduce the percentage of quartz in the ground product to between 15 and 20 per cent for the standard grade, as shown by analyses 3 and 4 of the table above.

As in most pegmatite bodies there is very little regularity in the distribution of the different minerals (see p. 22), a deposit that is of excellent quality commercially as regards feldspar may grade within a short distance and in a wholly irregular manner into pegmatite that is worthless because of its large percentage of quartz or its abundance of biotite, black tourmaline, or garnet.

MINING.

The methods of mining feldspar are very simple. The excavations are nearly all open pits, most of them of rather irregular form, the valueless portions of the pegmatite being avoided wherever it is possible in mining. In a few Pennsylvania quarries where the pegmatite masses are rather flat lying and are overlain by a roof of worthless rock short tunnels have been driven from the open pits.

In Maine, Connecticut, and New York the pegmatite is usually firm and undecomposed, even in the surface outcrops, and it is necessary to sink drill holes and blast out most of the material. In Pennsylvania and Maryland, however, most of the pegmatite is much decayed at the surface and can be excavated with picks, shovels, and crowbars. In a few of these quarries kaolin produced by the decay of the feldspar has been found in the past in sufficient quantities to be of commercial importance, though none is now produced. This difference in the character of the pegmatite deposits in the two regions is due to the fact that the Pennsylvania-Maryland region is unglaciated, whereas in the more northerly region glacial ice has planed off most of the products of rock decay.

In some of the smaller quarries, where the rock is firm, drilling is done by hand, but in most of the larger quarries steam drills are used. The large masses are then broken with sledges into pieces 6 inches or less in size. If the material is to be used as poultry grit or for the manufacture of roofing materials no sorting is necessary, but material used for making pottery is hand-picked at the quarry to remove the more micaceous and quartzose parts and the portions carrying iron-bearing minerals. In most of the Pennsylvania and Maryland quarries where the weathered materials near the surface can be excavated with pick and shovel, screening or even washing may be necessary to free the spar from dirt. In some of the larger and deeper quarries derricks and drags are used in hoisting the spar to the surface, the material being then loaded into wagons and hauled either to the railroad for shipment or to the mills for grinding. In some quarries the wagons descend into the pit along an inclined roadway. At two important quarries wire tramways connect quarry with mill.

The cost of actual mining at most of the quarries producing feldspar of pottery grade is reported at from $2 to $2.50 per long ton. At certain quarries where pegmatite is quarried for ready roofing, poultry grit, etc., where cobbling and hand sorting are unnecessary, and where the work is conducted on a large scale, the cost may be as low as 50 cents per ton. Hauling by team from mine to mill or shipping point in most of the feldspar districts may, under ordinary conditions, be estimated at a contract price of 35 to 40 cents per long ton per mile.

COMMERCIAL AVAILABILITY OF DEPOSITS.

Whether it will pay to work a given feldspar deposit depends upon a number of factors, chief among which are (1) the distance from the railroad or navigable water, (2) the freight rates to principal markets, (3) the quantity and quality of the material available, (4) the cheapness with which the feldspar can be mined, and (5) the market conditions. Favorable conditions with respect to some of these factors may offset unfavorable conditions with respect to others. The principal markets for the better grades of feldspar are the great pottery centers—Trenton, N. J., and East Liverpool, Ohio—so that the mines of Connecticut, Pennsylvania, and Maryland have the advantage over those in Maine and northern New York of being much closer to these markets. This superiority in position makes wagon hauls of 6 or 8 miles from mine to shipping point permissible in the Middle Atlantic States, whereas in Maine or in the Adirondack region only a much shorter haul allows a fair degree of profit. Pegmatite sold for roofing or poultry grit commands prices so small that hauls of more than 1 or 2 miles from mine to shipping point would in most places be prohibitive. The freight rates on feldspar from a number of the quarrying districts to Trenton, the principal feldspar milling center, are given below:

Freight rates per hundredweight on feldspar for carloads having a minimum weight of 40,000 pounds, May, 1909.

Bath, Me., to Trenton, N. J................................... $0. 15
Cathance, Me., to Trenton, N. J............................... .17
Auburn, Me., to Trenton, N. J................................. .16

The requirements of the potter's trade demand that in general the percentage of free quartz associated with the feldspar used shall not exceed 20 per cent in the ground product, and certain potters demand a spar which is nearly pure, containing probably less than 5 per cent of free quartz. In order to be profitably worked, in most feldspar mines between one-fourth and one-half of the total material excavated should contain less than 20 per cent of free quartz. Freshness of the feldspar is not essential.

A factor of the utmost importance in the mining of pottery spar is the quantity of iron-bearing minerals (black mica, hornblende, garnet, or black tourmaline) which is present and the manner in which these minerals are associated with the feldspar. The requirements of the pottery trade demand that the spar be nearly free from these minerals, which if present produce, upon firing, brown discolorations in white wares. In order that a deposit may be profitably worked, these minerals, if present in any appreciable quantity, must be so segregated in certain portions of the deposit that they can be separated from the spar without much more hand sorting and cobbing than is necessary in the separation of the highly feldspathic material from that which is highly quartzose or rich in muscovite. A number of pegmatite deposits of coarse grain are rendered worthless for pottery purposes by the abundance of one or more of these iron-bearing minerals. The presence here and there of minute flakes of white mica (muscovite) is characteristic even of the highest grades of commercial feldspar, and chemically this mineral is not injurious. It is, however, exceedingly difficult to pulverize the thin, flexible mica plates to a fineness equal to that attained by the feldspar, and it is therefore necessary in mining to separate carefully as much of the muscovite as possible from the spar.

Operation on a large scale with the aid of modern machinery reduces the mining cost. Favorable topographic position—a situation, for instance, that will permit the material to be excavated from a hillside opening instead of being hoisted from a pit—also reduces the cost.

MILLING.

The methods used for grinding feldspar for pottery, enamel ware, etc., are similar in a general way in all of the Eastern States and are very simple. The soda spar quarried in southeastern Pennsylvania is first burned in kilns, which serves to fracture it and thus to facilitate grinding. Most feldspar, however, is fed just as it comes from the quarry into a chaser mill consisting of two buhrstone wheels, 3 to 5 feet in diameter and 1 to 1½ feet thick, attached to each other by a horizontal axle, as are the wheels of a cart. The horizontal axle is attached at its center to a rotating vertical shaft, which causes the buhrstone wheels to travel over a buhrstone bed, the feldspar being crushed between the wheels and the bed. In a few mills the spar before going to the chaser mills is crushed in a jaw crusher.

The material as it comes from the chasers is screened, the tailings being returned to the chaser mills for recrushing, while the fines go to tube mills for final grinding. The tube mills consist of steel cylinders revolving on a horizontal axis. The cylinders are generally lined either with hard-wood blocks or with blocks made of natural or artificial siliceous brick and are charged with Norway or French flint pebbles 2 to 3 inches across. The type of tube mill used by most feldspar grinders is 6 to 7 feet long and grinds from 2 to 3 tons of spar at one charging. Certain millers, however, claim to effect a considerable saving in power by the use of larger mills, which grind from 4 to 6 tons at one charge.

Feldspar for pottery purposes is usually ground four to six hours, and in that time most of it is reduced to a fineness of less than 200 mesh. Screen tests made by the writer on four samples of commercial ground pottery spar collected personally from the bins at three feldspar mills showed that from 99.3 to 99.8 per cent of the material would pass through a 100-mesh screen and from 96.7 to 98.2 per cent would pass through a 200-mesh screen. A sample of No. 3 spar, used only in making glass and enamel ware, was notably coarser, 94 per cent passing through a 100-mesh screen, and 74 per cent through a 200-mesh screen. This grade is ground only for two to three hours. Some feldspar prepared for use in abrasive soaps is ground for ten hours.

After grinding, the spar is ready for shipment either in bulk or in bags. The red spars from Bedford, N. Y., and Bedford, Ontario, have a faint pinkish tint when ground, but the cream-colored and white spars grind to a pure white. In a few mills the ground spar is allowed to settle slowly in water, so as to separate the finer from the coarser material, but this method is now rarely used.

In mills for grinding feldspar for poultry grit and roofing purposes the spar is first crushed in jaw or rotary crushers and then between steel rolls. It is then screened over vibrating screens, usually of the Newago or Jeffrey type, to the various sizes desired.

USES.

The principal consumers of feldspar are the pottery, enamel-ware, enamel-brick, and electrical-ware manufacturers, its most important use being as a constituent part of both body and glaze in true porcelain, white ware, and vitrified sanitary ware, and as a constituent of the slip (underglaze) and glaze in so-called "porcelain" sanitary wares and enameled brick. The proportion of feldspar in the body of vitrified wares usually falls between 10 and 35 per cent. Its melting point being lower than that of the other constituents, it serves as a flux to bind the particles of clay and quartz together. In glazes the percentage of feldspar usually lies between 30 and 50. The trade demands that feldspar for pottery purposes be nearly free from iron-bearing minerals (biotite, garnet, hornblende, tourmaline, etc.), and that it contain little if any muscovite. The requirements in regard to the percentage of free quartz vary with different potters. A few manufacturers of the finer grades of pottery demand less than 5 per cent of free quartz and may even grind the spar themselves so as to be sure of its quality, preferring to insure a constant product even at higher cost by themselves mixing the requisite quantity of quartz with the spar. Most potters get satisfactory results with standard ground spar carrying 15 to 20 per cent of free quartz, and in some acceptable spars the percentage runs even higher. In the finely ground mixture as it comes from the mills it is difficult to separate the quartz from the feldspar by physical methods on account of the extreme fineness of the material. Chemical analysis seems to be the readiest means of determining whether its percentage is high or low.

Feldspar is also used in the manufacture of emery and carborundum wheels as a flux to bind the abrading particles together.

Small quantities of feldspar are used in the manufacture of opalescent glass. The feldspar used for this purpose is ranked as No. 3 by the miners. This generally contains more free quartz and muscovite than that used for pottery purposes, and most of it contains also fragments of iron-bearing minerals. Most of the spars known to the writer which are used for opalescent glass are rich in soda. They are not ground so fine as the pottery spars (p. 128).

Small quantities of carefully selected pure feldspar are used in the manufacture of artificial teeth. Some is used in the manufacture of scouring soaps and window washes, the fact that feldspar is slightly softer than glass rendering these soaps less liable than soaps which contain quartz to scratch windows or glassware. Two firms in New York State and one in Connecticut crush feldspar for poultry grit and for the manufacture of ready roofing.

Much interest has recently been aroused in the use of potash feld-spar as a fertilizer. Potash is an important plant food, which, in fertilizers, has usually been supplied in the form of wood ashes or imported from Germany in easily soluble potash salts (sulphate, carbonate, or chloride). The Department of Agriculture has recently made preliminary experiments to determine the availability of finely ground potash feldspar as a substitute for the more soluble potash salts. The following statement is quoted from the report on these tests:[a]

The evidence so far obtained appears to indicate that under certain conditions and with certain crops feldspar can be made useful if it is ground sufficiently fine. On the other hand, it is highly probable that under other conditions the addition of ground feldspar to the land would be a useless waste of money. At the present stage of the investigation it would be extremely unwise for anyone to attempt to use ground rock, except on an experimental scale that would not entail great financial loss.

If further experiment shows that ground feldspar has a wide efficiency as a fertilizer, it will undoubtedly lead to the utilization of many of the pegmatite deposits which, because of insufficient coarseness, too large a percentage of quartz, or too great an abundance of iron-bearing minerals, are not valuable as a source of pottery material. Deposits of this kind, favorably situated with respect to the railroads, are numerous, especially in the vicinity of the active feldspar quarries. An equally important result will be the utilization of much material that is now discarded at feldspar quarries.

A number of processes have been patented in this country for the dissociation of potash feldspar to obtain the more readily soluble potash salts, but none of these have yet been successfully applied on a commercial scale. What is, perhaps, the most promising method effects the decomposition through electrolytic methods.[b]

GRADES AND PRICES.

Most dealers recognize three grades of commercial feldspar—No. 1, No. 2 (sometimes called standard), and No. 3. From quarries in granite pegmatite, where most of the spar is of the potash variety, these are usually graded as follows: No. 1 is carefully selected, free from iron-bearing minerals, largely free from muscovite, and contains little or no quartz, usually less than 5 per cent. Analysis 6 of the table, on page 123, shows the character of material of this grade, the feldspar analyzed having been imported from Canada. No. 2 is

---

[a] Cushman, Allerton S., The use of feldspathic rocks as fertilizers: Bull. Bureau Plant Ind. No. 104 U. S. Dept. Agr., 1907, p. 31.

[b] Cushman, A. S., Extracting potash from feldspar: Min. World, June 22, 1907; also United States patent, No. 772612, October 18, 1904.

largely free from iron-bearing minerals and muscovite, but usually contains when ground from 15 to 20 per cent of quartz. No. 3 is not carefully selected and contains a little higher percentages of quartz, muscovite, and iron-bearing minerals. Spar from the soda pegmatites of southeastern Pennsylvania and adjacent parts of Maryland, being wholly free from quartz, is graded entirely on the basis of its freedom from iron-bearing minerals, principally hornblende. No. 1 is carefully selected and is practically free from such impurities. No. 2, though less carefully selected, is still fairly free from them. No. 3 is not carefully selected and carries hornblende in quantities large enough to render it unfit for use in the manufacture of pottery. It is utilized principally in making glass. Crushed pegmatite from New York State, used for poultry grit and for coverings for surfaces to give them the appearance of granite, and feldspar from Minnesota, used mainly for abrasive purposes, are graded according to coarseness.

The prices of feldspar fluctuate with general market conditions and local conditions of competition, but in general are about as follows:

Prices of feldspar f. o. b. mills.

	Crude, per long ton.	Ground, per short ton.
Maine: No. 2 or standard	$2.50-$3.00	....
Northern New York: Crushed pegmatite for ready roofing, poultry grit, etc.	....	$3.00-$3.50
Southern New York:		
No. 1	4.24- 4.50	8.50- 9.00
No. 2, or standard	3.50- 4.00	6.00- 6.50
Connecticut: No. 2, or standard	3.50- 4.00	5.50- 6.50
Pennsylvania: No. 2, or standard (potash feldspar)	3.75- 4.50	7.50- 9.00
Maryland: No. 2, or standard (potash feldspar)	3.50- 4.00	....
Trenton, N. J.:		
No. 1, Canadian	5.50	10.50
No. 2, or standard	5.00- 5.25	9.00- 9.50

Crude No. 1 feldspar usually brings from 50 cents to $1.50 a ton more than No. 2, and crude No. 3 brings about the same amount less. Ground No. 1 brings from $2 to $4 a ton more than No. 2. With finer grinding, such as is demanded by some scouring-soap manufacturers, the prices are proportionally higher. Very pure carefully selected potash feldspar, for use in the manufacture of artificial teeth, usually sells at from $6 to $8 a barrel of 350 pounds.

PRODUCTION.

The tables below show the recent production of feldspar in the United States.

Production of feldspar (exclusive of abrasive feldspar) in 1907 and 1908, by States, in short tons.

State.	Crude.		Ground.		Total.	
	Quantity.	Value.	Quantity.	Value.	Quantity.	Value.
1907.						
Maine.................	45	$110	16,428	$157,224	16,473	$157,334
New York.............	3,909	15,825	11,500	40,500	15,409	56,325
Connecticut...........	10,663	28,433	8,380	51,770	19,043	80,203
Pennsylvania.........	7,367	28,169	12,206	108,678	19,633	136,847
Maryland.............	7,169	23,672	3,895	34,081	11,064	57,753
Other States.........	1,927	5,607	1,000	5,000	2,927	10,607
	31,080	101,816	53,469	397,253	84,549	499,069
1908.						
Maine.................	168	375	13,751	123,034	13,919	123,409
New York.............	504	1,350	14,109	51,798	14,613	53,148
Connecticut...........	7,775	27,753	6,425	38,506	14,200	66,259
Pennsylvania.........	3,616	13,226	10,473	90,276	14,089	103,502
Maryland.............	6,217	21,076	3,517	30,774	9,734	51,850
Virginia and Minnesota............	560	2,000	125	750	685	2,750
	18,840	65,780	48,400	335,138	67,240	400,918

Total production of feldspar in 1907 and 1908, in short tons.

	Crude.		Ground.		Total.	
	Quantity.	Value.	Quantity.	Value.	Quantity.	Value.
Production of feldspar (exclusive of abrasive) in 1908.................	18,840	$65,780	48,400	$335,138	67,240	$400,918
Production of abrasive feldspar in 1908.....................	....	....	3,234	27,635	3,234	27,635
Total production of feldspar in 1908...................	18,840	65,780	51,634	362,773	70,474	428,553
Total production of feldspar in 1907.	31,080	101,816	60,719	457,128	91,799	558,944

The production of feldspar (exclusive of abrasive feldspar) from 1903 to 1908 is given in the following table:

Production of feldspar (exclusive of abrasive feldspar), 1903-1908, in short tons.

Year.	Crude.		Ground.		Total.	
	Quantity.	Value.	Quantity.	Value.	Quantity.	Value.
1903..................	13,432	$51,036	28,459	$205,697	41,891	$256,733
1904..................	19,413	66,714	25,775	199,612	45,188	266,326
1905..................	14,517	57,976	20,902	168,181	35,419	226,157
1906..................	39,976	132,643	32,680	268,888	72,656	401,531
1907..................	31,080	101,816	53,469	397,253	84,549	499,069
1908..................	18,840	65,780	48,400	335,138	67,240	400,918

QUARTZ.

GENERAL STATEMENT.

Quartz, the most abundant of all minerals, occurs in nature in a great variety of forms and is utilized commercially in many different ways. Sand consisting mainly of quartz is used for building, molding, and in glass and pottery manufacture. Tripoli, used for abrasive purposes, and sandstone and quartzite, used for building and other purposes, are also composed largely of quartz. The present discussion, however, deals only with the massive crystalline and gem varieties which occur in the pegmatite deposits.

Chemically pure quartz is an oxide of silicon of the formula SiO_2. It is too hard to be scratched with a knife and will itself scratch glass. It is generally translucent to transparent and ranges from colorless to dark gray, and in the gem varieties from amethyst to pale pink. It is brittle and without well-defined cleavage, fracturing irregularly with lustrous glassy surfaces. Most of the quartz of the pegmatites occurs in large pure masses without crystal outline. Quartz with crystal form is developed principally in the pockets. The form of most of the crystals is that of a six-sided prism terminated by an equal number of faces forming a pyramid. The mineral is difficultly fusible and is unaffected by acids under ordinary conditions.

MASSIVE CRYSTALLINE QUARTZ.

Occurrence.—Massive crystalline quartz is usually white, but some is rose-colored or smoky. It occurs in veins or dikelike masses, unmixed with other minerals, or as a constituent of pegmatite. In the latter form it is usually produced as an accessory in the mining of feldspar. The States producing massive crystalline (vein) quartz in commercial quantity in 1908 were Connecticut, Maryland, New York, Pennsylvania, Wisconsin, Tennessee, Montana, Colorado, and Arizona. Small quantities were formerly marketed from Maine, but these quarries are so far from the principal markets that there is very little profit in handling the material. Quartz of excellent grade occurs in considerable quantities at nearly all of the feldspar quarries of Maine and in a few is saved, though not shipped regularly. It is allowed to accumulate in stock piles until a favorable sale can be made.

The Connecticut localities at which quartz is mined were described in detail in the writer's report on the production of quartz and feldspar in 1907.[a] The quarries of Westchester County, N. Y., have also been previously described by the writer.[b]

Milling.—In the grinding of the massive forms of quartz two general processes are used, the wet and the dry.

[a] Mineral Resources U. S. for 1907, pt. 2, U. S. Geol. Survey, 1908, pp. 846–847.
[b] Bull. U. S. Geol. Survey No. 315, 1907, pp. 294–309.

In the wet process the quartz may be crushed just as it comes from the quarry, or it may first be highly heated in kilns and then fractured by turning upon it a stream of cold water. The first crushing is effected by jaw crushers, or if the quartz has previously been burned it may be crushed in chaser mills. In a few mills the chasers revolve in wet pans and are periodically stopped to allow the crushed quartz to be shoveled out. After crushing, it is ground in "wet pans" provided with a pavement of flat-faced quartz or quartzite blocks over which move several large blocks of similar material, the crushed quartz being pulverized between these blocks and the pavement. The grinding in wet pans usually occupies about twenty-four hours, the load ground in a single pan varying from 1,200 to 1,800 pounds. From the wet pans the pastelike mass of quartz and water is drawn into settling troughs, the first settlings being in some cases returned to the pans for finer grinding. From the settling troughs it is shoveled out upon drying floors heated by steam or hot air, or else it is dried in small pans which are placed tier on tier on heated racks constructed of steam pipes. Finally the dried material is bolted to various degrees of fineness and packed in bags for shipment, or it may be shipped in bulk.

In the dry method of treatment the quartz is usually crushed first in a jaw crusher and then between crushing rolls. Quartz to be used for filters and for abrasive purposes is then screened to various degrees of fineness and is packed in bags for shipment. In the manufacture of the finer grades for use in pottery, wood fillers, scouring soaps, etc., the material after leaving the roll crushers is ground in tube mills, either of the continuous or of the intermittent type. It is then graded to various sizes either by bolting or by a pneumatic process whereby the quartz powder is carried by a strong air current through a series of tubes and receptacles, the distance to which the quartz is carried being dependent upon its fineness. There are no quartz mills in Maine. Those nearest to that State are in Connecticut.

Uses.—Quartz is used for a great variety of purposes, the principal uses being in the manufacture of wood filler, pottery, paints, and scouring soaps. In pottery the quartz serves to diminish shrinkage in the body of the ware; it is used also in many glazes. Quartz for these purposes should contain in general less than one-half of 1 per cent of iron oxide. Finely ground quartz is used in paints in various proportions up to one-third of the total pigment used. Its chemical inertness prevents it from combining with other constituents of the paint and increases the resistance of the paint to the weather. Crystalline quartz is superior to silica sand for this purpose because the ground particles are highly angular and tend to attach themselves more firmly to the painted surfaces, thus giving the paint what is known as a "tooth" and after some wear affording a good surface for repainting. This angularity of the grains also renders the ground crystalline quartz superior to silica sand in the manufacture of wood fillers. In scouring soaps and polishers ground crystalline quartz is preferred to silica sand, not only because of its greater angularity, but because of its superior whiteness.

Massive quartz, crushed and graded to various degrees of fineness, is extensively used in sandpaper, sand belts, scouring agents, sand blasts, etc. The qualities which render it particularly serviceable for these purposes are its hardness (No. 7 in the Mohs scale), which is slightly greater than that of steel, and its conchoidal fracture, the absence of definite cleavage planes causing it to crush to fragments with sharp angular edges and corners. For such abrasive purposes massive quartz is far superior to sand or crushed sandstone, since the grains of the latter are likely to be more or less rounded. Blocks of massive quartz and quartzite are used in the chemical industry as a filler for acid towers and to some extent as a flux in copper smelting. Much ground quartz is used in filters, and some of the most finely pulverized grades are used in tooth powders and in place of pumice as a cleaner by dentists.

Within recent years crystalline quartz and also sand has been used to some extent in the manufacture of silicon and of alloys of silicon with iron (ferrosilicon), copper (silicon copper), and other metals. Ferrosilicon is largely produced in the electric furnace by using coke to reduce the quartz to the metallic state, and some iron ore or scrap iron to alloy with the silicon. The percentage of silicon in these alloys varies from about 10 to 80 per cent, according to the uses of the product. Ferrosilicon has been employed in the manufacture of steel as a deoxidizer and to prevent the formation of blowholes in steel ingots. Silicon is also produced in the electric furnace.[a] It is a brittle crystalline body with a dark silver luster. Its specific gravity is about 2.4 and its melting point 1,430° C. The commercial product contains small percentages of iron, carbon, and aluminum. The great affinity of silicon for oxygen renders it useful for the reduction of metals such as chromium and tungsten in the electric furnace. It can readily be cast into rods, and because of its high electrical resistance, which is about five times that of carbon, it is used in the manufacture of rheostats and electrical heaters. Its resistance to nearly all acids, combined with the fact that it can be cast into molds, makes it possible also to use it in the manufacture of chemical ware. Silicon copper is used as a deoxidizer in making castings of copper and copper alloys.

Quartz may be fused in the electric furnace and molded into tubes, crucibles, dishes, and other articles which can be used for certain

a Tone, F. J., Production of silicon in the electric furnace: Trans. Am. Electro-Chem. Soc., vol. 7, 1905, p. 243.

purposes in the chemical laboratory instead of porcelain and platinum wares. The fused quartz expands only very slightly when heated, its coefficient of expansion being about one-twentieth of that of glass, and in consequence may be plunged suddenly, red hot, into cold water without being cracked. These wares soften only above 1,400° C. (2,552° F.). The principal drawback to their use, especially in quantitative chemical work, is that the somewhat rough surface makes it difficult to wash all the material from the dishes.

Production.—Statistics showing the production of quartz in the United States are given below.

Production of quartz (exclusive of abrasive quartz) in the United States in 1908, by States, in short tons.

State.	Crude.		Ground.		Total.	
	Quantity.	Value.	Quantity.	Value.	Quantity.	Value.
1908.						
Connecticut and New York..........	980	1,750	9,227	56,700	10,207	58,450
Pennsylvania and Maryland........	25	99	4,160	31,670	4,185	31,769
Other States a.........................	22,500	30,594	1,933	17,833	24,433	48,427
	23,505	32,443	15,320	106,203	38,825	138,646

a Includes Arizona, Colorado, Montana, Tennessee, and Wisconsin.

Abrasive quartz was produced in 1908 in Connecticut, Maryland, Massachusetts, New York, Pennsylvania, and Wisconsin. The total, together with the total production of all quartz, is shown in the following table:

Total production of quartz in 1908, in short tons.

	Crude.		Ground.		Total.	
	Quantity.	Value.	Quantity.	Value.	Quantity.	Value.
Quartz (exclusive of abrasive quartz)	23,505	$32,443	15,320	$106,203	38,825	$138,646
Abrasive quartz.....................	2,973	4,876	5,518	46,635	8,491	51,511
	26,478	37,319	20,838	152,838	47,316	190,157

Production of quartz (exclusive of abrasive quartz) in the United States, 1903–1908, in short tons.

Year.	Crude.		Ground.		Total.	
	Quantity.	Value.	Quantity.	Value.	Quantity.	Value.
1903.............................	40,046	$38,736	15,187	$118,211	55,233	$156,947
1904.............................	41,490	28,890	10,780	71,700	52,270	100,590
1905.............................	39,555	33,409	11,590	70,700	51,145	104,109
1906.............................	41,314	37,632	25,383	205,380	66,697	243,012
1907.............................	5,618	4,282	17,359	152,812	22,977	157,094
1908.............................	23,505	32,443	15,320	106,203	38,825	138,646

Prices.—Pure crystalline quartz for use in the manufacture of pottery, abrasive soaps, paints, wood fillers, etc., brings usually from about $2 to $3.50 per long ton, crude, f. o. b. quarries, and the ground material brings from $6.50 to $10 per short ton f. o. b. mills, the price varying with fineness of grinding, distance from markets, etc. The purer varieties of quartzite used for similar purposes and for sand-papers sell, as a rule, at somewhat lower prices, the crude bringing from about $1 to $2 per long ton f. o. b. mines, and the ground from $6 to $8 per short ton f. o. b. mills. The finest grades of crystalline quartz ground to an impalpable powder and used for tooth powders, etc., may bring as high as $20 per ton f. o. b. mills. Imported French flints cost from $3.50 to $4 per long ton f. o. b. Philadelphia, and can be delivered in Trenton, N. J., for less than $5 per long ton.

SMOKY QUARTZ.

Smoky quartz has somewhat the appearance of smoked glass, though varying from a faint tint of gray or yellowish brown to nearly black. The shade commonly varies considerably from point to point in the same crystal.

Transparent crystals have been found in a number of the pegmatite masses of Maine and some are of value as museum specimens and as gems. In 1884 a mass weighing over 6 pounds, with clear spaces several inches across, was found on Blueberry Hill in the town of Stoneham, Oxford County, and a broken crystal that weighed over 100 pounds and another 4 inches long and 2 inches across, very clear in parts, were found near Mount Pleasant in Oxford County. On the southwestern slopes of Mount Apatite in Auburn, Androscoggin County, a large pocket in coarse pegmatite has yielded considerable quantities of fine crystals. Transparent quartz of pale amber-brown color has been observed by the writer at the Berry quarry, a short distance south of Mount Apatite in Poland, one mass showing a clear portion 3 by 5 inches in size.

The nature of the coloring matter is not known, but on heating the smoky varieties generally become first yellow and finally colorless. Some yellow quartz produced in this way is cut as a gem under the name of "Spanish topaz" or "citrine," though the true citrine is a natural occurrence of transparent yellow quartz. Crystals or irregular masses of transparent smoky quartz found in any of the feldspar or gem quarries should be preserved, for they may prove of value and interest to the mineral or gem collector.

ROSE QUARTZ.

Most of the rose quartz found in Maine is somewhat paler in tint than that commonly utilized as a gem stone, though occasionally some of deeper tint is obtained. The principal supplies of this material at present come from South Dakota and Colorado. In Maine it forms irregular masses in the pegmatite and usually grades into white quartz; it has not been found in distinct crystals. It occurs in a number of the smaller pegmatite bodies of Oxford County, notably at Tubbs Ledge in Norway, Frenchs Mountain in Albany, and occasionally at Mount Mica in Paris, but so far as known very little has been marketed. In a few places the pale-rose varieties show a milky opalescence and are very beautiful when well polished.

Rose quartz from the Red Rose mine in South Dakota is reported to have sold in 1908 at from 3 to 25 cents per pound, according to depth of color and number of flaws or seams. Selected material brought from $8 to $12 per pound.

AMETHYST.

Amethystine quartz, or amethyst as it is commonly called, is a transparent purple or violet variety of quartz and is one of the semiprecious stones. It must not be confused with the oriental amethyst, which is a rare purple variety of corundum and is much more precious. Deer Hill in the extreme northwestern part of the town of Stow, Oxford County, has furnished large numbers of amethyst crystals, but nearly all of them are of a pale tint and of little value as gems. They occur in pockets in the coarse pegmatite and also in the soil on the southeast slope of the hill, where the pegmatite is associated in a most irregular manner with fine-grained granite. Recently George Howe, of Norway, Maine, has found some remarkably fine specimens of amethyst on Pleasant Mountain, in the town of Denmark, Oxford County. By transmitted daylight these stones are a deep royal purple, but by lamplight they are a rich wine red.

As in the case of most other Maine gems, the retail prices obtained within the State for Maine amethysts are considerably higher than those prevailing in the New York market. They range up to $10 a carat for well-cut stones of the paler varieties, and from $10 to $18 a carat for those showing the deep colors.

MICA.

Types.—Mica is a group name comprising a number of mineral species, the most important of which, economically, are biotite (brown mica), muscovite (white mica), phlogopite (amber mica), and lepidolite (pink or lilac mica). Though biotite is occasionally ground for commercial purposes, it is so intimately intergrown with other constituents in the Maine pegmatites as to be unavailable even for such treatment. Lepidolite from Mount Mica, usually intergrown with some albite feldspar, has been cut into slabs and polished for paper weights, and has also been used to some extent as a source of lithium

MUSCOVITE FROM TOPSHAM, SHOWING WEDGE STRUCTURE.

A, Front view.   *B*, Side view.   *C*, End view.   Natural size.

salts; its use, however, is sporadic and it commands no steady market price. Phlogopite, which is produced in large quantities in Canada and is used for the same purpose as muscovite, is not found in commercial amounts in the United States. Muscovite is the only mica variety of commercial importance produced in Maine.

Physical and chemical properties.—Muscovite is a hydrous silicate of alumina and potash with a little water and usually a little iron. The hardness of the mineral is between 2 and 3; that is, mica is generally soft enough to be scratched with the finger nail. It is practically infusible at ordinary temperatures. The color is usually a silver gray or light yellow, and the mineral is generally transparent. It is attacked with difficulty by reagents and in nature successfully resists decomposition for long periods. Few minerals are so widely distributed. In small flakes it is a common constituent of a great variety of rocks, but in large crystals, such as can be used commercially, it is generally confined in Maine, as elsewhere, to pegmatite deposits. Its most striking physical characteristic is its highly perfect basal cleavage, which causes it to split into tough, flexible sheets whose thickness may be less than a thousandth of an inch. The crystals as they occur in the pegmatite thus resemble, in a rough way, thick pads of paper or books. The name "books" is, indeed, frequently used in the trade as a convenient descriptive term for the mica crystals. A few of the books show regular hexagonal borders, but as a rule their outlines are irregular.

Muscovite may exhibit certain characteristics not mentioned above, which may seriously affect its commercial value. These may be enumerated as follows:

By far the commonest defect noted in the muscovite of the Maine pegmatites is what is usually termed A structure. This appears to be due to a wedging out of the mica folia in two directions inclined to each other at 60°. It is recognized in a mica book by the presence of two sets of striations at 60° to each other and parallel to the directions of the "ruling." In most of the Maine quarries such A structure is repeated by twinning with the production of what is commonly termed "fish-bone" or "herring-bone" structure (Pl. XIX). Muscovite showing A and fish-bone structure is generally used only as scrap mica. The material obtained at the Black Mountain mine in Rumford was wholly of this type, and material showing these characters is found in nearly all the pegmatite deposits which have been worked commercially either for feldspar, mica, or gems, and even in deposits where good plate mica is also found.

A second defect frequently met is commonly termed "ruling" and consists in the presence of sharp, straight fractures parallel to the sides of the crystal and thus highly inclined to the plates. These are in fact the secondary or less perfect cleavage directions and they commonly divide a mica mass into a number of long narrow ribbon-shaped strips. Many large clear books which otherwise could be cut into large pieces of mica are, because of this ruling, rendered no more valuable than much smaller books which are free from this defect. In some crystals instead of actual cleavage there is a folding or wrinkling of the mica laminæ parallel to the secondary cleavage directions, which suggests that both wrinkling and actual cleavage may be developed in some cases as the result of strains to which the mica books have been subjected. In specimens from the Hibbs mine in Hebron the secondary cleavage has produced a multitude of fractures so close together that their intersection with the principal cleavage planes reduces the mica to a mass of fine fibers.

Plate mica which might otherwise be of good quality is sometimes injured by the presence between the laminæ of thin crystals of magnetite and other minerals usually showing more or less regular radiating or dendritic forms. Some of the crystals of magnetite occurring in this way are so extremely thin that they are transparent. The presence of these magnetite crystals injures the mica for electrical insulating purposes, as they form a path for the current and may lead to a puncturing of the plate and short-circuiting. Some such mica is, nevertheless, used to some extent in the electrical industries.

Perfectly colorless mica bears the highest value, though a slight tinge of color is for most purposes not regarded as a defect.

Occurrence.—In some places, as at the Waterford quarries and Black Mountain mica mine in Rumford, Oxford County, the muscovite is more or less evenly distributed throughout the coarser portion of the pegmatite mass. At Black Mountain it is all of the wedge variety, some of the spatulate mica books being 3 feet in length and $1\frac{1}{2}$ feet in maximum width. In most localities, however, though present to some extent in all parts of the pegmatite mass, muscovite is much more abundant along certain zones. The commonest mode of occurrence is illustrated in Plate IX, *A*, and has been described on page 26. More or less rounded aggregates of small muscovite plates occurring in certain feldspar quarries have also been described (p. 115). At the Hibbs mica and feldspar mine in Hebron, muscovite, mostly of the wedge variety, occurs sparingly throughout the whole pegmatite mass, but the plate mica is almost wholly confined to a zone 3 to 4 feet in width along the southwest wall of the pegmatite body. It makes up about 10 per cent of this zone, the other minerals being feldspar and quartz. The books are variously oriented; some of them have a width of 30 inches, though the average is about 5 inches.

Mica is not now being mined in Maine and the efforts to mine it in the past have for the most part proved unprofitable because of the small amount or poor quality of the material obtainable as compared with other mica-producing districts. It seems probable that a few of the Maine deposits could be worked in a small way with profit, but the industry can never be of much magnitude unless there is a marked increase in the demand for scrap mica. Localities where it has been mined are Albany, Hebron, Peru, Black Mountain in Rumford, and Waterford, all in Oxford County. The mines are described in the locality descriptions. Deposits of mica have been found in about twenty States of the United States, and have been worked profitably in a number of them. Among the States where mica has been actively mined are North Carolina, South Dakota, New Hampshire, Colorado, Virginia, Alabama, South Carolina, Idaho, and New Mexico.

Mining and manufacture.—The mica mining at the Hibbs mine in Hebron is accessory to the mining of feldspar, both minerals being loosened by hand drilling, succeeded by blasting. At the Black Mountain mine in Rumford the material, which was all scrap mica, was loosened by steam drilling and blasting and was then picked over so as to free it entirely from fragments of quartz or feldspar or other minerals. It was then placed in 100-pound bags, hauled to the railroad, and shipped to Gildersleeve, Conn., for grinding.

At the Beach Hill mine in Waterford the mica, after being thoroughly cleaned of adhering matter, was split up with a stout knife into plates averaging about one-sixteenth of an inch in thickness. If these plates showed fractures or creases they were then cut into two or more pieces, the knife following the cracks or creases so as to eliminate the imperfections and at the same time leave as large perfect plates as possible; this process is known as thumb trimming. Most of the plate mica was marketed in this form, though some of the output was further trimmed to various standard market sizes.

Uses.—The following account of the uses of mica is quoted from a report by Douglas B. Sterrett:[a]

The principal use for mica during recent years has been and still is in the manufacture of electrical apparatus; formerly its application in stove manufacture consumed the bulk of the production. The glazing industry still consumes much of the finest grades of sheet mica in the manufacture of windows for coal, gas, and oil stoves, gas-lamp chimneys, and in many minor uses, as lamp shades, fronts for fancy boxes, etc. The use of mica as an insulating material in electrical apparatus and machinery is extensive. Many forms of dynamos, motors, induction apparatus using high voltage, switchboards, lamp sockets, etc., have sheet mica in their construction. For practically every purpose of electrical insulation, with the exception of commutators of dynamos and motors, the domestic mica is as satisfactory as any other. For insulation between the copper bars of commutator segments, however, no mica produced in the United States is as satisfactory as the "amber" or phlogopite mined in Canada and Ceylon. This is due to the fact that the "amber" mica wears down evenly with the copper segments, while the ordinary white or muscovite mica, through its greater hardness, does not wear down so rapidly and is left in ridges above the copper, causing the

---

a Mineral Resources U. S. for 1908, pt. 2, U. S. Geol. Survey, 1909, p. 751.

motor to spark. Much of the sheet mica used in electrical apparatus is first made up into large sheets of mica board or micanite. In this form it is available for use in most of the purposes for which ordinary sheet mica can be used. It can be bent, rolled, cut, punched, etc. Bending is accomplished during baking, or by heating to soften the shellac used in the manufacture of the mica board. Insulation for commutators is generally cut from "amber" mica board.

Scrap mica, or mica too small to cut into sheets, and the waste from the manufacture of sheet mica are used in large quantities commercially. The greater part is ground for the manufacture of wall papers, lubricants, fancy paints, molded mica for electrical insulation, etc. Ground mica applied to wall papers gives them a silvery luster. When mixed with grease or oils mica forms an excellent lubricant for axles and bearings. Mixed with shellac or special compositions, ground mica can be molded into desired forms, and is used in insulators for wires carrying high potential currents. Ground mica for use in molded mica for insulation purposes should be free of metallic minerals. For lubrication purposes it is necessary that gritty matter be eliminated, either after grinding or by using only pure mica for grinding. For wall papers and brocade paints a ground mica with a high luster is required. This is best obtained by using a clean light-colored mica and grinding under water.

Coarsely ground or bran mica is used to coat the surface of composition roofing material, especially that manufactured by the Western Elaterite Roofing Company, of Denver, Colo. The mica serves the purpose of keeping the material from sticking when rolled for shipping or storage.

In the Western States the dry process is the common practice in grinding mica, but in the mica regions of the Eastern States the greater part of the mica is ground under water. In dry-grinding machines the mica is pulverized by the beating action of teeth or bars on cylinders revolving at a high rate of speed. In wet-grinding machines the mica is beaten and torn under water by teeth or spikes mounted in wheels or cylinders revolving at a comparatively slow rate of speed. The capacity of the dry-grinding machines or pulverizers is considerably greater than that of the wet-grinding machines. The dust of fine mica scales from the pulverizers is often a cause of annoyance to workmen around the mills, as it is very irritating to the throat and lungs when breathed. It is claimed that mica ground under water is better than that ground dry. Some consumers demand the wet-ground mica, claiming a greater purity and more brilliant luster. It is possible that the same effect could be obtained by thoroughly washing dry-ground mica and floating the product.

PRICES AND PRODUCTION.

The following statements in regard to the price of mica are also quoted from Sterrett's report:

The average price of sheet mica in the United States during 1908, as deduced from the total production, was 24.1 cents per pound, as compared with 33 cents per pound in 1907 and with 17.7 cents in 1906. The average prices per pound of sheet mica as reported in the production from several States were as follows: Virginia, 44.2 cents; South Carolina, 35.7 cents; South Dakota, 33.3 cents; Alabama, 24 cents; North Carolina, 19.1 cents. These average values vary greatly from year to year, a result caused in part by variation between the proportion of rough and trimmed sheet mica sold by the producers and in part by variation in the size of sheet produced.

The prices of several sizes of selected mica quoted in the price list of a large mica company of New York during 1908 were as follows:

Prices per pound of selected sizes of sheet mica at New York in 1908.

2 by 2 inches	$0.87	3 by 4 inches	$3.25
2 by 3 inches	1.10	4 by 6 inches	4.75
2 by 5 inches	1.70	6 by 8 inches	6.75
3 by 3 inches	2.75		

In most years the importations of mica into the United States are largely in excess of the domestic production in value. They come mainly from India and Canada.

TOURMALINE.

Chemical and physical properties.—Tourmaline is a complex silicate of boron and aluminum containing various amounts of either magnesium, iron, or the alkali metals. The form of the more perfect crystals is commonly that of a three-sided prism, the sides of the prism usually being striated and channeled (Pl. XV). In many crystals the three-sided form is somewhat modified by the combination with it of a hexagonal prism. The latter is usually subordinate and has the effect of merely somewhat rounding the angles of the triangular prism. Many crystals are terminated by three planes forming a low pyramid, but in others the number of terminal planes is very large. The hardness (7 to 7.5) is slightly greater than that of quartz. There is no well-defined cleavage.

The mineral exhibits a great variety of colors, ranging from black through brownish-black and blue-black to blue, green, red, pink, and colorless. The red varieties go under the name of rubellite; the blue varieties are known as indicolite and the colorless as achroite. A crystal may be green at one end and red at the other or in cross section may show a blue center, then a zone of red, and then one of green. Some of the crystals from Paris, Oxford County, grade from white at one termination to emerald green, then light green, then pink, and finally are colorless at the other termination. The color is dependent on the chemical composition, the green, blue, pink, and colorless varieties generally being rich in lithium and manganese and the dark opaque varieties being particularly rich in iron. The color in the transparent varieties varies with the direction in which the light penetrates the gem; thus a crystal which, when viewed from the side, is a transparent green, may be opaque or yellow-green when viewed along the length of the prism. Because of this property of dichroism, as it is called, it is usually necessary in cutting gem tourmalines to make the "table" of the stone parallel to the long axis of the crystal. Another distinctive quality of the mineral is that it becomes electrified when warmed slightly and is then capable of picking up ashes, small scraps of paper, etc.

Occurrence.—Tourmaline occurs in small crystals in a great variety of rocks and may be either an original crystallization or the result of metamorphic processes. Large crystals and those which are of gem value occur only in the pegmatite deposits. The black varieties occur almost exclusively in the solid pegmatite associated with quartz and feldspar and without any regularity in arrangement. The black varieties may contain from 3 to nearly 20 per cent of oxides of iron and must be carefully separated from feldspar which is to be used for pottery purposes. The colored varieties occasionally are found also in the solid pegmatite, as at the Newry mine (p. 76), but where occurring in this way seldom yield much gem material because of the difficulty of removing them unfractured from their matrix. The colored tourmalines showing the greatest perfection in crystal form and yielding most of the gem stock occur in pockets in the coarse pegmatite bodies. For a detailed description of their mode of occurrence the reader is referred to the description of Mount Mica (pp. 81–93).

Outside of Maine gem tourmalines are produced in the United States in important amounts only in Connecticut and California. Abroad they are found in Brazil, in the Ural Mountains, and in Ceylon.

Mining, prices, etc.—Mount Mica in Paris and Mount Apatite in Auburn are the only localities where systematic mining for tourmalines is now being carried on, although a few gem tourmalines are occasionally found at certain of the feldspar quarries. The quarries have been described in the detailed locality descriptions. In general, the excavation must proceed with great caution; the drilling must be done in a most careful manner, much of it by hand; and heavy charges of explosives must be avoided because of the liability of shattering valuable gem material.

Most of the gem tourmalines now mined in Maine, when not preserved for museum purposes, are cut within the State by lapidaries whose workmanship is said often to equal that of the best New York cutters. The size and general character of the finest gems which have been cut is described in the discussion of Mount Mica. The great bulk of the cut tourmalines marketed are, however, below 3 carats in size. Rubellites and stones of a color approaching an emerald green are the most valuable.

The prices obtained in Maine are higher than those current in New York City, because most are sold at retail to residents of the State or to summer tourists and have an enhanced value as souvenirs. Rubellites and emerald-green varieties bring at retail from $8 to $20 per carat. The indicolite and olive-green varieties bring from $6 to $18 a carat.

BERYL.

CHEMICAL AND PHYSICAL PROPERTIES.

Under the name beryl are included the opaque beryl found in nearly all the pegmatite dikes and the much rarer gem varieties, emerald, aquamarine, golden beryl, and cæsium beryl. In chemical composition beryl is a silicate of beryllium and alumina having the general formula of $Be_3Al_2Si_6O_{18}$ or $3BeO.Al_2O_3.6SiO_2$, but with the beryllium oxide replaced in some varieties by soda, lithia, or calcium oxide. The mineral has a hardness of $7\frac{1}{2}$ to 8; that is, it can not be scratched with a knife. The color varies from emerald green through pale green, light blue, and golden yellow to white and pale pink. The crystals are generally hexagonal prisms, many of them striated vertically, and most of them terminated by a single flat plane at right angles to the long axis of the prism. Some pyramidal terminations also occur. There is no marked cleavage, only an imperfect one parallel to the basal planes. Beryl is fusible only with difficulty and is not attacked by acids.

OPAQUE BERYL.

The commoner varieties of beryl are light blue or green in color, and are opaque, though portions of some crystals are transparent and may even yield gems. Opaque crystals are quite common in most of the coarser pegmatite deposits of Maine, where they occur as more or less regular prisms embedded in the solid pegmatite. Some of these reach remarkable dimensions: one found in the Maine Feldspar Company's quarry at Mount Apatite in Auburn was described as having a diameter equal to that of a hogshead. One from the Noyes gem mine in Greenwood, Oxford County, was so large that a man could barely reach around it with his arms. From Acworth, N. H., one crystal 6¼ feet long and another estimated to weigh over 2½ tons were quarried. A peculiar beryl from Auburn is described by Kunz as follows: [a]

In the state cabinet in Albany, N. Y., is a curious beryl found by S. C. Hatch at Auburn, Maine. It is of imperfect structure and broken diagonally across, showing the structure to advantage. It is 8⅘ inches (30 centimeters) high, 8⅔ inches (22 centimeters) wide, and has 50 different layers, 25 of beryl, the remaining 25 of albite, quartz, and muscovite. All the corners of the hexagonal prism are carried out in full, giving the beryl an asteriated appearance and making it a striking and interesting specimen.

The opaque varities of beryl are of little commercial value, though prized for museum collections when they show perfect crystal forms.

EMERALD.

Transparent beryl of deep-green color is the gem emerald, but it must not be confused with the oriental emerald, which is a green variety of corundum. Emeralds are of rare occurrence in the pegmatite deposits of Maine. One crystal of light grass-green color embedded in quartz was observed by the writer at the Dunton gem quarry in Newry, Oxford County. It was a prism half an inch across and 1½ inches long but was so badly fractured as to be valueless for gems. Parker Cleveland [b] mentions having seen several emeralds from Topsham, Sagadahoc County, of a lively green color and

a Kunz, G. F., Gems and precious stones, pp. 91–92.
b Mineralogy and geology, 1822.

comparable in beauty to the Peruvian emeralds, but none are now in the museums and none, so far as the writer knows, have since been found. In the United States emeralds are found in important quantities only in North Carolina. Abroad they are obtained in Colombia, the Urals, Austria, and upper Egypt.

AQUAMARINE.

The light-blue to sky-blue and light-green transparent varieties of beryl known as aquamarine are more abundant than any of the other gem varieties of beryl found in Maine, and specimens of remarkable size and beauty have been obtained. The prismatic crystals lie in various positions in the solid pegmatite masses and are more commonly associated with quartz than with the other constituents. Few of them occur in pockets. Their position in the solid ledge renders it difficult to obtain the crystals without more or less fracturing. Some few crystals come from quarries which are worked primarily for feldspar or for tourmalines, but the principal supply, like that of golden beryl, is obtained by gem collectors who work small prospects, using hand drills and light blasts of powder.

Most of the gem material has come from Oxford County. Some has been obtained from what is known as the Emmons mine in the southwestern part of Greenwood, from Frenchs Mountain in Albany, Sugar Hill in Stoneham, and Lovell, Bethel, and other towns. A fine sea-green aquamarine weighing about 7 carats was found near Sumner. Recently some good gems have been obtained on the Dudley farm in Buckfield.

The price obtained at retail for the cut stones ranges from $4 to $15 per carat for perfect stones, depending on the size and color. Most of the stones now obtained in Maine are cut and marketed within the State.

GOLDEN BERYL.

Beautiful transparent golden-yellow beryls have been obtained in the pegmatites at various points in Oxford County, at Edgecomb Mountain in Stoneham, in Albany, and recently good gem material of a straw yellow has been obtained from the west side of Speckled Mountain in Peru. They are mined sporadically by gem collectors, mostly from small prospects. The retail prices obtained for flawless cut stones of this variety vary from $10 to $25 per carat, depending upon the size and color. Nearly all that are found are sold to residents or to visitors, and as native Maine gems command a higher price than they would in the general markets.

CÆSIUM BERYL.

A colorless to bluish-white or pinkish-white variety of beryl containing a small percentage (1.66 per cent to 3.6 per cent) of oxide of cæsium was first discovered in Hebron, Oxford County, but has since been found to occur at a number of other pegmatite localities in the western part of the State, notably at Mount Mica in Paris, at the Dudley farm in Buckfield, Oxford County, and at the feldspar quarry of Mr. A. R. Berry in Poland, Androscoggin County. Generally it occurs in somewhat irregular masses in the solid pegmatite, but in some occurrences shows regular crystal forms. When cut it makes a stone of high brilliancy which as a night stone is considered by some to be superior to many diamonds. It is valued chiefly because of its resemblance to the diamond. Flawless cut stones of moderate sizes sell at retail at present at from $5 to $20 a carat.

TOPAZ.

Topaz is a silicate of alumina containing fluorine and having about the composition $Al_{12}Si_6O_{25}F_{10}$. It may be colorless, straw yellow, or wine yellow, or may show faint tints of gray, green, blue, or red. Its hardness is 8, and it is thus capable of scratching quartz. It is also much heavier than quartz, having a specific gravity of 3.4 to 3.65. The mineral belongs to the orthorhombic system and its crystals are usually prismatic in form, with one end terminated by crystal faces. It possesses a perfect cleavage at right angles to the prism axis. Transparent smoky quartz is frequently called smoky topaz, and the so-called Spanish topaz is simply smoky quartz heated until it assumes a yellow color. Clear, colorless quartz is also sometimes sold under the name of topaz.

So far as known to the writer, topaz in any considerable amounts has been found in Maine only at Harndon Hill in Stoneham, Oxford County. (See p. 100.)

INDEX.

A.

	Page.
Abrasives, feldspar for	129
quartz for	135
Alaska, graphic granite from	24
Albany, pegmatites in	70
Amblygonite, occurrence and character of	88
Amethysts, occurrence and character of	102, 138
Andover, pegmatites in	71
Androscoggin County, pegmatites in	46-61
Apatite, definition of	16
occurrence and character of	52-53, 58, 60, 88, 101
Appleton, rocks near	69
Aquamarines, occurrence and character of	99, 146
A-structure, explanation of	139
Auburn, graphic granite in, plate showing	22
pegmatites in	11, 46-59
plate showing	10
Auburn Falls, pegmatites at	46
Auburn reservoir, pegmatites near	46-47

B.

Bay Point Peninsula, pegmatites on	108-109
Beech Hill mine, description of	104-105
mica of	104-105, 141
Bennett prospect, mica at	70
Berry, A. R., quarry of	59-61
Beryl, definition of	16
occurrence and character of	52, 60, 70, 78, 92, 98-99, 101, 144-147
See also particular varieties.	
Beryllonite, definition of	16
occurrence and character of	99-100
Biotite, definition of	17
See also Mica.	
Black Mountain mine, description of	95-97
mica in	95-96, 140
Boothbay Harbor, pegmatites near	12, 14, 19, 35, 64-70
pegmatites near, figure showing	14
Brunswick, pegmatites in	12, 13, 61-62
Buckfield, pegmatites in	71
Bygden, A., on graphic granite	40

C.

Cæsium beryl, occurrence and character of	147
Calcite, definition of	16
occurrence and character of	68-69
Calkins, F. C., on graphic granite	24
Cathance, pegmatites near	112-114
Cavities, gems in	32-33
See also Miarolitic cavities.	
Chemical apparatus ware, quartz for	135-136
Citrine, occurrence and character of	137
Cobble Hill, pegmatites near	78-79

	Page.
Colombite, occurrence and character of	101
Contact-metamorphic effects, occurrence and character of	33-35
Crocker Hill, pegmatites at and near	11, 79-81
Crystallization, differences in, effects of	28-36, 45-46
temperature of, effect of	36-39
Cumberland County, pegmatites in	61-63
Cumberland Mills, pegmatites at	62-63
Cushman, A. S., on feldspar as fertilizer	130

D.

Dale, T. N., on fluidal cavities	21
Danville Corners, pegmatites near	47-48
Danville Junction, pegmatites near	48-49
Deer Hill, amethysts at	102
Diabase dike, view of	98
Dikes. See Pegmatite dikes.	
Diorite, lenses of, plate showing	12
Dunton tourmaline mine, description of	76-78

E.

Edgecomb, pegmatites in	63-64
Electrical apparatus, mica for	141
Emerald, definition of	17
occurrence and character of	145-146
Emmons, W. H., on Mount Mica	36, 83
Eutectics, importance of, in rock formation	39-43, 46

F.

Feldspar, analyses of	51, 106, 123, 124
commercial availability of deposits of	126-127
composition of	119-125
definition of	17
impurities in	127
intergrowths of, with quartz, plate showing	24, 124
milling of	127-128
mining of	125-126
cost of	126
prices of	130-131
production of	132
quarries of	51, 63-64, 72-73, 86, 105-108, 110-117
uses of	129-131
Feldspar brushes, occurrence and character of	23-25
Ferrosilicon, quartz for	135
Fertilizer, feldspar for	130
Field work, extent of	9
Fisher, J. A., quarry of	112-113
quarry of, graphic granite from, analyses of	124
Fluidal cavities, bands of, plate showing	18

149

Fluidal cavities, figures showing............ 20,77
   occurrence and character of.......... 19-21,77
Fluorine minerals, distribution of........... 43
Fluorine phase, description of.............. 21
Foliates, definition of...................... 11
   origin of................................ 11-13
   pegmatite intrusions in................. 11-13
French Mountain, beryls at.................. 70

G.

Garnet, definition of....................... 17
   occurrence and character of..... Passim 52-119
Gaseous constituents, effect of, in crystalliza-
   tion................................... 30-32,45
   effect of, on viscosity.................. 30-36
Gems, occurrence and character of.......... 26-27,
   52,53,55-56,58,60-61,74,89-92,98-102,116
   See also Tourmalines.
Geology, account of........................ 10-46
Georgetown, pegmatites in................. 105-109
   pegmatites in, plate showing........... 10
Georgetown Center, pegmatites at.......... 105
Glass, feldspar for......................... 129
Gneiss, flow structure in, plate showing..... 12
   foliation of............................. 12-13
Golden beryl, occurrence and character of.... 146
Grain, variations in........................ 10,22
Granite, distribution of, map showing..... Pocket
Goldings quarry, feldspar at............... 105-108
   intergrowths at, plate showing......... 120
Granite, pegmatite intrusions in........... 13-15
   figure showing......................... 14
Grant quarry, pegmatites in............... 61
Graphic granite, analyses of............... 124
   composition of...................... 40-42,124
   diagram showing...................... 40
   occurrence and character of.......... 22-23,
   118-119,124-125
   plate showing......................... 22
Graphite mine, rocks at..................... 11
Greenwood, pegmatites in.................. 71-72

H.

Hamlin, E. S., Mount Mica deposits found by. 81
   work of.............................. 82,83,85
Hamlinite, occurrence and character of.... 101-102
Hancock County, pegmatites in............. 63
Harndon Hill, gems at..................... 100-102
Hebron, pegmatites in..................... 72-76
   structure in, figure showing............ 73
Hibbs farm, quarry on..................... 72-74
   quarry on, mica in...................... 140
   section on, figure showing.............. 73
Hinckleys Landing, pegmatites at.......... 105

I.

Iddings, J. P., on crystallization........... 30,45
Igneous foliates, nature of................. 12
Injection gneiss, occurrence of............. 11
   plate showing.......................... 10
Intergrowths, occurrence and character of... 22-26,
   42-43
Intrusives, forms of....................... 35
Iron minerals, injurious effects of.......... 127

J.

Johanssen, H. E., on graphic granite........ 40

K.

Keewaydin Lake, rocks near............... 15,98
Kennebec Point, pegmatites in............. 109
Knopf, Adolph, on graphic granite.......... 24
Kunz, G. F., on beryl...................... 145
   on Harndon Hill........................ 100
Kunzite, occurrence and character of....... 71

L.

Larsen, E. S., and Wright, F. E., on quartz
   crystallization.............. 36-39,45-46
Lee, L. A., aid of.......................... 98
Lepidolite, definition of.................... 17,
   occurrence and character of............ 52
   57-58,77,87,138-139
Lewiston, pegmatite from.................. 46
   pegmatite from, photomicrograph of.... 10
Lime-soda feldspars, composition of........ 120-123
   qualities of............................ 121-123
Lincoln County, pegmatites in............. 63-70
Lithium phase, description of.............. 21
   distribution of......................... 43

M.

McKown Point, pegmatites at............. 65,69
McMahons Island, pegmatites on, plate
   showing............................... 10
Maine, cooperation of...................... 9
   map of part of........................ Pocket
Maine Feldspar Co., quarries of.......... 50-54,115
   quarries of, pegmatites in............. 53
Map of part of Maine..................... Pocket
Metamorphism, occurrence and character of.. 11-12
   See also Contact metamorphism.
Miarolitic cavities, occurrence and character
   of.................................... 32-33
Mica, injurious effects of.................. 127
   intergrowths of, plate showing.......... 120
   occurrence and character of............ 26,
   Passim 51-119,138-139
   types of............................... 138-139
   wedge structure in, plate showing....... 138
   See also Muscovite.
Microcline, composition of................. 119
Mills quarry, description of................. 76
Mineral composition, character of.......... 15-22
   effects of, on crystallization........... 28-29,45
Mineralizers, definition of................. 32
Minerals, effect of, on crystallization...... 29-30,45
   list of................................. 16-18
   proportions of...................... 18,28-29
Minot, pegmatites in....................... 59
Montana, graphic granite from............. 24
Mount Apatite, gems at.................... 49-50
   pegmatites at.......................... 49-50
   quarries on............................ 50-59
Mount Ararat, quarries on........ 110-112,117-119
Mount Mica, gems from................... 89-92
   gems from, plates showing............. 88,90
   mine at, description of................. 81-93
   plates showing......................... 82,84
   pegmatite pockets at, plates showing.... 26,86
   structure at, figure showing............ 84

Page.

Mount Rubellite, gems at................. 74
Muscovite, defects in................. 139–140
  defects in, plate showing......... 138
  manufacture of................ 140–141, 142
  mining of...................... 140–141
  prices of...................... 142
  production of.................. 143
  occurrence and character of.... Passim 51–112,
                                        139–141
  uses of........................ 141–142
  See also Mica.
Muscovite phase, description of............ 22

N.

Newry, pegmatites in.................. 76–78
New Mexico, graphic granite from......... 24
North Topsham, feldspar quarry at........ 116–117
Norway, pegmatites in.................. 78–79
  rocks at, plate showing............... 18

O.

Orthoclase, composition of.................. 119
Oxford County, pegmatites in.............. 70–105

P.

Paints, quartz for............................ 134
Paris, pegmatites in.................. 33–34, 79–93
  schists in, structure of, plate showing....
  structure in, figures showing............. 19, 84
Pegmatite, age of........................... 14–15
  character of............................. 15–27
  definition of 10
  distribution of.......................... 10, 43–45
    map showing....................... Pocket
  fluorine phase of......................... 21
  lithium phase of 21
  muscovite phase of 22
  origin of................................ 27–46
  photomicrographs of....... 10, 24, 26, 34, 120, 124
  quartzose phase of....................... 18–19
    figure showing......................... 19
  relation of, to bordering rocks........... 10–15
  schist fragments in...................... 35–36
  sodium phase of......................... 21
  texture of.............................. 22–27
Pegmatite dikes, structure of............. 11, 13
  structure of, figure showing............. 11
Pemaquid Point, rocks at, plate showing.... 10
Penobscot Bay quadrangle, rocks in........ 15, 44
Perry Basin, rocks near.................... 15
Peru, pegmatites in......................... 93
Pingree, C. P., mica prospect of........... 70
Plagioclases, composition of.............. 120–123
Pockets, gem-bearing, occurrence and charac-
    ter of.................................. 27,
            53, 58–59, 71–72, 74, 82–86, 89, 116
  views of................................. 26, 86
Poland, pegmatites in..................... 59–61
Potash-soda feldspars, composition of...... 119–120
Pottery, feldspar for.................. 127, 128, 129
  quartz for.............................. 138
Poultry grit, feldspar for................. 129
Pulsifer, P. P., quarry of................. 56–59

Q.   Page.

Quartz, crystallization of, temperature of.. 36–39
  definition of............................ 17
  intergrowths of, with feldspar, plate
    showing.............................. 24, 124
  milling of.............................. 133–134
  occurrence and character of.. Passim 50–119, 133
  prices of............................... 137
  production of........................... 136
  uses of................................. 134–136
  vein of, view of........................ 98
Quartz, rose, occurrence and character of... 137–138
Quartz, smoky, occurrence and character of. 137
Quartzose phase, description of............ 18–19

R.

Rare minerals, effect of, on crystallization.. 29–30
Raoult's law, statement of................. 31
Rockland quadrangle, rocks in............. 44
Rose quartz, occurrence and character of.. 137–138
Ruling, defects in mica due to........... 139–140
Rumford, pegmatites in............. 26, 35, 93–97
Rumford Falls, pegmatites at and near. 34, 35, 94–95
  schist at, feldspar in, plate showing.... 34

S.

Sagadahoc County, pegmatites in........ 105–119
St. George River, rocks on................. 12
Schaller, W. T., on California pegmatites.. 42
Schists, foliation of..................... 11–12
  structure of, plate showing............. 34
Scouring, feldspar for.................... 129
  quartz for............................. 134
Silicon, quartz for....................... 135
Small Point feldspar quarry, description of.. 108
Sodium phase, description of.............. 21
South Glastonbury, Conn., quartz vein at,
    view of............................... 98
Southport, rocks near..................... 14
South Waterford mica prospect, description
    of.................................. 103–104
Spanish topaz, nature of.............. 137, 147
Spence Hills, pegmatites in............... 98
Spodumene, definition of................. 18
  fluidal cavities in..................... 77, 88
  figure showing......................... 77
Spence Point, pegmatites near............. 66
Standish, pegmatites in.................. 98
Sterrett, D. B., on mica............... 141–142
Stoneham, diabase dike in, plate showing ... 98
  pegmatites in 98–102
Stoves, mica for......................... 141
Stow, pegmatites in...................... 102
Streaked Mountain, pegmatites of..... 35–36, 74–75
Sugar Hill, gems at................... 99–100
Sweden, graphic granite from............. 125
Syenite porphyry, occurrence and character
    of................................... 69

T.

Teeth, artificial, feldspar for.............. 129
Texture, photomicrograph showing.......... 10
  variations in........................... 10

Page.

Todds Bay, feldspar quarry near.......... 105–108
Topaz, definition of......................... 18
    occurrence and character of............ 100, 147
Topsham, feldspar and quartz at, plate
        showing......................... 24
    pegmatites in.............. 12, 23, 41, 42, 109–119
        plate showing...................... 26
Tourmaline, definition of.................... 18
    occurrence and character of.....Passim 50–119,
                                    143–144
Tourmalines, gem, definition of............. 18
    occurrence and character of....:....... 49,
            52, 58, 60, 71, 72, 78, 81–92, 96, 144
    mining of............................... 144
    prices of............................... 144
    views of................................ 88, 90
Towne, J. S., quarry of..................... 55–56

Page.

Trenton Flint and Spar Co., mill of......... 117
Tubbs Ledge, gems at........................ 78
Turner, E. Y., quarries of.................. 54–55

V.

Viscosity, effects of gas on................ 30–36
Vogt, J. H. L., on graphic granite........ 39–40, 42

W.

Waterford, pegmatites in.................... 102–105
Westbrook, pegmatites in.................... 62–63
Willes, G. D., quarry of.................... 115–116
Willes, William, quarry of.................. 113–114
Woodside quarry, pegmatites in............. 13, 61
Wright, F. E., and Larsen, E. S., on quartz
        crystallization............ 36–39, 45–46

O

Lightning Source UK Ltd.
Milton Keynes UK
UKHW030621060519
342177UK00009B/1952/P